EMOTIONAL DEVELOPMENT
FROM INFANCY TO
ADOLESCENCE

Emotional Development from Infancy to Adolescence: Pathways to Emotional Competence and Emotional Problems offers a chapter-by-chapter introductory survey of all aspects of emotional development from infancy to adolescence, from delight, surprise and love to anger, distress and fear. Taking a chronological approach, each chapter focuses on a specific emotion and covers the theories and research relating to its development, from infants' emotional capabilities to the changes in self-understanding and self-conscious emotions of adolescence.

Hay integrates the approaches of classic developmental differentiation and differential emotions theory to create a comprehensive textbook with a unique approach to the subject matter, showcasing a range of research linking emotions to biological underpinnings and early experiences. This wide-ranging book also includes coverage of differences in temperament, developmental psychopathology, emotion regulation and development of emotional understanding and attachment.

It is core reading for students of developmental psychology, health psychology, child welfare and social work, as well as anyone taking a course on social and emotional development. It will also be of interest to practitioners working in educational and clinical psychology and child psychiatry.

Dale F. Hay is Professor Emerita of Developmental Psychology at Cardiff University. She has led a major longitudinal study to understand the origins of developmental disorders. She has taught developmental psychology, with special emphasis on social and emotional development, developmental psychopathology and developmental research methods.

International Texts in Developmental Psychology

Series editor: Peter K. Smith, Goldsmiths College, University of London, UK

This volume is one of a rapidly developing series in International Texts in Developmental Psychology, published by Routledge. The books in this series are selected to be state-of-the-art, high level introductions to major topic areas in developmental psychology. The series conceives of developmental psychology in broad terms and covers such areas as social development, cognitive development, developmental neuropsychology and neuroscience, language development, learning difficulties, developmental psychopathology and applied issues. Each volume is written by a specialist (or specialists), combining empirical data and a synthesis of recent global research to deliver cutting-edge science in a format accessible to students and researchers alike. The books may be used as textbooks that match on to upper level developmental psychology modules, but many will also have cross-disciplinary appeal.

Each volume in the series is published in hardback, paperback and eBook formats. More information about the series is available on the official website at: https://www.routledge.com/International-Texts-in-Developmental-Psychology/book-series/DEVP, including details of all the titles published to date.

Published Titles

An Introduction to Mathematical Cognition
Camilla Gilmore, Silke M. Göbel, and Matthew Inglis

Emotional Development from Infancy to Adolescence
Pathways to Emotional Competence and Emotional Problems
Dale F. Hay

For a full list of titles in this series, please visit www.routledge.com

EMOTIONAL DEVELOPMENT FROM INFANCY TO ADOLESCENCE

Pathways to Emotional Competence and Emotional Problems

Dale F. Hay

Routledge
Taylor & Francis Group

LONDON AND NEW YORK

First published 2019
by Routledge
2 Park Square, Milton Park, Abingdon, Oxon OX14 4RN

and by Routledge
52 Vanderbilt Avenue, New York, NY 10017

Routledge is an imprint of the Taylor & Francis Group, an informa business

© 2019 Dale F. Hay

British Library Cataloguing-in-Publication Data
A catalogue record for this book is available from the British Library

Library of Congress Cataloging-in-Publication Data
Names: Hay, Dale F., author.
Title: Emotional development from infancy to adolescence : pathways to emotional competence and emotional problems / Dale F. Hay.
Description: Abingdon, Oxon ; New York, NY : Routledge, 2019. | Includes bibliographical references and index.
Identifiers: LCCN 2018059890 (print) | LCCN 2019002667 (ebook) | ISBN 9781315849454 (Ebook) | ISBN 9781841691862 (hardback) | ISBN 9781848720145 (pbk.)
Subjects: LCSH: Emotions in children. | Child psychology.
Classification: LCC BF723.E6 (ebook) | LCC BF723.E6 H379 2019 (print) | DDC 155.4/124—dc23
LC record available at https://lccn.loc.gov/2018059890

ISBN: 978-1-84169-186-2 (hbk)
ISBN: 978-1-84872-014-5 (pbk)
ISBN: 978-1-31584-945-4 (ebk)

Typeset in Bembo
by Apex CoVantage, LLC
Printed by CPI Group (UK) Ltd, Croydon CR0 4YY

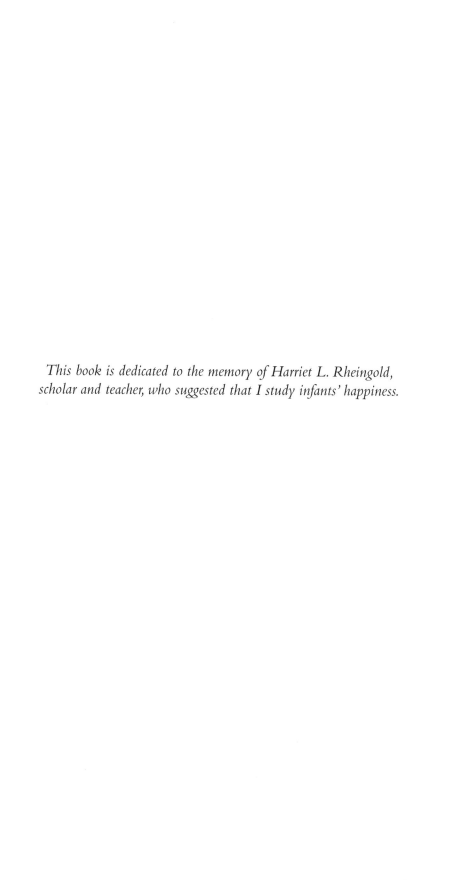

This book is dedicated to the memory of Harriet L. Rheingold, scholar and teacher, who suggested that I study infants' happiness.

CONTENTS

ACKNOWLEDGEMENTS

I am very grateful to many colleagues and students who have helped me study children's emotional development, especially within the context of the Cardiff Child Development Study, which was supported by the Medical Research Council, the Medical Research Foundation and the Waterloo Foundation. Special thanks go to Salim Hashmi and Cerith Waters for their comments on the manuscript. I am grateful to Stephanie van Goozen, Ross Vandewert and Sarah Gerson for supplying photographs of children's expressions of emotion.

1

MORE THAN A FEELING

The study of emotion and its development

Trying to define emotion

The aim of this book is to examine the features and possible causes of children's emotional development, from infancy to adolescence. Yet what exactly does that entail? Although most of us know what we're talking about when we talk about our own emotions, it is notoriously difficult for psychologists to define the concept of emotion. The definitions they offer often seem rather abstract. For example, in their authoritative review of studies of emotional development in the *Handbook of Child Psychology*, Saarni, Campos, Camras, and Witherington (2006) proposed the following 'working definition of emotion': 'Emotion is . . . the person's attempt or readiness to establish, maintain, or change the relation between the person and his or her changing circumstances, on matters of significance to that person' (p. 227; quoted from Campos, Frankel, & Camras, 2004). Saarni and her colleagues go on to distinguish the concept of *feeling* from the concept of *emotion*, and argue that what laypeople refer to as their feelings is not the core of emotion.

It is certainly true that the student of emotional development must study many different things, beyond an individual's self-reported feelings. Emotion is felt and expressed through physiological reactions and physical actions, and interpreted through thoughts and words. Nonetheless, there is some danger that, when acknowledging the complexity of the process of emotional development, we might lose sight of its distinctive content. Furthermore, the very general definitions are somewhat circular: How do we determine what is significant to a person without any indication of an emotional reaction? Therefore, in this book, we shall not dwell at the outset on definitional complexities. Rather, this book takes an empirical approach to the study of emotion, by focussing on particular categories of emotions, more or less in the sequence in which they consolidate from infancy to adolescence. We will then return to the vexing definitional issues in the final chapter.

Differentiation theory and its critics

The organisation of the book has been influenced by the classic theory of the differentiation of emotion offered by Katherine Banham Bridges (1932). Bridges, who was born in Sheffield, UK in 1897, became the first person to pursue an honours degree in psychology at Manchester University. After moving to Canada, she became the first woman to receive a PhD in psychology from the University of Montreal. Bridges argued that the original emotion experienced by infants is excitement, which becomes differentiated into interest and distress (Figure 1.1). On the basis of her observations of 62 infants in a foundling hospital in Montreal, Bridges argued that:

> The earliest emotional reactions are very general and poorly organized responses to one or two general types of situations. As weeks and months go by the responses take on more definite form in relation to more specific situations . . . in the course of genesis of the emotions, there occurs a process of differentiation. . . . In this manner slowly appear the well known emotions of anger, disgust, joy, love, and so forth. They are not present at birth in their mature form.
>
> *(p. 324)*

The differentiation hypothesis put forth by Bridges was in line with more general theories of emotion set forth by her contemporaries. For example, Allport (1924) claimed that 'At the beginning . . . of the life of feeling there is little to differentiate the emotional states beyond the mere qualities of pleasantness and unpleasantness.

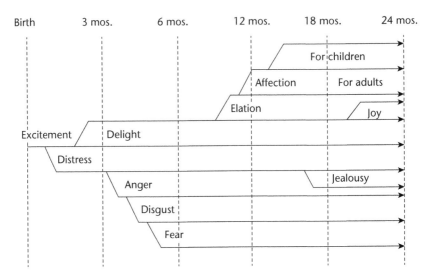

FIGURE 1.1 Katherine Banham Bridges' classic model of emotional development

The child has feelings of unpleasantness, but not yet definite unpleasant emotions' (p. 93).

In the pages that follow, I shall draw on the classic scheme presented by Bridges as an organisational framework for this book. Bridges claimed that the 'original emotion' (p. 325) was *excitement* (a term that subsequent emotion theorists might equate with *arousal*), which soon differentiated into two general tendencies, *interest* and *distress*. According to Bridges, distress then differentiated into the primary negative emotions (fear, anger, disgust and sadness). Accordingly, we shall first examine infants' initial expressions of distress and pleasure (crying and smiling) and then the primary negative emotions, before proceeding to discuss more complex emotions, including the so-called moral emotions that emerge later in childhood and are bound up with the development of a sense of self.

A few decades after Bridges undertook her study of infants, the issue of differentiation of emotion over time became a matter of considerable controversy. Later theorists working within an evolutionary perspective, such as Silvan Tompkins (1963), Paul Ekman (Ekman, Friesen, & Ellsworth, 1972) and Carroll Izard (1971), disagreed with Bridges' differentiation theory. They proposed instead the theory that discrete facial expressions of emotions such as fear, disgust or anger have been selected for in evolution. They claimed that these expressions of distinct emotions were seen across human cultures and already shown by young infants, even in the first months of life (e.g., Ekman, 1993; Izard, Huebner, Risser, & Dougherty, 1980). This latter approach became known as the *differential emotions* theory. A body of work testing differential emotions theory has focussed on patterns of emotional expression that could be discerned across ages and cultures.

Over the last few decades, the differential emotions approach set forth by Ekman, Izard and their colleagues has shaped much research on emotional development in infancy. However, in recent years, it has received some criticism. Some psychologists claim that emotional development does not entail the emergence of discrete emotions nor entirely undifferentiated ones but rather the consolidation of different components of emotions over time (e.g., Witherington, Campos, Harriger, Bryan, & Margett, 2009). Still other theorists question whether very young infants can experience emotion at all, because they cannot yet distinguish between themselves and other people (Sroufe, 1995).

One analysis of children's understanding of emotion concepts, as measured by their spontaneous references to different emotions and their performance on discrimination tasks (Widen & Russell, 2008), returned to an updated *differentiation model* of emotional development that echoes Bridges' earlier theoretical framework. Widen and Russell's circumplex model features two orthogonal dimensions, one measuring the degree of a person's arousal and the other the degree of pleasure/displeasure he or she experiences (Figure 1.2). In Widen and Russell's model, surprise is an emotion that reflects a high degree of pure arousal. The negative emotions of fear, anger and disgust also show high arousal, whereas sadness reflects low arousal. The positive emotion of happiness reflects a moderate level of arousal. Their empirical analyses of children's understanding of emotion labels during early

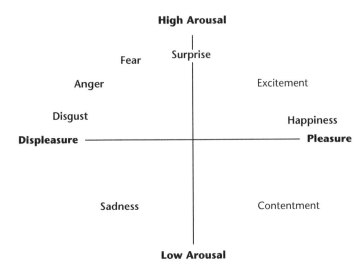

FIGURE 1.2 A two-dimensional model of children's understanding of emotions

Source: Widen & Russell, 2008

childhood also show a gradual differentiation from a basic distinction between positive and negative emotion to a more nuanced understanding of the different negative emotions (Widen & Russell, 2008). Thus, although Bridges theorised about infants' observed expressions of emotion, and Widen and Russell focussed on children's use of emotion language, both theories point to a gradual differentiation of negative emotional experience.

My own use of Bridges' classic account of emotional development as an organising framework for this book certainly does not imply unqualified acceptance of this early theory. Although criticisms have been levelled against the theory of differential emotions in recent years (e.g., Camras & Shutter, 2010), and some elements of Bridges' differentiation theory may be worth revisiting, caution is still needed. Children's emotions may not differentiate in the exact way that Bridges proposed, and, if they do, the underlying processes that lead to differentiation may reflect learning and emotional socialisation, as well as biological maturation. What is most important, however, is the fact that Bridges' account was a *developmental* theory, resting on the premise that important developmental changes take place in both the expression and understanding of emotion over infancy and childhood. For example, children's abilities to associate felt emotions with bodily sensations show considerable development between childhood and adulthood (Hietanen, Glerean, Hari, & Nummenmaa, 2016).

Therefore, because it sets out an explicitly developmental perspective, Bridges' scheme still provides a useful conceptual framework in which to consider what actually happens during emotional development. We shall return to the issue of developmental processes that underlie emotional development in the final chapter of this book.

Key dimensions of emotional development

Within and across these different domains of emotional experience, fundamental questions must be asked about what a child's emotional development actually entails. In this book, we shall concentrate attention on three important components to the development of emotion: the *expression of emotion* (and its relation to inner emotional experience), the *understanding of emotion* (one's own emotions and those of other people) and the *regulation of emotion*. Emotion is regulated both through internal physiological and cognitive processes and through learning about the social rules that control displays of emotion in particular families and cultures. Developmental psychologists have provided evidence for *change over time* and *continuity of individual differences* with respect to each of these three components of emotional development.

The expression of emotion

In humans, emotion is expressed through different channels: the face, the voice, the hands and the physiological reactions of the body. Ever since Darwin's (1872) treatise *The Expression of Emotion in Man and Animals* was published, emotion researchers have debated evidence about the universality of human emotion and its biological basis. Given the prominence of differential emotions theory in the latter part of the twentieth century, much empirical work has been conducted within the theoretical framework of evolutionary theory, focussing on specific configurations of the facial musculature that are associated with primary emotions such as anger or sadness. These distinct patterns of facial configurations can be discerned across cultures (Ekman, 1972) and identified as early as the first year of life (Field, Woodson, Greenberg, & Cohen, 1982), which supports claims from the differential emotions theorists that the morphology of the human face and its underlying muscles has been selected for in the course of evolution.

Such studies of infants' facial expressions draw attention to the early origins of emotion; however, they also raise the theoretical question of whether outward emotional expressions provide direct evidence for inner emotional experience. For example, does the child who shows a typical expression of facial anger (Figure 1.3) experience rage in the same way an adult would? Is the outward expression a veridical index of inner experience? Or does the facial expression precede a more mature understanding of anger, which in turn informs the inner experience? Should the adults who care for the child interpret the expression as being a true indication of anger, as an adult would understand that, or is it more helpful to consider it a signal of more global distress?

FIGURE 1.3 Is this child expressing anger?

In the chapters that follow, we shall consider this thorny issue with respect to the primary negative emotions that emerge from initial distress: disgust, fear, anger and sadness. Bridges' theory of a differentiation process is still germane to our understanding of the emergence and subsequent development of these negative emotions.

Emotional understanding

In any given situation, how do we know what we're feeling? On what basis do we guess what other people are feeling? Emotional experience clearly has a cognitive, interpretational dimension.

Understanding our own emotions

In a classic account of the nature of emotion (the James–Lange theory), it was argued that our observation of our own reactions to emotion-provoking situations tells us what we are actually feeling (James, 1894). For example, if we are walking down a deserted street, late at night, hear footsteps behind us, and begin to hurry along, breaking into a run, it could be argued that we interpret our emotions in accordance with the physical and physiological reactions of our own bodies. In other words, if we're running, we must be afraid.

Although the James–Lange theory was challenged by early neuroscientists (Cannon, 1927), who demonstrated that animals whose cerebral cortices had been removed still expressed emotion, the James-Lange legacy is still felt in more modern theories that emphasise people's cognitive construction of their own emotions (e.g., Russell, 2003). However, contemporary emotion theorists must attempt to reconcile cognitive perspectives on emotion with the findings emerging from affective neuroscience, in particular, neuroimaging studies of alert human brains. This new body of evidence draws attention to relations between brain structures that underlie physiological responses to emotion-provoking stimuli and cognitive representations of emotional experience.

Understanding other people's emotions

Human beings pay attention to each other's emotions from the first days of life onwards: Even newborn infants are sensitive to each other's cries (Sagi & Hoffman, 1976). However, infants do not yet possess a *theory of mind*, i.e., an understanding that other people have thoughts, feelings and intentions. Understanding that other people have emotions and desires appears to develop before understanding that other people have thoughts and beliefs (Wellman & Woolley, 1990), which further underscores the salience of emotion in infants' worlds. It has long been thought that infants' growing understanding of their own mental life is influenced by their growing understanding of the mental lives of others, in a reciprocal and dialectical fashion (Baldwin, 1895), and so the understanding of other people's emotions may help children to understand their own. This process is apparent in the phenomenon of *social referencing*, which occurs when infants who are confronted with a situation that could be pleasant or dangerous consult the emotional expressions of their caregivers before expressing their own emotion; the caregivers' expressions guide the infants' choices to approach or avoid the ambiguous situation (e.g., Campos, Thein, & Owen, 2003). We shall return to this topic of understanding other people's emotions when discussing the social emotion of empathy for another person's feelings in Chapter 9.

Emotion regulation

Physiological regulation

The important organs of our bodies are all involved in the experience and regulation of emotion; when we talk about our emotional reactions to the things that happen to us, we say that we feel things 'in the pit of our stomachs'; we may feel 'breathless,' or 'break out into a sweat,' or feel 'tears coming to our eyes.' The experience of emotion is bound up with these bodily reactions, and the reactions are regulated by the autonomic nervous system (ANS), the pathways of neural connections that transmit information from the brain to the visceral organs and back again. The ANS includes the sympathetic and parasympathetic divisions. It has long been thought that the sympathetic system mobilises the individual to react to threatening events, with 'fight or flight' (reacting to threat with anger and aggression versus fear and attempts to escape), whereas the parasympathetic system helps restore calm. For example, in response to threatening events, the sympathetic system works to increase heart rate; when threat has passed, the parasympathetic system slows the heartbeat and restores the individual to a homeostatic balance. Thus, the two systems have traditionally been seen as working in a reciprocal fashion, serving to activate and regulate the expression of emotion. More recent research has shown that sometimes both systems work together, under the control of higher brain processes as well as brainstem mechanisms (Berntson & Cacioppo, 2009). The study of emotional development must include investigation of the development of these physiological processes that contribute to the expression and regulation of emotion.

Display rules and emotional socialisation

As children grow older, their emotions are regulated by social learning and their growing understanding of the world. Although discrete facial expressions of emotion have been identified across culture (Ekman, 1972), there exist cultural constraints on the circumstances under which emotions are expressed; the cultural norms governing the expression of emotion are referred to as 'display rules' (Ekman & Friesen, 1969). Even in early childhood, children learn to mask emotion, in accordance with the rules of their culture (e.g., Cole, 1986). Within a culture, emotional socialisation often differs for girls and boys, with different display rules governing emotional behaviour in the two sexes.

Coping

Clinical psychologists have drawn attention to the issue of regulating one's emotion when coping with stress and other adversities (Lazarus & Folkman, 1984), making a distinction between *problem-focussed* and *emotion-focussed* coping strategies. There is some evidence that problem-focussed attempts to tackle the problem causing the stress are more effective than emotion-focussed attempts to distract oneself or improve emotional states through use of substances; however, it is likely that effective problem-solving also reduces negative emotion, and so there is not always a clear distinction between problem-focussed and emotion-focussed coping (Folkman & Moskowitz, 2000). Much more needs to be learned about the development of both types of coping strategies in childhood.

Individual differences

The concept of temperament

While many theories of emotional development focus on universals, e.g., the age at which particular emotional expressions appear, or general trends over time in emotional understanding, important differences amongst individuals can be discerned in early infancy: Different infants have different emotional reactions to the world, and different patterns of emotionality is an important component of individual *temperament* (Allport, 1924). Different dimensions of human temperament have been remarked upon since ancient times, when the physician Galen drew attention to different emotional tendencies (e.g., melancholia), thought to be related to different humours of the body. In the twentieth century, developmental psychologists who were attempting to chart age-related change over time also became aware of extensive differences amongst infants (e.g., Shirley, 1933). In the 1960s, in reaction to strong environmental claims about the effects of early child-rearing on infants' development, some investigators began to document the effects of infants on their parents (Bell, 1968; Rheingold, 1969) and to note important differences amongst infants, even in the newborn period (e.g., Birns, 1965). In this context, several different research groups attempted to measure various dimensions of individuality in infancy, which in turn has led to different approaches to the measurement of temperament (e.g., Buss & Plomin, 1975; Kagan & Moss, 1962; Thomas, Chess, & Birch, 1970). Information about temperament is obtained from parents' reports (e.g., McDevitt & Carey, 1978; Rothbart, 1986), experimental assessments (e.g., Gagne, van Hulle, Aksan, Essex, & Goldsmith, 2011) and psychobiological measures (e.g., Gunnar & Vazquez, 2000; Porges, Doussard-Roosevelt, & Maiti, 1994). These different measurement strategies have led to a rich but complex literature; however, across the different definitions and approaches to measurement, there is clear evidence for a biological basis to infant temperament. Temperament in infancy is linked to dimensions of personality in later childhood and adulthood (e.g., Caspi et al., 2003).

Developmental psychopathology

The studies of temperament document normal variation in emotionality and emotional regulation. However, some children experience emotional problems to such a degree that they actually meet diagnostic criteria for mental health problems. *Developmental psychopathology* refers to the study of such problems, in terms of identifying the genetic and environmental influences that set children on a path to psychopathology. It has become clear that adult psychological problems derive from a combination of genetic risk and adversity in family environments (e.g., Caspi et al., 2003). What is even more surprising is the fact that clinical conditions such as depression and anxiety first appear in early childhood (e.g., Egger & Angold, 2006). Therefore, it is important to examine the development of such clinical disorders against the background of normal variation in emotional development.

   The study of developmental psychopathology relies on a number of different research methods. What we know about children's mental health problems, including anxiety disorders, largely comes from three types of studies: (1) *case studies*, which are detailed qualitative reports on the features of and possible causes of particular children's symptoms; (2) *clinical studies*, in which groups of children who have been referred for assessment or treatment of mental health problems are contrasted with children who are free of such problems, or those who are showing symptoms of a different type of disorder; and (3) *community studies*, in which an entire population of children is assessed with questionnaires and diagnostic interviews for possible symptoms and disorders, to determine how commonly such disorders occur. The latter type of study is sometimes referred to as an *epidemiological* study, because the method of surveying a large population for the occurrence of particular diseases comes from the large-scale studies of epidemics of infectious illness. Studies of clinical samples allow for the study of a sufficient number of children with serious problems, for example, to explore possible causes of their fears and anxiety. Such clinical samples can also be used to create *clinical trials*, which test the effectiveness of particular medical and psychological interventions. In contrast, community studies produce information about how common the problem is and what factors are associated with particular disorders in a large population. All of these methods provide information that is relevant to the emergence of children's psychological disorders.

In the chapters that follow, we will chart the course of emotional development and the emergence of clinically significant disorders. In each chapter, we will first focus on developmental trends, then examine individual differences and, finally, identify clinical conditions such as anxiety, obsessive-compulsive disorder, oppositional-defiant disorder, depressive disorder and conduct disorder, which reflect the extreme end of the continuum of individual differences in emotional experience.

Organisation of the book

In Chapter 2, we begin by examining infants' first manifestations of emotion, in terms of infants' expression of distress and delight. In Chapters 3–7, we then examine facets of primary emotional experience that follow on from that basic distinction between positive and negative emotion: surprise and disgust, fear, anger, sadness and happiness. For each type of emotion, we shall examine evidence for its age of onset and then examine its developmental course over the childhood years.

In Chapters 8–10, we examine more complex emotions that play an important role in our relationships with other people, sometimes referred to as social or moral emotions: love and jealousy, empathy and callousness, and shame and guilt. These latter emotions are defined not by immediate physiological and behavioural reactions, but rather are informed by knowledge, memory and the interpretation of other people's behaviour and mental states.

Finally, in Chapter 11, having investigated the development of each of these different emotions, we return to our primary question: How do emotions develop? We once again consider the advantages and disadvantages of Bridges' original proposal that emotions differentiate over the first years of life, as opposed to the competing differential emotion theory, which suggests that primary emotions are already present in infancy. The account of emotional development offered in this

book will draw upon both nativist and empiricist perspectives on human development, as manifested across nearly a century of relevant studies.

Throughout this book, terms relating to a child's age are defined in accordance
with the scientific literature in developmental psychology. The word 'infant' refers
to children under the age of 24 months, with somewhat older children (up to 36
months) often referred to as 'toddlers.' Early childhood is the term used for children
between 3 and 5 years (sometimes referred to as 'preschool children'), and middle
childhood corresponds to the primary school years (approximately 5 to 11 years).

2

DISTRESS AND DELIGHT IN INFANCY

Under ordinary circumstances, as they move through their daily routines, adults do not often express strong emotion. At intervals, they experience events that evoke joy or despair, and they may encounter situations that elicit fear or anger. However, most mentally healthy adults have acquired strategies of emotion regulation – they keep their emotions under control.

The same cannot be said of the newborn infant, whose very first act is to cry. During the early months of life, infants and the adults who care for them are wedded to the infants' expression of negative emotion – its intensity, its duration, its rhythmic patterns and its responsiveness to all the attempts adults make to soothe their crying infants. During the first couple of months after birth, infants move between states of calm alertness, restlessness and full-blown distress, and their caregivers must react accordingly. After a month or two, infants become able to express positive emotion: They begin to smile, and their caregivers acquire a clearer understanding of their infants' capacity for delight as well as distress (Bridges, 1932).

The development of crying and its regulation

Crying as an expression of emotion: the first social signal

In contrast to other mammals, members of our species are born with reasonably acute perceptual abilities but limited motor skills. Unlike some young mammals, they can see and hear, but they cannot voluntarily move away from alarming or dangerous situations. Nevertheless, because they are born with the ability to cry, young humans have an inborn ability to draw other people's attention to their needs and take any necessary action to provide comfort or help. This ability is of course not unique to humans – vocal distress calls are given by birds and other mammals.

However, perhaps because crying in older children and adults signals deeply felt emotion, parents and other caregivers typically respond to the newborn's cry as an *emotional signal*, not just as a reflexive act indicating a physical need. The overall time infants spend crying declines over the course of the first year (Bell & Ainsworth, 1972), and bouts of crying reduce in length (Hubbard & van IJzendoorn, 1991), perhaps because older infants have developed other ways of expressing their needs. A meta-analysis of diary studies of crying suggested that the average duration of crying dropped after the first two months of life (Wolke, Bilgin, & Samara, 2017).

Parents often report that they can distinguish different types of crying, which help them figure out what exactly their infants need or want, e.g., whether the infant is hungry, in pain or needs a nappy change. Experimental studies have shown that parents are better than other people at interpreting their own infants' cries (e.g., Sagi, 1981).

Developmental psychologists have sought to identify the precise acoustic features of infants' crying that corresponds to parents' perceptions of different types of cries, in particular distinctions between the cry at the time of birth, cries of pain and hunger cries. The pitch of the infant's cry, which is measured in terms of the fundamental frequency (F_o) of the tones the crying infant is producing, has been the focus of much attention. High-pitched crying is often perceived as more urgent and also more annoying to the listener (e.g., Dessereau, Kurowski, & Thompson, 1998; Gustafson & Green, 1989). Adults often perceive high-pitched crying as a sign of infants' pain, and indeed male infants undergoing circumcision emit very high-pitched cries (Porter, Miller, & Marshall, 1986), in parallel to facial expressions and physiological reactions to the stressful event (Lehr, Zeskind, Ofenstein, Cepeda, & Aranda, 2007; Porter, Porges, & Marshall, 1988). It is not just the average pitch of an infant's cry but also variation in pitch (what acoustic scientists term 'jitter') that induces adults' negative perceptions of the cry (Protopapas & Eimas, 1997). Automated systems that support more systematic analysis of various acoustic properties of infants' crying can detect differences between expressions of pain and other types of crying (Sheinkopf, Lester, & Silverman, 2015). Acoustic patterns that together are referred to as 'vocal roughness' reveal infants' pain reactions in response to being immunised with two different vaccines as well as differences between immunisation and the everyday discomfort experienced when given their baths (Koutseff et al., 2018).

Infants' cries can be analysed for features other than pitch, and these other dimensions of crying also influence adults' perceptions of the cry. Duration of crying affects adults' reactions to the sound of infant crying (Dessereau, Kurowski, & Thompson, 1998; Gustafson & Green, 1989). Infants' crying is a dynamic process, showing a rhythmic pattern, with bursts of crying and pauses to take a breath (Zeskind, Parker-Price, & Barr, 1993). Over the course of a long episode of crying, punctuated by these bursts and pauses, the acoustic properties of the cry changes, as infants become more or less aroused (Green, Gustafson, & McGhie, 1998). Experimentally manipulated increases in the length of infant's bursts of crying (and comparable reduction of the pauses in between cries) makes adults perceive the cry as more annoying but also more important and informative (Zeskind, Klein, & Marshall, 1992). These experimental studies demonstrate that the properties of human infants' cries affect many adult participants, not just experienced parents, although parents and other adults may be sensitive to different dimensions of infants' cries (Irwin, 2003).

Individual differences in the quality of infants' cries

No two infants are exactly alike, and despite the common features of crying, different infants cry in different ways, and thus send different signals to their caregivers. Indeed, the particular features of an infant's cry is one of the first signs of individuality. By one month after childbirth, when they listen to audiotapes of different infants' cries, parents can recognise their own infants (Green & Gustafson, 1983). A number of dimensions contribute to variability in infants' crying patterns, which together provide a distinctive 'cry signature' for an individual infant (Gustafson, Sanborn, Lin, & Green, 2017).

Some investigators have claimed that infants growing up in different language environments cry in different ways; for example, acoustic differences have been reported for the cries of newborn infants who were being cared for by French-speakers vs. German-speakers (Mampe, Friederici, Christophe, & Wermke, 2009). However, in a comparison of infants who were growing up in English-speaking or Mandarin Chinese-speaking language environments, group differences were no longer significant when the individual newborns' 'cry signatures' were taken into account (Gustafson et al., 2017).

Colic

Some infants cry much more than others, which poses challenges for their caregivers. Persistent, paroxysmal crying for more than three hours a day, three or more days a week, is characterised as 'infant colic,' which is often attributed to gastrointestinal distress. The causes of colic are still not completely known, although it is now thought to originate in dysregulation of the 'microbiota-gut-brain axis' (Partty & Kalliomaki, 2017, p. 529). A recent randomised control trial, in which the mode of feeding the infants (by breast or bottle) was taken into account, revealed that colic was associated with inflammation of the gut (Rhoads, Collins, Fatheree, Hashmi, Taylor, et al., 2018).

The sustained bouts of crying in 'colicky' infants are perceived as more intense and urgent, and do not easily abate in response to care. A recent systematic review of studies of infants' crying and the prevalence of colic concluded that cases diagnosed with colic were at the extreme end of the distribution of time spent crying (Wolke et al., 2017). However, the unpredictability and unsoothability of infants' cries may be more indicative of colic than the length of crying per se (St James Roberts, Conroy, & Wilsher, 1996).

There is disagreement about whether infants diagnosed with colic cry in distinct ways. Some argue that the crying associated with colic does not have distinctive acoustic features, being distinct in its resistance to soothing rather than in pitch or duration of the cries (St James Roberts, 1999). Other work suggests that colicky infants' crying after an evening feed shows higher pitch and longer bursts of crying (Zeskind & Barr, 1997).

Developmental and medical problems

Infants who have experienced medical complications and illness may take longer to cry and when they do cry, may produce very high-pitched cries (Shinya, Kawai, Niwa, & Myowa-Yamakoshi, 2014). Preterm infants' cries differ from those emitted by full-term babies (Goberman & Robb, 1999). A recent computerised analysis of acoustic features of the cries of preterm infants identified ten key parameters that distinguished the preterm group from other infants, including but extending beyond the fundamental frequency of the cry (Orlandi, Garcia, Bandini, Donzelli, & Manfredi, 2016). The features of infants' crying predict later developmental outcomes for infants who are born prematurely (Lester, 1987), which suggests that the acoustic features of crying may provide a measure of the integrating of the developing nervous systems of preterm infants (e.g., Grauel, Hock, & Rothganger, 1990).

There are some indications that infants who will later show atypical neurodevelopment may cry in ways that differ from typically developing infants. Longitudinal studies have shown that, as infants get older, their cries become less high-pitched; analysis of home videos suggests that this decline in high-pitched crying is not evident in infants who go on to be diagnosed with autism, whose cries are perceived as more distressing (Esposito & Venuti, 2010; Esposito, Nakazawa, Venuti, & Bornstein, 2012). Acoustic analyses have identified some differences in the cry signatures of infants who are at risk for autism. For example, in a study of the younger siblings of children already diagnosed with autism, the infants with autistic siblings showed higher-pitched cries in response to pain than those shown by infants in the comparison group (Sheinkopf, Iverson, Rinaldi, & Lester, 2012).

It is not just the pitch or duration of crying but also infants' readiness to cry that may indicate medical problems. Infants who take a long time to cry may show other biological problems, such as poor startle reflexes, that suggest their nervous systems are compromised (Zeskind, Marshall, & Goff, 1996).

Prenatal experiences

Individual differences in the extent and pattern of crying in infancy may be influenced by the infants' experiences prior to birth. For example, mothers' anxiety and depression prior to birth predict infants' distress in response to novel situations after birth (Davis et al., 2004). Mothers' anxious and depressed feelings during pregnancy are linked to her production of the stress hormone cortisol, which can cross the placenta and influence her child's own stress response (Talge, Neal, & Glover, 2007). Infants whose mothers produced more cortisol during the pregnancy were more likely to cry during the first five months after birth (de Weerth, van Hees, & Buitelaar, 2003).

The substances mothers use during pregnancy may also have an impact on their infants' crying. Infants' crying is influenced by the mothers' use of alcohol (Zeskind et al., 1996) and cocaine (Beeghly, Frank, Rose-Jacobs, Cabral, & Tronick, 2003). Infants exposed to alcohol and cocaine in pregnancy may cry *less* than other infants, i.e., are *less* able to signal their distress to adult caregivers. In contrast, infants exposed to tobacco in utero are reported to show excessive levels of crying (Reijneveld, Lanting, Crone, & van Wouwe, 2005).

Irritable temperament

The concept of 'colic' usually refers to a tendency that infants are expected to grow out of; however, some infants show a tendency to become distressed in response to new situations, or in response to frustration, that appears to consolidate into a general way of dealing with the world. Infants who become distressed easily were initially described as showing 'difficult temperament' (Thomas et al., 1970; Bates & Bayles, 1984) or 'irritability' (Lemery, Essex, & Smider, 2002), a tendency that endures over time from infancy to childhood (e.g., Gartstein & Rothbart, 2003). Prenatal factors, such as exposure to the hormone cortisol, influence infants' irritability, although the nature of the effect may depend on the infant's gender (Braithwaite et al., 2017).

Infants with irritable temperament are thought to be at risk for later emotional and behavioural problems, although the evidence for this is mixed; irritability in early childhood, as opposed to infancy, is a more robust predictor of later problems (Leibenluft & Stoddard, 2013). Even during the period of infancy itself, such irritable infants pose particular challenges for their parents.

Parents' responses to infants' crying

In general, infants' behaviour has strong effects on their parents and other caregivers; in the same way that parents influence their children, so infants' behaviours help teach their parents how to care for them properly (Rheingold, 1969). Infants' cries affect parents' behaviour and also the reactions of their brains (e.g., Feldman, 2015). Experimental studies have demonstrated that the readiness with which adults try to provide care for a crying infant depends on the acoustic features of the cry, but also on contextual information, such as whether the infant is in need of a nap (Wood & Gustafson, 2001); adults' decisions to offer care also depend on the duration of the cry (Zeifman, 2004).

Do infants try deliberately to manipulate their caregivers' responses?

When does crying become an intentional signal, a means by which infants can deliberately communicate with their parents and other caregivers? Longitudinal studies suggest that, over the course of the first year of life, infants' reflexive crying transforms into more intentional vocalisations. For example, one study of four infants over the course of the first year showed that the infants' 'hunger cries' increased in pitch as the infants grew older, which may be evidence for older infants' modulating their signals to get a response from caregivers.

Some parents believe that infants cry intentionally, in order to seek attention from their parents. In the 1970s, this issue was a subject of vigorous debate between a learning theorist, Jacob Gewirtz, who argued that crying was a learned response, reinforced by parents' attentive responses, and an ethological attachment theorist, Mary Ainsworth, who argued that sensitive responsiveness to infants' crying actually led to less distress as infants grew older (Bell & Ainsworth, 1972; Gewirtz & Boyd, 1977). The debate centres on whether it is best for parents to ignore their infants' cries, so as not to reward the baby for crying for attention. In a classic longitudinal study of 26 infants, observed repeatedly over the first year of life, Bell and Ainsworth measured the extent to which mothers ignored or responded to their infants' cries and other milder forms of expressing distress, by fussing or whingeing. They found that the more mothers ignored their infants' cries in early infancy, the more infants were likely to cry later on. In other words, if parents ignored crying, its frequency went up, not down. More recent research in a large sample of infants confirmed and extended Ainsworth's claims, showing that parents' sensitivity when their infants were distressed appeared to reduce the infants' risk for developing behavioural problems (Leerkes, Blankson, & O'Brien, 2009). Furthermore, in that sample, even when infants had more irritable temperament, parents' sensitive responses to their distress led to fewer instances of distressed emotion in early childhood.

The implications of this line of research is that parents who fail to respond to infants' distress because they do not want to reward crying may actually be faced with more, not less crying in the future. It seems best for parents to treat crying as a communicative signal, not a simple operant behaviour that can easily be extinguished.

Smiling and laughing

Infants' crying is without doubt an important signal to their caregivers, but their abilities to express positive emotion are equally important. In contrast to crying, which may upset or annoy parents, as they try to figure out what the infants want or need, infants' smiling and laughter are gratifying to their parents and to other people as well, particularly in mid-infancy when it becomes clear that smiling is a social signal that acknowledges the infants' own pleasure when interacting with other people.

Smiling

The development of the ability to smile

The physical ability to smile is present in the full-term neonate, months before smiling can be safely interpreted as an intentional social signal. Emotion researchers who study the musculature of the human face have distinguished two main types of smiles: simple smiles with the lips only versus facial expressions known as Duchenne smiling, which involve the muscles of the cheeks and eyes as well as the lips (Figure 2.1). By 10 months of age, the two types of smiles are associated with different patterns of brain activity (Fox & Davidson, 1988). The extent to which infants produce each type of smile is also associated with cultural factors (e.g., Camras et al., 1998).

Both types of smiles can be seen in newborns, when they are asleep as well as awake; smiling is especially likely to occur during active sleep with rapid eye movements (Dondi et al., 2007). It is generally agreed that newborn infants' smiles reflect inborn tendencies, not imitation of adults' facial expressions; even congenitally blind infants produce such smiles (e.g., Freedman, 1964; Troster & Brambring, 1992). However, infants do smile in response to social input, even shortly after birth. For example, in a study of newborn infants' responses to contingent and non-contingent stimulation (Cecchini et al., 2013), adults gave the infants their fingers to hold and responded contingently to the infants' own hand movements,

FIGURE 2.1 A toddler's wide-eyed, smiling face

by gently squeezing back. In other conditions, adults did not respond to the infants' movements or did not engage in sustained contact with them. The infants were likely to smile and less likely to cry when the adults responded contingently over a period of time.

Smiling in the context of social interaction

The social nature of infants' smiling

Over the first months of life, the early reflexive smiling of infants becomes more social and intentional and more responsive to their social environments. Young infants' smiles are responsive to rewards and reinforcement schedules (Brackbill, 1958); for example, in one study, infants smiled more when they were rewarded by being picked up (Brossard & Decarie, 1968). The frequency of infants' smiling increases slightly over the first 2 months of life, while other forms of positive social behaviour become more common (Murray et al., 2016).

Infants are interested in other people's smiles. By 4 months of age, infants can detect differences in adults' expressions of positive and negative emotion (Montague & Walker-Andrews, 2001). In an experiment conducted in their own homes, infants looked longer at photographs in which people smiled broadly than they did at photographs with neutral facial expressions or slight smiles (Kuchuk, Vibbert, & Bornstein, 1986). In that study, infants' preferences for broad smiles were associated with their own experiences of social interaction, which in turn suggests that smiling is an important social signal for both infants and their parents. Subsequent research suggests that infants' preference for smiling over other types of facial expression is particularly marked when they are looking at female faces, especially when they have the experience of being most often cared for by a woman (Bayet et al., 2015).

The infant's ability to smile is an important component of social interactions between infant and caregiver, when each partner's behaviour is directly related to the other's, producing a sequence of interaction that is like a nonverbal dialogue. Such *behavioural contingencies* between mother and infant can be discerned shortly after birth, when the newborn infant is being fed (e.g., Kaye & Wells, 1980), but the study of somewhat older infants' smiling in response to parents' smiles (and vice versa) reveals the development of a capacity to share positive emotions with other people. A comparison of mothers and 2- to 3-month-old infants in Germany with those in Cameroon showed that this type of reciprocal smiling between mother and infant is present across cultures (Wormann, Holodynski, Kartner, & Keller, 2012).

When analysing such contingent interactions between infants and parents, researchers calculate *conditional probabilities*, i.e., the chance that an infant will smile, given that the parent has just smiled, or vice versa. In the course of such interactions, which emerge by 8 weeks of age (Symons & Moran, 1994), infants learn to respond to their parents' smiles and also become aware when the parents have responded to their own smiles. Such structured, contingent interactions that parents engage in with their infants often take on the feel of a playful game, generating the positive affect that produces smiles (e.g., Watson, 1972). Exchanges of smiles are underpinned by consistency in both parents' and infants' facial expressions, as well as their influence on each other (Beebe et al., 2016).

However, interaction between parents and infants is not always perfectly synchronised. If the parent's response does not occur immediately (e.g., within a few seconds of the infant's signal), then the infant may not detect any connection between the two events. The general level of contingency in infants' interactions with their parents influences their reactions to new people. In one study, infants smiled more often at their mothers than at unfamiliar people, but they were most likely to respond positively to new people whose responsiveness was at about the same level as their mothers' contingent responding (Bigelow, 1998). These findings suggest that infants' ability to use smiling as a general form of communication with other people is shaped by their particular social experiences.

Recognising other people's smiles

By the middle of the first year of life, infants can tell the difference between smiles and other types of facial expression. For example, in a study of 7-month-olds (Kestenbaum & Nelson, 1990), the infants demonstrated the ability to distinguish smiling faces from ones that were showing anger or a neutral expression. However, they were less able to do so when the faces were shown to them upside-down. Infants who were able to recognise smiling faces in photographs were also likely to show signs of approach, gesturing and moving toward the pictures; infants who were shown angry faces were rather more likely to shrink away from those photographs (Serrano, Iglesias, & Loeches, 1995). By 5 months of age, infants taking part in a habituation study showed sensitivity to differences in the intensity of smiles across photographs of the same person, while also showing discrimination of familiar and novel faces and of smiles versus fearful expressions (Bornstein & Arterberry, 2003).

When do infants' smiles become intentional forms of communication?

Although it is possible to detect contingency in smiling in the course of early parent-infant interaction, mothers may smile, even when their infants have not just smiled, whereas infants may not smile, just because their mothers have smiled at them (Symons & Moran, 1994). The intentionality of infants' communications is easier to detect a few months later, when they can crawl or walk some distance away from the people who are looking after them and when their interactions with parents often involve a topic beyond gazing at each other's faces (Bakeman & Adamson, 1986). For example, when infants are enjoying playing with a toy at some distance from their parents, they often begin to smile to themselves, then turn their faces toward their parents to share their pleasure. Such *anticipatory smiling* to parents and to other people is related to the infants' understanding of cause and effect (Jones & Hong, 2001; Venezia, Messinger, Thorp, & Mundy, 2004), which suggests that, by this age, infants have become aware that their smiles will produce certain effects on others. Infants smile most often when they are in the presence of attentive people, both their parents and other individuals (Jones, Collins, & Hong, 1991).

Parents' responsiveness to their infants' smiles

As we have seen, parents may differ in the extent to which they respond to their infants' smiles (Bigelow, 1998). Findings from a brain imaging study suggested that mothers perceive their own infants' smiling (but not sad) faces as rewarding; presentation of photographs of happy infants was associated with activation of dopaminergic brain regions associated with processing of rewards (Strathearn, Li, Fonagy, & Montague, 2008). In an experimental study (Mizugaki, Maehara, Okanoya, & Myowa-Yamakoshi, 2015), first-time mothers watched videos of their own infants, which had been recorded one week earlier. All mothers watched a clip of their infants crying. In one condition, the next clip showed the infant smiling and in the other, the clip showed the infant's calm, neutral face; the mothers' stressful reactions (as measured by their skin conductance) were recorded in response to the crying segments and in each follow-up condition. The mothers showed elevated skin conductance in response to the videos of their infants crying, and that reduced more when they next saw their infants smiling, as opposed to showing neutral affect.

There is individual variability in parents' responsiveness to infants' smiling, linked to characteristics of both infants and parents. For example, one study indicated that parents with a history of child maltreatment showed a physiological stress response in reaction to infants' crying but also in response to infants' smiles (Frodi & Lamb, 1980). However, a meta-analysis of such studies suggested that links between maltreatment and parents' stress responses were not so striking in subsequent research (Reijman et al., 2016).

Laughing

Infants' ability to laugh appears to emerge somewhat later than their ability to smile, although some vocalisations that sound like laughs have been reported in the second month of life (Rothbart, 1973). By 4 months of age, however, infants clearly engage in laughter, and their companions try to do things that make babies laugh. In such situations, it is possible that the infant's laughter is actually evoked by the parent's own laughing while trying to be silly. In a short-term longitudinal study of infants observed at 5, 6 and 7 months of age, parents were asked to alternate laughing or expressing neutral emotion while clowning around with their infants (Mireault et al., 2015). The parents were asked to blow 'raspberries' toward their infants; observers checked that the parents really did not laugh in the neutral condition. The infants' tendencies to laugh increased with age, and as they grew older, they were more likely to laugh if their parents were also laughing.

The relationship between laughter and arousal

Just as there are different types of smiles, so there are different types of laughs, and not all of them express positive emotion. People sometimes laugh when they are faced with things they do not comprehend or in social situations where they are not necessarily comfortable. The cognitive theorist Berlyne (1960) discussed laughter and humour more generally in relation to the state of psychological arousal, and noted that the relationship between laugher and arousal is evident in infancy:

> During the first year of life, inexhaustible giggling and chuckling can be occasioned by stimuli that are slightly and briefly startling or frightening: tossing the infant into the air and catching him, making sudden noises or movements, and, above all, the peekaboo game or hiding and reappearing. Later comes an appreciation of incongruity, e.g., the sight of an adult with something strange on his head.
>
> *(Berlyne, 1960, p. 258)*

Further evidence on the things that make babies laugh was provided by two cross-sectional and one longitudinal study of infants in the first year of life (Sroufe & Wunsch, 1972). Experimenters enacted 30 different behaviours, categorised as social, visual, tactile and auditory, and the infants' responses were recorded. Older infants laughed more frequently and laughed at different things. The youngest infants were most likely to laugh when experimenters kissed their stomachs or proclaimed 'I'm going to get you!' These behaviours continued to amuse 12-month-olds, who also laughed when the experimenters covered their faces or stuck out their own tongues (Sroufe & Wunsch, 1972). By 6 months of age, infants' laughter in response to games like peek-a-boo is bound up with their cognitive expectations; deviation from prior expectations may not necessarily lead to laughter at this age (Parrott & Gleitman, 1989).

When infants are aroused, it is very easy for laughter to turn into tears. Adults' attempts to amuse infants might provoke laughter or elicit crying. The temperament theorist Mary Rothbart (1973) set out a model that describes the likelihood that potentially arousing stimuli – those that are intense, sudden, or in some way discrepant from the infant's expectations – are interpreted as dangerous or harmless and, if harmless, amusing. The infant would need to be aroused sufficiently for laughter as opposed to mere smiling to occur, but not so aroused to cry or shrink back in fear. Support for Rothbart's model was found in a condition that compared potentially laugh-provoking behaviours, delivered by parents or unfamiliar people, when infants were more or less aroused; at high levels of arousal, infants were more likely to laugh if the behaviours were displayed by their parents, not by people they had not met before (Macdonald & Silverman, 1978). There appears to be a fine balance between being aroused enough to find things funny and being so aroused that it is impossible to laugh.

Laughter, temperament and physiology

The extent to which infants express positive emotion, i.e., laugh and smile, has been described as a dimension of individual temperament, reported reliably by parents and other informants (e.g., Gartstein & Rothbart, 2003). Infants' temperamental smiling and laughter is related to more adaptive processing of novel experiences, as measured by brain evoked potential responses to pictures of faces and expression of the stress hormone cortisol (Gunnar & Nelson, 1994).

Laughter as an element of infants' social interactions

Just as the infant's ability to smile contributes to interactions with parents and other people, so laughter on the part of infants and their parents plays a role in early interactions. Parents may deliberately tease infants to elicit laughter; there is some evidence that infants may vary their behaviour to obtain laughter from their parents (Reddy, 2001).

In an intensive longitudinal study of infants observed weekly throughout the first year of life and biweekly thereafter, infants laughed more often and for longer periods of time as they grew older, and they became less likely to laugh on their own and more likely to laugh while interacting with their mothers (Nwokah, Hsu, Dobrowolska, & Fogel, 1994). In that study, infants' laughter often triggered mothers' laughter, leading to periods of simultaneous laughter. Infants' laughter in response to peek-a-boo is associated with mothers' own expression of positive emotion during the game (Dawson et al., 1992). Longitudinal observations reveal that as infants grow older, mothers change the nature of their games to incorporate actions or events that might promote infants' amusement (Mireault et al., 2012).

Infants also laugh when interacting with less familiar people, particularly in the context of social games involving mutual engagement, repetition and alternation of turns. For example, in one study where a social game had been established and the experimenter disrupted the game by failing to take a turn, the infants stopped laughing and instead behaved in ways that might induce the experimenter to continue with the game (Ross & Lollis, 1987).

Smiling and laughing in children with developmental disorders

Children who are developmentally delayed in general may be slower to develop the abilities to smile and laugh, compared to typically developing children (Kopp, Baker, & Brown, 1992). For example, a study of young children with Down syndrome revealed that the developmental sequence with which they found things funny was the same as that shown by typically developing children, but delayed by several months (Cicchetti & Sroufe, 1976). In samples of children who are experiencing some developmental delay, the age at which children develop the ability to laugh is a good predictor of their subsequent functioning. For example, infants with Down syndrome who first began to laugh before the age of 10 months showed higher levels of symbolic play as toddlers (Motti, Cicchetti, & Sroufe, 1983).

Recent studies designed to look at early predictors of Autism Spectrum Disorder (ASD) often compare the younger siblings of children with diagnosed ASD and comparison children; in longitudinal designs, it is also possible to compare the younger siblings of children with ASD who go on to experience the disorder with those younger siblings who do not go on to meet criteria for the disorder. In one such study (Filliter et al., 2015), those infant siblings who went on to develop ASD had shown a lower rate of smiling at 12 months of age than infants in the other groups. In a similar study, in which infants' laughter was measured within a broader category of non-speech sounds, infant siblings at risk for ASD were *more* likely to produce such vocalisations, but that category included sounds of distress as well as laughter (Paul, Fuerst, Ramsay, Chawarska, & Klin, 2011).

Summary

Infants' abilities to signal both negative and positive emotions, by crying versus smiling and laughing, develop over the first half of the first year of life and are subsequently refined in interactions with their caregivers. Infants' expressions of emotion are underpinned by biological and cognitive processes. Early crying, smiling and laughing represent important dimensions of individuality, contributing to individual temperament and, eventually, personality. In the next chapters, we move beyond early infancy and focus on developmental change and individual continuity in the experience, expression and understanding of different types of positive and negative emotion.

3

SURPRISE AND DISGUST

Knowledge, expectations and emotion

The studies of infants' distress and delight show how infants respond to their immediate circumstances with positive, negative or neutral affect. However, infants' emotional reactions to situations and events soon come to reflect what they have already learned about the world. In infancy, children acquire an understanding of their familiar environments and respond in different ways to unfamiliar events – sometimes with interest, other times with apprehension. As they interact with both the social and the non-social world, infants begin to have expectations of what things should be like (e.g., Stahl & Feigenson, 2015), and the violation of those expectations may provoke two distinct types of emotion: *surprise* and *disgust*.

Surprise and disgust are each considered to be a primary emotion, accompanied by very distinct patterns of facial expression. It is important to note, however, that both of these emotions are not simply responses to immediate circumstances but rather are dependent on the capacity for memory, the growth of knowledge and the infants' abilities to compare their current experience with their expectations. As infants come to know more about the worlds they inhabit, their expectations will change. Nonetheless, even as children grow older, they are still capable of being surprised, and some experiences will provoke disgust.

Surprise

As we have seen in Chapter 1, surprise is an emotion that indicates high arousal, as noted in the circumplex model of different emotions presented by Widen and Russell (2008). Thus, infants experience surprise at the physiological level, as well as expressing it in their faces and voices.

Facial expressions of surprise in infancy

Investigators who study facial expressions have pointed to some key indicators of surprise in adults' and children's faces: raised eyebrows, wide eyes and sometimes an open mouth (see Figure 3.1). These movements of the face are apparent in early infancy and identified reliably by adult observers (Oster, Hegley, & Nagel, 1992). They are also observed in response to situations designed to violate expectations and thus induce surprise, e.g., experimental procedures in a study of infants that led to a toy being switched or vanished entirely (Hiatt, Campos, & Emde, 1979).

However, experiments designed to create a surprise do not always actually elicit such facial expressions (e.g., Scherer, Zentner, & Stern, 2004). Rather, when their expectations are violated, infants may simply continue to watch what is going on or freeze in response to the unexpected event (Scherer et al., 2004). Furthermore, there may be cultural variation in the individual components of the surprised expression, such as raising the eyebrows (Camras et al., 1998). Even if infants' facial expressions do not express surprise in the stereotypical way, however, electroencephalogram (EEG)

FIGURE 3.1 Some components of the facial expression of surprise

recordings reveal that the infants' brains are reacting to unexpected events (Kouider et al., 2015).

Recognising other people's expressions of surprise

Children only gradually acquire the ability to recognise surprise. For example, a study of children's discrimination of different facial expressions of emotion (Gao & Maurer, 2010) asked the participants to sort pictures of faces showing different emotions by placing the pictures into different houses (each house being associated with a different primary emotion). The findings from that experiment showed that intense surprise was more easily discriminated from other types of emotion than were mild expressions of surprise (see Figure 3.2 for a comparison of surprised faces at different levels of intensity). However, that experiment also showed that in general, 5-year-old children were less likely than older children and adults to discriminate surprise, even at high intensity levels.

The ability to recognise expressions of surprise appears to develop gradually between early childhood and adulthood (Herba & Phillips, 2004; Widen, 2013). Younger children are more likely than older children to confuse expressions of surprise and fear (Rodger, Vizioli, Ouyang, & Caldara, 2015).

Children can detect emotion in people's voices as well as their facial expressions. As they grow older, children become better able to tell when other people are surprised, based on the nonverbal sounds they make and the inflections in their speech (Sauter, Panattoni, & Happe, 2013).

Children's understanding of the context of surprising events

Children's understanding of the contexts in which people might become surprised has been explored through the use of narratives about story characters and unexpected events. For example, in one study, 3-year-old children were told a story about a child who went to get a toothbrush and instead found an elephant in the bathroom (Wellman & Banerjee, 1991). This work suggests that children's

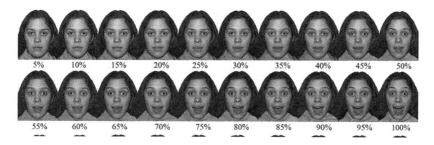

FIGURE 3.2 Varying intensity of surprise in experiment on identification of emotion

Source: Gao & Maurer (2010)

understanding of the situations that surprise other people depends on the children's understanding of people's beliefs and therefore the violation of prior expectations. Put the other way around, children's understanding of surprise relates to their understanding that people can have false beliefs, and thereby provides a measure of their theory of mind skills. This has led to the development of measures of children's understanding of false belief that present stories about nice versus nasty surprises (e.g., Hughes et al., 2005).

Disgust

Surprise has traditionally been seen as a neutral or possibly positive emotion (e.g., Hiatt et al., 1979). In contrast, disgust has long been recognised as a fundamental negative emotion. Allport (1924) described disgust as one of the basic emotions characterised by unpleasant feelings, and noted that it was similar to pain in being a 'relatively simple condition' (p. 86), perhaps because of the crucial role of disgust as well as pain in preventing injury and death. The survival advantages associated with feelings of disgust are seen in relation to its role in encouraging people to avoid contaminated food (Rozin, Fallon, & Augustoni-Ziskind, 1985) and to stay away from individuals with contagious illness (Curtis, De Barra, & Aunger, 2011). Many of the stimuli that most commonly elicit feelings of disgust are also likely to transmit disease (Oaten, Stevenson, & Case, 2009).

Early signs of disgust

In the emotion differentiation theory proposed by Bridges (1932), disgust was thought to emerge gradually over the first six months of life, differentiating from general distress along with fear and anger. In contrast, the differential emotions theorists have claimed that distinct signs of disgust can be identified in quite young infants (e.g., Ekman, 1993; Izard, 1994).

In adults, disgust is considered to be a basic emotion that is expressed via distinct muscle movements. The prototypical 'disgust face' in adults is characterised by wrinkling of the nose and raising of the upper lip, which further wrinkles the nose (Ekman & Friesen, 1978; see Figure 3.3). Perhaps because of the obvious difference in the length of adult and infant noses, the expression of disgust appears to be somewhat harder to identify in young infants.

Within the perspective of differential emotions theory, Izard and colleagues (1980) undertook a systematic investigation of observers' detection of 1- to 9-month-old infants' expressions of emotions, including disgust; they used different techniques to analyse video records of the infants in a number of pleasant and unpleasant situations. Initially, disgust was recorded less accurately than some other emotions. However, in that study, training observers in the recognition of particular muscle movements in the face improved accuracy.

FIGURE 3.3   Signs of disgust in an adult's face

Subsequently, Izard and colleagues conducted a longitudinal study of the facial expressions shown by infants between 2.5 and 9 months of age, in relation to two different contexts for mother-infant interaction (summarised in Izard, 1994); infants showed distinct facial expressions of anger and sadness in that sample from an early age and stability in the way they expressed those emotions over time. Discrete expressions of disgust were also observed but did not occur often enough to permit statistical analysis.

In the literature on infants' expressions of emotion, different researchers have used different observational coding systems, such as the Maximally Discriminative Facial Movement Coding System (MAX; Izard, 1983) and the Facial Action Coding System (FACS; Ekman & Friesen, 1978). There appears to be some lack of concordance in identifying expressions of disgust, depending on which system is being used and whether an adult or infant version is being deployed (Camras & Shutter, 2010). For emotions that occur less often, such as disgust, this discrepancy in coding definitions could lead to inconsistent results across studies.

One approach to the study of disgust has been to provide infants with different tastes and observe how they react. One such study provided evidence for some expressions of disgust soon after birth. Newborn infants were presented with water, either plain, sweetened with sucrose or made sour with citric acid (Fox & Davidson, 1986). The newborns made expressions of disgust (as coded using the MAX system) in response to both plain water and the sour taste of the citric acid. Moreover,

EEG analysis showed that the different tastes evoked different patterns of brain response. Infants' negative reactions to bitter tastes increase in the months after the newborn period (Kajiurwa, Cowart, & Beauchamp, 1992).

More recent work on infants' expressions of disgust has suggested that, even when observers are not just making subjective judgements but actually coding muscle movements, it may be difficult to apply adult criteria for disgust to infant faces. Even adult observers may interpret elements of the 'disgust face' shown by infants as general, undifferentiated distress or as a blend of different negative emotions (Oster et al., 1992).

As children grow older, they communicate their experiences of disgust with words and expressive vocal sounds, such as 'Eugh!' or 'Yuck!', as well as with their faces. Such vocal signs of disgust may often be made in response to disliked food. For example, in a study of video records of family mealtimes, such expressions of disgust occurred at least once an hour in observations of children between 1 and 4 years of age (Wiggins, 2013).

Children's recognition of other people's expressions of disgust

In evolutionary accounts of emotional development, the ability to recognise and react to other people's expressions of disgust is thought to be critical for children's avoidance of sources of contagion and contamination in the environment (Izard, 1994). This process would constitute a form of social referencing, enabling children to avoid touching or eating substances that might make them ill. This implies that children might be able to recognise the standard 'disgust face' at early ages. However, despite the argument for the evolutionary advantages of sensitivity to other people's expressions of disgust, children are less likely to be able to label the 'disgust face' than other expressions of emotion.

Indeed, in early childhood, many children confuse disgust with other emotions, especially anger (Gagnon, Gosselin, Hudon-ven der Buhs, Larocque, & Milliard, 2010). Five- to six-year-old children perform better on matching tasks than labelling tasks (Vicari, Reilly, Pasqualetti, Vizzotto, & Caltagirone, 2000). However, when children are provided with a narrative that puts the facial expression of disgust into context, they are more likely to recognise disgust (e.g., Nelson, Hudspeth, & Russell, 2013).

Bridges' (1932) differentiation theory proposed that the specific emotion of disgust emerges from the broader feeling of distress (see Figure 1.1). Given that proposal, it is interesting that children's recognition of other people's facial expressions follows a similar pathway, from recognising distress to recognising more specific negative emotions. The available cross-cultural evidence suggests that younger children generally perceive the disgust face as distressed or unhappy, but they do not necessarily recognise the pure emotion of disgust separately from the broader category of negative emotion (Widen & Russell, 2013). However, perceiving the disgust face as negative may still induce even young children to avoid whatever has upset another person (Moses, Baldwin, Rosicky, & Tidball, 2001).

Some children and teenagers have particular problems in recognising disgust in others. For example, teenagers with longstanding behavioural problems – those that began earlier in childhood – show difficulties in recognising expressions of disgust as well as fear, anger and happiness (Fairchild, van Goozen, Calder, Stollery, & Goodyer, 2009).

Moral disgust

Adults sometimes use the word 'disgusting' to refer to moral transgressions as well as physical stimuli. Although this use of the word may simply be metaphorical, people sometimes respond to hypothetical moral transgressions with the facial expression of disgust (Cannon, Schnall, & White, 2011). Some investigators have also attempted to show that physically disgusting stimuli and moral transgressions evoke similar patterns of brain activity; the evidence for this claim is mixed (see review by Chapman & Anderson, 2013).

Five- to nine-year-old children who were asked whether certain activities could be considered to be disgusting were most likely to give that label to physically disgusting things; they were also somewhat likely to refer to some activities that violated moral rules as disgusting, but they did so significantly less often (Danovitch & Bloom, 2009). The same pattern of findings was observed in a subsequent experiment when the word 'disgusting' was not mentioned, but children were asked to point to pictures of different facial expressions; they were more likely to point to a picture of the 'disgust face' when referring to physically rather than morally unpleasant activities, although some children did associate moral transgressions with the facial expression of disgust.

Obsessive-Compulsive Disorder and the experience of disgust

Some individuals are particularly likely to experience disgust, a phenomenon known as *disgust sensitivity*, which is often a feature of Obsessive-Compulsive Disorder (OCD). Symptoms experienced by children with OCD often focus on issues of dirt, contamination and disease (Swedo, Rappoport, Leonard, Lenane, & Cheslow, 1989). Children who show heightened disgust sensitivity are more likely to experience symptoms of anxiety and phobias, as well as symptoms of OCD (Muris, van der Heiden, & Rassin, 2008). In a clinical sample of adolescent patients, disgust sensitivity was associated with more severe symptoms of OCD (Olatunji, Ebusutani, Kim, Riemann, & Jacobi, 2017). Cognitive behaviour therapy has been found to reduce disgust sensitivity as well as core symptoms of disorder in children who are being treated for OCD and other anxiety disorders (Taboas, Ojserkis, & McKay, 2015).

These findings regarding the relationship between heightened sensitivity to disgust and symptoms of OCD and other anxiety disorders suggest that fear and disgust may intertwine to produce particular phobias and the obsessions and compulsions characteristic of OCD. In the next chapter, we will examine what is known about the development of fear and its relation to anxiety disorders.

4

FEAR AND ANXIETY

When do children first feel fear? 'Fear' is defined in the *Oxford English Dictionary* as 'the emotion of pain or uneasiness caused by the sense of impending danger, or by the prospect of some possible evil' (p. 973). In other words, fear has a cognitive component: To feel fear, infants must sense or know that something unpleasant is about to happen. They must understand the physical properties of the world well enough to know when they are in possible danger.

Fear is a primary emotion that is experienced in the moment, elicited by signs of danger in the world. In contrast, anxiety requires the cognitive ability to imagine a dangerous future – to anticipate what dangers might be encountered in particular places, with particular people, at particular times. With increasing age, children are more likely to imagine future possibilities and so begin to express worries as well as fears. For some children, this tendency to worry about things that might happen consolidates into clinically significant anxiety disorders.

The first signs of fear in infancy

Studies of infants' depth perception

Defensive reactions to looming stimuli

Much of what we know about the very early development of fear comes from vision scientists' studies of infants' depth perception, in particular studies of very young infants' responses to looming objects and studies of older infants' reactions to a perceived drop-off in the surface they are crawling on. It is clear that infants soon become sensitive to one form of danger. In a set of experiments on looming, investigators presented young infants with displays of dots that were manipulated to look as though they are moving toward or away from the infants. One- to two-month-old infants tracked the pattern of the dots with their eyes but did not seem to perceive an impending collision. In contrast, 4-month-old infants show a defensive reaction, blinking when the dots appear to be about to hit them in the face (Yonas et al., 1977). By 6 to 7 months of age, infants who are presented with looming stimuli blink in a pattern that shows they are sensitive not only to the visual angle of the stimulus but also to the likely time of collision (Kayed & van der Meer, 2000). Is this one of the first signs of fear? Similar studies of adults show that participants react more quickly to looming stimuli when the stimuli are threatening, for example, snakes and spiders as opposed to rabbits and butterflies (Vagnoni, Lourenco, & Longo, 2012), which implies that people's reactions to looming stimuli have an emotional component.

EEG studies show that infants' defensive reactions to looming stimuli are associated with brain activity in the visual cortex (van der Weel & van der Meer, 2009), particularly for younger infants (van der Meer, Svantesson, & van der Weel, 2012). Insofar that classic work with rhesus monkeys has shown that the perception of looming stimuli are associated with fear responses, infants' defensive reactions to both visual and auditory stimuli that appear to be approaching them reveal the beginnings of the development of fear.

Reactions to the visual cliff

Early signs of fear are also measured using the 'visual cliff.' The visual cliff is a piece of apparatus originally designed to study the development of depth perception in human infants and members of other species:

> It consists of a board laid across a large sheet of heavy glass which is supported a foot or more above the floor. On one side of the board a sheet of patterned material is placed flush against the undersurface of the glass, giving the glass the appearance as well as the substance of solidity. On the other side a sheet of the same material is laid upon the floor; this side of the board thus becomes the visual cliff.
>
> *(Gibson & Walk, 1960, p. 67; see Figure 4.1)*

Infants' reactions to the deep and shallow sides of the cliff depended on whether or not the infants had already learned to crawl; analyses of infants' heart rate (HR) showed that 5-month-olds showed HR deceleration, a sign of attention and interest, whereas 9-month-olds showed HR acceleration, a sign of emotional arousal (Schwartz, Campos, & Baisel, 1973). These reactions to the visual cliff show that infants express their discomfort in behavioural and physiological ways.

It is clear that the development of locomotion fosters infants' understanding of possible dangers in the world, as measured by the studies that use the visual cliff. But infants' wariness of heights does not appear as soon as they achieve independent movement. Learning to crawl promotes the ability that vision scientists refer to as *visual proprioception*, that is, the ability to perceive yourself moving around the

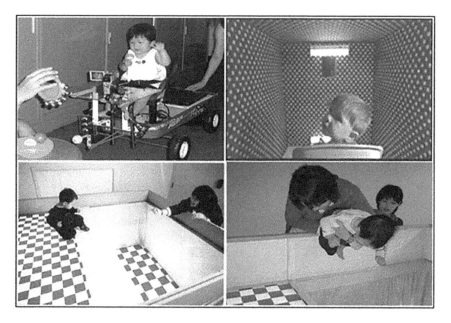

FIGURE 4.1   Experience with self-propelled movement in a 'baby go-cart' and sensitivity to the visual cliff

Source: Dahl et al. (2013)

environment. The experience of self-propelled movement facilitates visual proprioception, even when infants have not yet mastered independent crawling. In one experiment (Dahl et al., 2013), infants who had not yet learned to crawl were randomly assigned either to a condition in which they were trained in the use of what the scientists referred to as a 'baby go-cart' (Figure 4.1) or one in which they did not receive this training. Infants who experienced moving around in the 'baby go-cart' showed stronger reactions to being placed on the deep side of the visual cliff.

Facial expressions of fearful emotion

During the first months of life, infants begin to show facial expressions that convey negative emotion. There is mixed evidence concerning whether these expressions map onto the operational definitions used to identify fearful expressions in adults (cf., Hiatt et al., 1979; Izard, 1994; Oster et al., 1992). In a cross-cultural study of 11-month-old European American, Chinese and Japanese infants, adult raters found it difficult to distinguish infants' expressions of negative emotion in two situations – arm restraint versus being presented with a growling gorilla – which were designed to provoke anger versus fear (Camras et al., 2007). In other respects, the infants responded differently to the two situations, struggling when their arms were restrained and freezing up in the face of the gorilla, but their facial expressions could not be differentiated. These data are compatible with Bridges' (1932) proposal that expressions of anger and fear both emerge from younger infants' generalised distress, and further suggest that different manifestations of these emotions emerge at different points in early development. The mixture of emotional signals seen in infants' faces has been discussed in terms of 'facial babbling,' analogous to the mixture of vocal sounds produced before infants speak with words (Cole & Moore, 2015).

Clearer facial expressions of fear, in response to novel situations, are seen in toddlers by the age of 24 months (Buss & Kiel, 2004). By that point, expressions of sadness, anger and fear are more clearly differentiated. Thus, although we cannot interview infants to determine if they are feeling fearful, there is converging evidence that when placed in highly novel or potentially dangerous situations, they show accelerated heart rate, avoidance of potential danger, vocal distress and facial expressions of emotion, all of which together suggest that they feel afraid.

Fear of new things and new people

Much classic research on infants' fears focussed on the question of whether or not infants were naturally afraid of new experiences. A fear of novelty – particularly new things that are coming right at you – is characteristic of many different species, not just humans; such fear in response to novel experiences is shown when animals startle at a strange sound or run away from strange objects (Bronson, 1968). Similar reactions to novelty are also shown by human infants, when they first begin to distinguish what is new from what is familiar. In this way, the development of fear can be seen as an early intellectual achievement.

However, it is also important to note that infants may be interested in and amused by the new things they encounter, and so they do not always respond with negative emotion. How they do respond depends greatly on the extent to which they have control over their encounter with new people and new things. Infants' positive and negative emotions to novelty were explored in a number of classic experiments that set up challenges that might provoke fear or more positive reactions from infants.

Fear of novel toys and novel environments

A good illustration of the importance of infants' control over a potentially fear-provoking object is provided by a study of 12-month-old infants who encountered a toy monkey who clanged cymbals together in a somewhat menacing way (Gunnar-von Gnechten, 1978). Half of the infants were able to control the monkey's actions by pressing a panel. The other infants did not have any control over the monkey's behaviour. Boys who did not have control over the monkey's actions were especially likely to be frightened by the monkey; in contrast, girls were generally less frightened by the toy, even when they had no control over its movements.

Another classic study of infants' degree of control over novel experiences shows that while infants may protest being separated from their parents, they may choose on their own initiative to leave their parents behind whilst they explore new environments. Infants exploring a novel and complex outdoor environment (a suburban garden in the United States) crept or toddled away from their mothers, the distance travelled by a particular infant being functionally related to its age (Rheingold & Eckerman, 1970). The researchers also found that, when 10-month-old infants were invited to explore an empty room by going through an open doorway, they were eager to do so; however, it was quite different when it was not the infants' own decision and they were placed in the same room, under the same condition, by their mothers who then returned to the first room (Rheingold & Eckerman, 1969). It was only under the latter condition that the infants showed what has traditionally been labelled 'fear of separation' by psychoanalytic theorists (Bowlby, 1969). Thus, what is frightening may become pleasurable if infants can choose to experience the novel environment or play with the novel toy.

Fear of unfamiliar people

The idea that 'fear of separation' is a normal developmental milestone is paralleled by the similar idea that infants become naturally afraid of strangers shortly before their first birthday, the time when they are developing focussed attachment relationships with their caregivers (Bowlby, 1969). Longitudinal observations of the same infants over time suggest that there is an increase in negative responses to unfamiliar people at this time (Sroufe, 1977). However, a critical review of the literature revealed little evidence for a normative 'fear of strangers' in infancy (Rheingold & Eckerman, 1973). Rather, once again, the nature of the infants' reactions when meeting new people depends on the degree of control they have and the behaviour of the people whom they meet.

For example, unfamiliar people who do not try to intrude on infants' personal space, but instead invite infants to come over to play with attractive toys, are not met with fear but with interest (Ross & Goldman, 1977). In that study, infants were more likely to approach active, sociable yet non-intrusive people than quiet, passive strangers who did not actively invite the infants to explore the toys. Thus, control over the situation but also the reassuring expressions of positive affect and interest by the strangers seemed to prevent fearful responses to new people.

As infants grow older, they may be more likely to show signs of fear of the unknown. For example, in one longitudinal study, 143 infants and their mothers were observed four times in the infants' first 1.5 years (Braungart-Rieker, Hill-Soderlund, & Karrass, 2010). At each age, the infant was approached by a stranger. On average, the infants showed a significant increase in fear reactions from 4 to 16 months of age, but the extent of the increase showed considerable individual variability.

FIGURE 4.2 Infants' emotional reactions to an unfamiliar adult and a large teddy bear were observed during a simulated birthday party

Source: Hay et al. (2017)

Many classic studies of infants' reactions to new places and new people are based on relatively small, selected samples of infants. However, a recent study of a nationally representative sample of British infants replicated the procedures advocated by Ross and Goldman (1977), in which an active but non-intrusive stranger invites 12-month-olds to play with toys. In a teddy bears' picnic scenario, a friendly, conversational stranger dressed as a fairy tale character invited the infants to help unpack a picnic basket filled with cups, dishes and play food (Hay et al., 2017).

Only 5% of the 250 infants tested were distressed at the beginning of the teddy bear picnic procedure, when the costumed fairy tale character set out the dishes and play food; an additional 5% showed some wariness. The other infants joined in the interaction with the stranger. These findings from a relatively large, representative community sample corroborated earlier evidence that a friendly, sociable stranger does not usually evoke signs of distress in infants (Ross & Goldman, 1977).

In contrast, when a second stranger arrived for this teddy bear's picnic – the eponymous life-sized teddy bear – 20% of the infants became very distressed, with another 15% showing some degree of wariness, although the majority responded to the bear with neutral or positive affect (Hay et al., 2017). Analysis of the stress hormone cortisol in the infants' saliva showed that the experience of meeting the teddy bear was challenging for the average infant but did not necessarily lead to overt distress (Waters et al., 2013).

Taken together, these findings confirm that infants at this age are not universally afraid of strangers. The levels of fear shown depend on what the strangers look like, what they do and the degree of control infants have over the interaction.

The emergence of specific fears in childhood

What kind of things frighten young children?

As children grow older and develop the ability to imagine things and events that are not immediately present in the environment (Harris, 2000), they become more likely to fear the unknown. Studies undertaken over the last century show some commonality in children's fears over the decades, as well as some responses to their current circumstances. In a classic study of 400 children between 5 and 12 years of age (Jersild, Markey, & Jersild, 1933), the majority of children interviewed reported fears of remote dangers, or imaginary or supernatural beings. Thirty years later, an interview study undertaken in the US revealed that many of children's fears were political in nature, with the children saying they were afraid of war and hostile takeover of their country (Croake, 1969). A subsequent study in which children were interviewed while they were drawing pictures also revealed fears of ghosts and monsters, although older children expressed more realistic fears of being injured or being exposed to physical dangers (Bauer, 1976).

In subsequent decades, primary school-aged children were likely to report being afraid of the dark, being in physical danger, animals and inoculations, but they also expressed fears of illness or punishment (Meltzer et al., 2009; Spence & McCathie, 1993). In a survey of British children in the 1990s, the most common fears were (in order): being hit by a car or lorry; not being able to breathe; bombings and invasions; fire; burglars; falling from a height; serious illness; earthquakes; being sent to the headteacher; death (Ollendick, Yule, & Ollier, 1991).

Fears are related to the growth of children's imaginations, as shown in their expressed fears of imaginary beings like ghosts and monsters. Ways of coping with these imagined fears change as children grow older. For example, preschool-aged children may use their pretend play abilities to cope with a fear of ghosts by pretending the ghosts they fear are friendly; older children are more able to reassure themselves that the ghosts or monsters they fear are not real (Sayfan & Lagatutta, 2009).

Although we have seen that, in one study, male infants were more likely than their female counterparts to be afraid of an uncontrollable toy (Gunnar-von Gnechten, 1978), and in another, larger sample, no differences between girls and boys were seen in overt fear (Hay et al., 2017), surveys of children's fears and phobias in the primary school years suggest that girls are more fearful than boys (e.g., Lichtenstein & Annas, 2000; Ollendick et al., 1991). A large study of developmental trajectories in fearfulness over the middle childhood years showed that girls commonly showed an increase and subsequent decrease in fearfulness, whereas boys showed more consistent levels of fear over those years (Côté, Tremblay, Nagin, Zoccolillo, & Vitaro, 2002). Conversely, fearless risk-taking is more common in boys than girls (Byrnes, Miller, & Schaefer, 1999; Côté et al., 2002).

Culture influences both the nature and the intensity of children's fears; for example, in a study of children living in the American West, Navajo children expressed more fears than did Anglo American children (Tikalsky & Wallace, 1988). In a large survey of the fears reported by children living in the US state of Hawaii, fears were expressed more often by children of Hawaiian or Asian background (Shore & Rapport, 1998). In a comparison of Finnish and Estonian children, some cultural differences emerged in the content of the children's fears but, in both countries, children expressed more fears than their parents reported (Lahikainen, Kraav, Kirmanen, & Taimalu, 2006).

These findings suggest that fear may play a different role in different cultures; it seems possible that children's fears are either endorsed or minimised by adult caregivers, depending on the cultural context. To the extent that normal levels of fear are adaptive in preventing children's potentially dangerous actions, cultural variation in the endorsement or suppression of fears may be related to children's risk-taking activities.

There may be some disparity between what children fear the most and what they worry about most often on a day-to-day basis. For example, American children in the 1990s reported their worries (in order) as: their health; issues to do with school; possible harm that might befall them; being asked to perform in front of other people; the unknown future; possible disasters; family problems; problems with their classmates; money problems; war; friendship issues; and their appearance (Silverman, La Greca, & Wasserstein, 1995). Some children worry more than others, and excessive levels of worry are often shown by children with clinically significant anxiety disorders. However, even before children acquire the verbal skills to articulate their fears and worries, there are individual differences in fearfulness and fearlessness that begin in infancy and may extend into later childhood and adolescence. These individual differences have a biological basis but are also susceptible to the influence of the family environment.

Individual differences in fearfulness and fearlessness

Within any culture and within both sexes, some children are more fearful than others. In recent years there has been considerable interest in describing and explaining individual differences in fearfulness and its converse, fearlessness, in childhood and adolescence. It is clear that these individual differences originate in infancy.

Fearful temperament in infancy

In Chapter 1, we already considered the developmental importance of individual temperament. Not all babies are alike in their emotional reactions to the world. Individual differences in fearfulness can be identified in two ways, using temperament questionnaires completed by parents and by using direct observation of infants confronted with novel, somewhat threatening environments in which alarming things might happen. Both parents' reports and direct observation of infants suggest that even in the first year of life, when some think that fears of separation and unfamiliar people are normative, some infants are more fearful than others (e.g., Goldsmith & Campos, 1990).

Laboratory studies of behavioural inhibition

Temperamentally fearful infants who freeze up in response to unfamiliar things are said to be showing *behavioural inhibition* (Kagan, Reznick, & Snidman, 1987). For example, in an initial study by Kagan and his colleagues, 305 parents were interviewed by telephone about their toddlers' temperament; 160 of the children were classified as extremely fearful or extremely fearless. Subsequently, 117 of them were brought into the laboratory, where they met strangers, were asked to take part in a difficult imitation task and played with unfamiliar toys, including a frightening robot. They also experienced separation from their mothers. On the basis of those direct observations of responses to the experimental challenges, 58 were classified as either extremely inhibited or extremely uninhibited in their reactions to the situation (Garcia-Coll, Kagan, & Reznick, 1984; Kagan, Reznick, & Snidman, 1984). The highest rates of behavioural inhibition were seen in response to the robot and separation from the mother.

In Kagan and colleagues' study, the children's observed behavioural inhibition in the laboratory correlated with the parents' independent reports of fearfulness, which suggested that these individual differences were stable across different situations. Similarly, mothers' earlier ratings of fearfulness on the Infant Behaviour

Questionnaire predicted toddlers' later behavioural inhibition in laboratory tasks (Braungart-Rieker et al., 2010).

Fearfulness in response to social challenges

Attempts have been made to distinguish children's reactions to robots and other sights and sounds in strange environments versus new people and social challenges. To the extent that behavioural inhibition in infancy might be associated with later shyness in childhood, we might expect to see a particular difficulty in response to the challenge of meeting someone new. To test this possibility, 108 toddlers were assessed during two laboratory sessions (Rubin, Burgess, & Hastings, 2002). In the first session, the toddlers met both a robot and a clown and were separated from their mothers. The social challenge – meeting a human clown, as opposed to a mechanical robot – was met with almost universal avoidance.

In the second session, the toddlers each met an unfamiliar peer and that child's mother. The children's inhibited behaviour was moderately stable from the first to the second sessions, suggesting that at least some of the toddlers were responding in a similar way to physical and social challenges. Individual differences in the laboratory measures of behavioural inhibition are associated with greater fear of strangers (Brooker et al., 2013), confirming earlier evidence that fear of strangers is not a universal developmental milestone (Rheingold & Eckerman, 1973), but rather an individual tendency that is bound up with more general fearfulness in response to novelty and emotional challenges.

Biological correlates of fearfulness in infancy

Subsequent studies by Kagan's research group and others sought to find physical correlates of behavioural inhibition, including eye colour (with children with blue eyes hypothesised to be more fearful; Rosenberg & Kagan, 1987; Coplan, Caldwell, & Rubin, 1998) and facial morphology (with children with narrow faces hypothesised to be more fearful; Arcus & Kagan, 1995). However, any attempt to identify physical markers of inhibited temperament must take into account the fact that individual variation in fearfulness is not restricted to humans. Similar variations in temperament are found in nonhuman species whose bodies differ from our own. For example, similar patterns of behavioural inhibition and associated physiological arousal can be identified in rhesus macaques (Figure 4.3; Suomi, Chaffin, & Higley, 2011).

The studies of behavioural inhibition in infancy have revealed biological underpinnings of the differences amongst individuals. As adults, when we feel afraid, we may feel our hearts beat faster or our hands grow cold. These reactions and others, which are linked to the autonomic nervous system, may also be experienced by infants. In their first studies of behavioural inhibition, Kagan and his colleagues (1987) argued that three possible systems that underpin individuals' reactions to

FIGURE 4.3   Rhesus macaques show similar patterns of behavioural inhibition as shown by human infants

novel and challenging events might be activated more readily in inhibited infants, namely, the reticular activating system, the hypothalamic-pituitary-adrenal (HPA) axis and the sympathetic nervous system. Their longitudinal analyses indicated the more fearful toddlers had higher and more stable heart rates, and those children with higher, more stable heart rates were more likely to remain shy and cautious when tested again as 5-year-olds.

Other work has linked infants' fearfulness with vagal tone and respiratory sinus arrhythmia (Blandon, Calkins, Keane, & O'Brien, 2010; Brooker & Buss, 2010; Graham, Ablow, & Measelle, 2010) and levels of the stress hormone cortisol (Buss, Davidson, Kalin, & Goldsmith, 2004; Kagan et al., 1987). Our study of 12-month-old infants' reactions to meeting a teddy bear during a birthday party showed that those infants who became overtly distressed were also more likely to be secreting higher levels of cortisol (Hay et al., 2017). Thus, children's experience of fear is related to underlying physiological processes.

Inhibited temperament may also reflect particular patterns of brain development. For example, in a longitudinal study in which infants' brains were scanned using magnetic resonance imaging (MRI), the brain scan yielded maps of connections in the brain that were associated with parents' reports of the infants' later behavioural inhibition at the age of 2 years (Sylvester et al., 2017). In particular, a lower level of connectivity in a brain network associated with attention predicted inhibited temperament at 2 years of age.

Prediction from behavioural inhibition in infancy to shyness in childhood

When children who have been characterised as showing behavioural inhibition were observed again some years later, their early fearfulness predicts more caution and shyness at the later time point. For example, children who are inhibited in experimental situations as infants or toddlers show more reticent, less engaged play with peers as 4- or 5-year-olds (Kagan et al., 1987; Rubin et al., 2002). Such shy behaviour is relatively stable from early to later childhood (Rapee & Coplan, 2010).

Family influences on fearfulness

Genetic influence and gene-environment interplay

It is well known that variations in infants' and toddlers' temperament is partly heritable (e.g., Goldsmith, 1996), and there is evidence from both behavioural and molecular genetic studies to suggest that fearfulness is affected by genetic factors. For example, in a study of 130 twins, monozygous (MZ) and dizygous (DZ) twin pairs were compared with respect to behavioural inhibition, as measured by informants' reports and direct assessments in the laboratory at 12, 18, 24 and 30 months of age (Matheny, 1989). If genetic influences are at work in determining an infant's degree of fearfulness, MZ twins who share all of their genes should be more similar to each other than DZ twins who on average would share half their genes. Indeed, the identical MZ twins were significantly more likely to resemble each other in their responses on the behavioural inhibition tasks than were the DZ twins.

A similar difference between MZ and DZ twins was found in a study of 157 two-year-old twins' behavioural inhibition during play with unfamiliar peers, thus further documenting genetic influence on fearfulness (Dilalla, Kagan, & Reznick, 1994). Analyses of a sample of 178 same-sex MZ and DZ twins similarly drew attention to genetic influences on extremely inhibited behaviour (Robinson, Kagan, Reznick, & Corley, 1992). Further analyses of that sample showed that, even though some infants changed in their levels of fearfulness over time, genetic factors played a role in the extent and nature of the change (Plomin et al., 1993).

The study of genetic influence on infants' fearfulness must also take into account the infants' experiences in their family environments. In a study of adopted infants, information was obtained about the biological mother's fearfulness (i.e., whether or not she had experienced social phobia) and about the adoptive mothers' and fathers' behaviour toward their adopted infants (Natsuaki, Leve, Neiderheiser, & Shaw, 2013). At 2 years of age, the infants were observed in a social situation, and their tendencies to show behavioural inhibition were observed. The birth mother's history of social phobia was associated with the 2-year-olds' behavioural inhibition, but that association was less evident when the adoptive parents had been emotionally and verbally responsive to the infant, as assessed one year earlier. These findings suggest that parents' responsiveness to infants does not increase 'clinginess' in new situations, but rather facilitates infants' abilities to cope, even when the infants may be genetically inclined to be fearful.

Prenatal and postnatal exposure to maternal cortisol

Biological influences on infants' fearfulness extend beyond genetic influence. Infants' experiences in the womb may have effects on their temperament and reactions to their postnatal environments. In particular, mothers' own experience of stress during pregnancy is associated with infants' fearfulness (e.g., Bergmann, Sarkar, O'Connor, Modi, & Glover, 2007). This effect may be due to the mothers' secretion of the stress hormone cortisol during the pregnancy, which can have direct effects on the foetus.

For example, in a small but intensively measured longitudinal sample, Dutch women experiencing pregnancy without medical complications were assessed for levels of cortisol during pregnancy and then followed up several times after their infants were born, when mothers and infants were observed whilst the infant was being given a bath (de Weerth et al., 2003). Younger infants were generally somewhat likely to be distressed by the everyday experience of taking a bath, but their fearful reactions tailed off over time. However, infants who had been exposed to higher levels of maternal cortisol during pregnancy were more irritable and fearful than other infants.

The pathway between mothers' secretion of cortisol and infants' fearful temperament may be complex. In a longitudinal study of 162 women who were undergoing amniocentesis in mid-pregnancy, the women's self-reports of stress were unrelated to the cortisol levels measured in their blood (Baibazarova et al., 2013). However, their plasma cortisol levels were correlated with the level of cortisol in the amniotic fluid, which in turn was related to the infants' subsequent birth weight. Birth weight in turn predicted infants' later fearfulness.

Birth weight is of course often associated with preterm birth, and both are linked to the functioning of the placenta. During pregnancy, the placenta releases corticotrophin-releasing hormone (CRH) which, at high levels, is associated with preterm birth. Low levels of CRH in mid-pregnancy is associated with lower levels of fearfulness after birth, although there seems to be a narrow time window when this prenatal influence holds sway (Poggi Davis et al., 2005).

Infants may also be affected by mothers' stress levels after birth, since maternal cortisol may be transferred to the infants' via breast milk. In a longitudinal study (N = 253) of pregnancy and infant outcomes (Glynn et al., 2007), the cortisol levels in mothers' blood were significantly associated with infants' fearfulness, but only in the case where the infants were being breast-fed. If infants were being fed formula, their mothers' cortisol levels were unrelated to the infants' fearful temperament. Analysis of the actual cortisol levels within samples of breast milk provided by 52 mothers similarly showed a significant relationship with infants' fearfulness, which was particularly striking for girls (Grey, Poggi Davis, Sandman, & Glynn, 2011).

Mother-infant interaction

Although it seems clear that biological factors influence infants' fearfulness, fearful reactions are also shaped by experiences in the postnatal environment. In particular, infants' experiences whilst interacting with their primary caregivers are important influences on the development of fearful temperament.

As we have seen, a longitudinal study of infants' reactions to unfamiliar people showed a significant increase in fearful reactivity from 4 to 16 months of age; however, the extent of fearful reactions was influenced by mothers' sensitivity to the infants' behaviour (Braungart-Rieker et al., 2010). Mothers' sensitivity to the infants' needs was measured independently, in the context of the mothers' and infants' mutual play with toys; sensitivity was defined in terms of the mothers' awareness of their infants' signals, acting 'in tune' with their infants' emotions and participation in contingent interaction with their babies. When mothers showed higher levels of sensitivity during play with toys, infants experienced a less sharp increase in fearful reactions to strangers. This suggests that more positive experiences with sensitive caregivers reduce fearful reactions to unfamiliar people and events.

Maternal sensitivity in early infancy is a well-known predictor of secure attachment relationships between infants and their caregivers (Ainsworth, Blehar, Waters, & Wall, 2015; de Wolff & van Ijzendoorn, 1997). Children's fearful reactions to novel events and their own secretion of cortisol is influenced by the security of their attachments to their caregivers; temperamentally fearful toddlers with less secure attachment relationships are likely to show greater cortisol levels in response to novel, fear-provoking events (Nachmias, Gunnar, Mangelsdorf, Parritz, & Buss, 1996). Children's security in their attachment relationships also influences whether or not they show elevated heart rate in response to novel challenges (Stevenson-Hinde & Marshall, 1999).

Rather than showing such sensitivity, some caregivers are intrusive or derisive when interacting with their infants. For example, they might laugh when their infants show fear of new people or objects. Mothers' intrusiveness and derision in response to their infants' fearful reactions appear to make it more likely that early signs of behavioural inhibition consolidate into later shyness and difficulties in interacting with peers (Rubin et al., 2002). Caregivers' sensitivity and intrusiveness are however linked to the caregivers' own emotional problems, including their experience of depression and anxiety disorders.

Links between parents' psychopathology and children's fearfulness

We have seen that infants' fearful reactions increase in rate over the first year of life (e.g., Braungart-Rieker et al., 2010); a sharper increase in fearfulness is shown by infants whose mothers are experiencing symptoms of depression (Gartstein et al., 2010). In the latter study, the association between mothers' symptoms of depression and infants' increasing fearfulness was noted when the infants' behaviour was directly observed in laboratory as well as when the mothers reported on the infants' behaviour; thus the relationship between mothers' and infants' emotions was not due to depressed women's possibly negative views of their infants.

Depression is an episodic illness; mothers who are depressed when their infants are young are likely to have been depressed before and likely to become depressed again. This means that there are many mechanisms whereby maternal depression may be related to infants' fearfulness, including biological ones. Genetic factors exert their influence across generations so that the infants of depressed parents may be prone to emotional problems, including fearfulness.

It is not always easy to disentangle genetic transmission from the influence of the family environment, because parents who experience depression pass on more than genes to their children; they also may provide riskier prenatal and postnatal environments. For example, mothers' depression or anxiety during pregnancy may be linked to their infants' prenatal exposure to the stress hormone cortisol, which as we have seen is correlated with infants' subsequent fearfulness (e.g., Baibazarova et al., 2013). After their infants are born, mothers who suffer from anxiety problems may show less sensitivity when interacting with their infants (Nicol-Harper, Harvey, & Stein, 2007), and we have already seen that maternal sensitivity reduces infants' fearfulness (e.g., Braungart-Rieker et al., 2010).

Infants of anxious parents may explicitly learn to be afraid of new things by watching their parents' discomfort when meeting new people or entering novel situations. This possibility was tested in one longitudinal study in which 4000 British women were screened during pregnancy for symptoms of social anxiety, with 105 meeting criteria for a clinical diagnosis of social anxiety disorder (Murray et al., 2008). A comparison group of women who had low levels of anxiety was also drawn from the population. The women and their infants were invited to the laboratory when the infants were 10 and 14 months of age. On each occasion, they met a stranger. The infants were also assessed for behavioural inhibition in response to fear-provoking, non-social toys and events. The women with anxiety disorders were less likely than other women to engage in easy conversation with the stranger. They were more likely to show overt signs of anxiety in that social situation. When the mothers and infants returned to the laboratory at 14 months, the infants of anxious mothers were significantly more likely than the other infants to avoid interacting with the stranger. These findings suggest that anxious parents' own discomfort when interacting with new people may transfer to their infants.

Emotion socialisation

Fearful children may either reduce or expand upon their fears over time, depending on the input they receive from their parents. Adults report that as children, they learned about emotion by observing their parents' reactions to their expressions of positive and negative affect; such retrospective reports suggest that emotions are socialised, and the nature of emotion socialisation depends on the gender of the child (Garside & Klimes-Dougan, 2002), as well as the gender of the parent (Hooven, Gottman, & Katz, 1995).

Emotion socialisation takes place in everyday situations when parents talk to their children. Parents' conversations with their children include *reminiscing* about past emotionally laden experiences and *planning* how to respond emotionally to present or future challenges, a process sometimes known as *emotion coaching* (e.g., Denham, Mitchell-Copeland, Strandberg, Auerbach, & Blair, 1997). Conversations with parents about emotion may be experienced differently by girls and boys. In particular, when talking about potentially frightening situations, girls use more emotion words than boys do (Fivush, Brotman, Buckner, & Goodman, 2000). In general, young children seem to find it harder to talk about fear than other negative emotions (Widen & Russell, 2003), which may impact upon the emotion socialisation that they receive. However, when given experimental challenges designed to elicit different emotions, young children do report being frightened in response to novelty, both human strangers and other unusual stimuli such as a pop-up snake (Durbin, 2010). In that study, children's reports of fear were linked to the facial expressions they made in response to the novel people and objects, which implies that even in early childhood, children can reflect on frightening experiences.

Gene-environment interaction

It is likely that genetic influences interact with environmental factors to influence children's levels of fearfulness. Scientific developments in the field of molecular genetics allow investigators to tests hypotheses about *gene-environment interaction* by comparing children with different combinations of alleles with respect to a gene that might affect their fearfulness in relation to different types of experience in their childhood environments. For example, much attention has been focussed on a particular genetic polymorphism, the serotonin transporter gene 5-HTT, which has two alleles (referred to as the long and short alleles). The presence of the 5-HTT short allele is associated with lower uptake of serotonin. Variation in the 5-HTT polymorphism is associated with differences in the attention people pay to negative information, a psychological process that is linked to fear and anxiety (Pergamin-Hight, Bakermans-Kranenburg, van IJzendoorn, & Bar-Haim, 2012).

Interaction between the presence of the short allele and the quality of caregiving an infant receives has been found to influence levels of fearfulness in infant rhesus macaques (Barr et al., 2004). Similar findings emerged in a longitudinal study of human children's fearful temperament (Fox et al., 2005). Seven-year-old children who had been assessed for behavioural inhibition at earlier ages were genotyped and observed with unfamiliar peers. Their levels of behavioural inhibition in response to the unfamiliar peers were significantly related to the interaction between their genotype and the levels of social support they experienced in their environment, even when controlling for earlier levels of fearfulness. If children had low levels of social support and also possessed the short 5HTT allele, they were more likely to show inhibition when interacting with peers. If, however, children who possessed the short 5HTT allele had adequate social support, they were less likely to show fearfulness in this novel social situation. Subsequent research has discovered similar patterns of interaction between the short 5HTT allele and levels of environmental stress, affecting a range of negative emotions, not just fear, in children and adolescents (for a meta-analysis of this work, see van IJzendoorn, Belsky, & Bakermans-Kranenburg, 2012).

Anxiety disorders in childhood

Clinical diagnoses of anxiety disorder

When does normal variation in the tendency to feel fear or worry about things turn into emotional problems of clinical concern? Clinical diagnostic systems devised for adults, such as the *Diagnostic and Statistical Manual* (DSM) and the *International Classification of Diseases* (ICD), include definitions of several anxiety disorders that are sometimes also seen in childhood. For example, in the DSM system, these include *Generalised Anxiety Disorder* (GAD), 'unrealistic and excessive anxiety . . . not linked to a specific situation or external stress'; Social Anxiety Disorder, 'pronounced and persistent fears of social and performance situations'; *Specific Phobias*, e.g., strong fears of particular things or situations, such as spiders or heights; and *Obsessive-Compulsive Disorder* (OCD), 'recurrent thoughts or behaviours that are time consuming, cause distress, and . . . (cause) impairment in the person's functioning' (American Psychiatric Association, 2013, see pp. 189–290). In addition, the DSM also highlights anxiety disorders that are especially likely to occur in childhood, including *Separation Anxiety Disorder* (SAD), 'obvious distress from and concern about being separated from those to whom the child is attached,' and *School Phobia*, a form of specific phobia to do with attending school.

Individual differences in risk for anxiety disorders in childhood

Community studies of children's mental health reveal that a small minority of children are already experiencing such high levels of fear or anxiety that they meet the diagnostic criteria for one or more anxiety disorders. The rate with which children experience clinically significant anxiety disorder seems to vary across cultures. For example, in a community sample of preschool-aged children in the southern United States, 10% of the children met DSM criteria for an anxiety disorder (Egger & Angold, 2006). In contrast, in a community sample of 4-year-olds in Norway, in which the same diagnostic interview was used, only 3% did so (Wichstrøm et al., 2012). However, the findings from both samples attest to the fact that even very young children may experience extreme levels of fear and anxiety, and their lives are impaired by their symptoms.

Children whose parents suffer from anxiety and related emotional problems are at particular risk to develop such problems, and that risk is exacerbated if, as infants, those children already showed behavioural inhibition in response to new situations and potentially frightening events. For example, a sample of 200 children whose parents had been diagnosed with panic disorder and/or major depressive disorder (most had both diagnoses) was compared with 84 comparison children whose parents were free of disorder (Biederman et al., 2001). The children were tested for behavioural inhibition as preschoolers and assessed for symptoms of anxiety disorder when they were over 5 years of age. In the sample as a whole, 5% of the children met diagnostic criteria for Social Anxiety Disorder. However, when children had a parent who experienced panic disorder and also had shown behavioural inhibition as preschoolers, they were at heightened risk: one out of four of such children were diagnosed with Social Anxiety Disorder (Biederman et al., 2001). In general, regardless of the parents' history of mental health problems, those children who had shown behavioural inhibition as preschoolers were significantly more likely than other children to be diagnosed with social anxiety in childhood.

Other longitudinal studies have corroborated this finding. In one major Australian study of temperament, where children were assessed on 10 different occasions, persistent shyness over childhood was found to be a significant predictor of anxiety symptoms in early adolescence (Prior, Smart, Sanson, & Oberklaid, 2000). More short-lived shyness was less predictive. In another large community sample from New Zealand, a pattern of increasingly fearful and withdrawn behaviours predicted later emotional disorders (Goodwin, Fergusson, & Horwood, 2004). Inhibited temperament in early childhood, coupled with mothers' history of anxiety, predicts social anxiety in particular, as opposed to other forms of anxiety disorder (Rapee, 2014).

However, other work suggests that it is important to take the context into account. There are some worrying or even dangerous situations in life where it is quite reasonable to be fearful. Under such conditions of high threat, some behavioural inhibition might be adaptive. In contrast, under conditions of low threat – when the situation is predictable and children have control over what they might have to see and do – behavioural inhibition is less likely to occur in most children. Toddlers who show fearful behaviour in such low-threat situations are more likely to develop anxiety symptoms (Buss, 2011). A child's tendency to see threat in the environment interacts with the child's past history of behavioural inhibition to promote anxiety disorder in later childhood (White et al., 2017). As we have seen, such attention biases to threat may reflect an interplay between the child's genetic heritage and family environment (Pergamin-Hight et al., 2012).

Not all fearful infants go on to experience anxiety disorders. A review of research on prediction from early fearfulness to later anxiety disorder has identified some key factors that protect inhibited children against the risk of more severe anxiety. These protective factors include: (a) being a girl, perhaps because it is more socially acceptable for girls to be shy; (b) having less intrusive parents who are more accepting of the child's shyness and caution; (c) having positive experiences in child care settings; and (d) having good attention skills (Degnan & Fox, 2007).

Stress disorders in childhood

We have seen from the surveys of children's fears and worries that children dread being caught up in disasters. What happens when children's lives are endangered, through accidents, weather-related disasters or exposure to warfare? Increasing attention is being paid to children's experiences of stress disorders, both acute stress disorder that occurs immediately after the traumatic events and posttraumatic stress disorder (PTSD) that may linger long after the event took place. PTSD is diagnosed when the child has directly experienced or witnessed a life-threatening event, when the event caused intense fear or horror, and when the child's reactions afterward involved some distortions of memory, e.g., flashbacks to the traumatic circumstances. PTSD can be accompanied by other disorders; for example, children caught up in road traffic accidents may have specific phobias involving driving or cars (Keppel-Benson, Ollendick, & Benson, 2002). However, children do experience the distinct pattern of symptoms of PTSD, and these may persist for very long periods of time.

A number of longitudinal studies have identified long-lasting symptoms of PTSD deriving from some of the terrible things that have happened to children in recent decades. Over half of the British school children on an educational cruise who survived the shipwreck of their ship, the *Jupiter*, were diagnosed with PTSD; 15% of them still showed symptoms seven years later (Yule, Bolton, Udwin, & Boyle, 2000). Children who were exposed to warfare in Bosnia were still showing symptoms of PTSD two years after peace was declared (Smith, Perrin, Yule, Hacam, & Stuvland, 2002).

When children experience life-threatening destruction, their symptoms of PTSD sometimes persist into later life. For example, children whose town was devastated by floods when a dam collapsed in the state of West Virginia in the United States were experiencing PTSD at a higher rate than other people in their geographical area 17 years after the actual disaster (Green et al., 1994).

Nearly half of the Welsh children whose primary school in the village of Aberfan was buried by a collapsing slag heap in 1966, with 116 of their classmates dying in the landslide, were still experiencing symptoms of PTSD in middle age (Morgan, Scourfield, Williams, Jasper, & Lewis, 2003). In that sample, the very distinct symptoms of PTSD persisted, even though the sufferers were not at heightened risk for other anxiety disorders, depression or substance misuse. This suggests that the environmental effect of exposure to a life-threatening disaster has particular effects on emotion and memory function, whether or not the person develops other forms of emotional problems.

Fearlessness and behavioural problems in childhood

In their initial studies of behavioural inhibition in response to novel events, Kagan and his colleagues drew attention to extreme fearlessness as well as extreme fearfulness in the infants and toddlers they studied (e.g., Kagan, Reznick, & Gibbons, 1989). Infants' fearless responses to the fear-provoking paradigms (e.g., meeting a robot) are sometimes referred to as 'exuberance' and discussed in terms of active sociability that persists over time (e.g., Fox, Henderson, Rubin, Calkins, & Schmidt, 2001). However, high levels of fearlessness in response to these emotional challenges are sometimes related to later disruptive behaviour (Degnan et al., 2011). Conversely, children who show more fearfulness on behavioural inhibition tasks may be less likely than other children to be diagnosed with a disruptive behaviour disorder, e.g., conduct disorder or oppositional-defiant disorder (Biederman et al., 2001). Infants on the pathway toward such disorders may also show higher levels of anger at an early age. In the next chapter, we shall discuss the development of anger and its relation to these later disorders.

5

ANGER

Fight vs. flight

In contrast to fear, which is manifested by attempts to escape from or avoid challenging situations, some emotion theorists see anger as an 'approach-related affect' (Carver & Harmon-Jones, 2009), which induces people to confront and deal with the frustrating or challenging situation that is eliciting their anger. This difference between avoidance and confrontation is summed up in the familiar phrase, 'fight or flight,' in response to challenge. Whilst anger certainly does not inevitably lead to overt aggression, it often leads to some form of active protest. Thus, whereas fearful children may withdraw from social interaction with other people, angry children may act on their feelings and confront the people and things that are frustrating or otherwise annoying them.

The development of anger

Adults express anger through many different channels, often using a combination of words (including swear words), nonverbal utterances, facial expressions, gestures and impatient actions. Infants begin to find similar ways of expressing their frustration and anger in the first years of life.

Vocal protest

In Chapter 2, we saw that infants spend less of their time crying as they approach their first birthdays. As crying becomes less frequent, it provides a clearer signal of what infants need and want, and therefore a clue as to what emotions they might be feeling on the inside. Crying becomes a form of protest when infants' actions are restricted, or when their parents or other people do things the infants find objectionable.

In her classic developmental model of the differentiation of emotions described in Chapter 1, Bridges (1932) hypothesised that anger was the first primary emotion to emerge out of more generalised distress. Based on her observations of infants in an orphanage in Montreal, she suggested that signs of anger first emerged between 3 and 6 months of age. But can infants so young truly be said to be feeling an emotion as complex as anger?

In a more recent attempt to determine when infants first express anger, my colleagues and I studied a nationally representative sample of 300 firstborn British infants whose parents had been recruited in pregnancy. When the infants were 6 months old, we asked mothers, fathers and a third family member or friend to complete questionnaires about the infants' behaviour, which included a list of 'developmental milestones': achievements in motor development, like sitting up or trying to stand up, and communicative behaviours like smiling or expressing affection. Two items measured possible signs of anger: angry moods and temper tantrums (Hay et al., 2010). Even at this early age, over half the infants sometimes experienced 'angry moods' though only a few showed anger often (Figure 5.1).

At first glance, these reports by parents and other people in infants' lives might be discounted. Perhaps some parents see their infants more negatively than others, and maybe that says more about the parents' own emotional states than the infants' true feelings. But some indication of what the family members were talking about could be corroborated in 30 seconds of observation of the infants' behaviour during an everyday frustration task, being strapped into a car seat. Those infants who

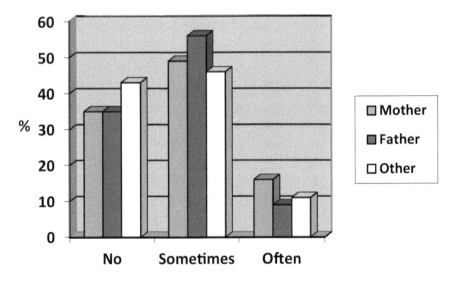

FIGURE 5.1 Percentage of mothers, fathers and other family members reporting that 6-month-old infants experience angry moods

Source: Hay et al. (2010)

cried or screamed when placed in the car seat had been independently reported to be angry and to hit out at or bite other people (Hay et al., 2010). This suggests that the capacity for angry crying has emerged by 6 months of age, but there are also individual differences in the tendency to express anger, even at this very early age.

Facial expressions of anger

As our observations of infants' reactions to being put in a car seat revealed, early expressions of anger are linked to frustration. Infants' angry emotions are conveyed by the face as well as the voice. In a classic experiment designed to elicit anger in response to frustration, 7-month-olds were offered a biscuit by an experimenter, who then snatched it away from them (Stenberg, Campos, & Emde, 1983). The infants were observed to show distinct facial expressions of anger, comparable to those seen in adults. The infants' faces also became red and flushed. Other types of facial expressions did not change when the rusk was taken away, which suggests that the experiment evoked anger, not a mix of other emotions.

Angry facial expressions are also seen when infants lose control over the production of an interesting event. In one experiment, 2- to 8-month-old infants who were trained on a contingency task (pulling a string to see a picture of children accompanied by the Sesame Street theme tune) showed joyful expressions while learning the trick and angry expressions when the contingency was extinguished (Lewis, Alessandri, & Sullivan, 1990). Within this age range, older infants expressed more interest in the task but also more anger when their efforts no longer worked. If infants expressed anger rather than sadness during the extinction procedure, they were more likely to maintain their interest in relearning the task (Lewis, Sullivan, Ramsay, & Alessandri, 1992).

Facial expressions of anger are also shown by older toddlers when they encounter frustrating circumstances. For example, in a study of young children in China, facial signs of anger were recorded when a toy was removed or the children were presented with a locked box; in that sample, the children's expressions of anger were accompanied by greater persistence in trying to overcome the frustrating conditions (He, Xu, & Degnan, 2011).

In general, these studies show that facial expressions connoting anger are likely to be seen under frustrating circumstances, when infants' enjoyment of food or an interesting activity has been interrupted. Facial expressions of anger in response to frustration occur proportionally more often in infants who have reached their first birthday than in younger infants (Kearney, 2004). However, other researchers advise caution in drawing conclusions from infants' facial expressions in a context in which the experimenters are only trying to elicit one particular emotion (Oster et al., 1992). They argue that infants' facial expressions may incorporate elements of different primary emotions, and it may be too easy to assume that the negative emotion elicited in response to restraint is pure anger. These more recent findings are thus in line with Bridges's (1932) original claim that the negative emotions only gradually differentiate from each other.

It has long been known that observers' inferences about infants' emotions draw on context as well as the details of the infants' reactions and are subject to the effects of professional experience (Sherman, 1927). However, it is also possible that in early infancy, distress in response to particular situations does incorporate a range of emotional experience, rather than the manifestation of a 'pure' emotion. As we shall see in Chapter 6, frustration elicits sadness and hopelessness, not just anger. Infants' facial expressions of positive emotion are more likely to take the form of discrete signals (such as smiling), not blended emotion, but their expression of negative emotion is more likely to show a mix of components associated with different discrete emotions (Matias & Cohn, 1993). This finding suggests that, while it is often useful to focus on one negative emotion at a time, as we are doing in this book, it is important to realise that people may often experience mixed feelings in response to their experiences and must therefore attempt to interpret their own reactions to themselves. This process begins in infancy.

Angry protests during conflict

Conflict with peers

In our longitudinal study of the early development of anger, the family members' reports of infants' anger were also associated with the infants' observed behaviour during conflicts with unfamiliar peers, six months later (Hay et al., 2010). Conflict – defined as social interactions in which one person objects to something another person has done (Hay & Ross, 1982) – often arises in the course of peer interaction when one infant attempts to touch the peer or grasp a toy the peer is holding. Infants often simply resist their peers' actions, but sometimes express their displeasure with vocal protests or retaliation against the peers.

When conflict first appears in infants' peer interactions in the last quarter of the first year of life, infants usually make their objections known through simple resistance (e.g., withdrawing a toy the peer is reaching for that is out of reach of the peer's grasp), rather than angry protest or the use of force (Hay, Nash, Caplan, Ishikawa, & Vespo, 2011). Older infants are more likely to react to peers' behaviour with vocal protest or the deployment of force, perhaps tugging on the toy in question or, more rarely, striking out at the peer's body (Hay, Hurst, Waters, & Chadwick, 2011).

Conflict with siblings

Angry protest also occurs when siblings, as well as peers, do things that infants find undesirable. Some degree of conflict between siblings is to be expected and may have positive consequences. For example, conflict between siblings may promote the development of theory-of-mind (Foote & Holmes-Lanergan, 2003), particularly if the siblings' conflicts are constructive and contain elements of positive emotion (Randell & Peterson, 2009); the presence of a younger sibling fosters social cognitive development in middle childhood, even when many other family factors are taken into account (Paine, Pearce, van Goozen, de Sonneville, & Hay, 2018).

However, while sibling conflict may have some positive effects, children's intense anger with their siblings can also be a harbinger of future problems. Five-year-old boys' highly angry, aggressive conflict with their siblings – sometimes referred to as 'destructive conflict' – predicted later behavioural problems, particularly in the context of less optimal parent-child relationships (Garcia, Shaw, Winslow, & Yaggi, 2000). Although constructive sibling conflict may foster the development of theory of mind, angry, destructive behaviour with siblings is inversely associated with understanding of other people's mental states (Howe, Rinaldi, Jennings, & Petrakos, 2002).

Conflict with parents

Children also display anger toward their parents. For example, infants show anger when their parents leave them, as happens in the Strange Situation, a laboratory assessment designed to measure individual differences in the security of attachment to the parent (Ainsworth, 1979). Analysis of infants' facial expressions during the separation episodes of the Strange Situation revealed that anger in response to the parent's departure was more common than sadness; secure children were no less likely than insecure children to express anger (Shiller, Izard, & Hembree, 1986).

Anger continues to be a component of parent-infant interaction in middle childhood. Parents and children do express anger toward each other, although detailed observations of 6-year-old children interacting with their parents showed that displays of positive emotion were six to seven times as likely to occur as expressions of all negative emotions, including sadness, fear and disgust as well as anger (Snyder, Stoolmiller, Wilson, & Yamamoto, 2003). However, individual differences were apparent. In Snyder and colleagues' study, the likelihood of a particular child becoming angry with his or her parents was stable over a week of observations.

Children may become angry with their parents because a sibling has arrived; sibling jealousy may provoke conflict with both the parent and the sibling. For example, in a longitudinal study, toddlers who had shown signs of being jealous of their father's attention to a younger sibling were more likely to engage in conflict with that sibling over two years later (Kollak & Volling, 2011).

The degree of angry conflict children experience with their parents and siblings may be influenced by parents' own emotional difficulties, including their symptoms of clinical disorder. For example, in an observational study of children whose mothers had or had not experienced depressive illness, conflict between siblings was most common for children whose mothers had not been ill and least common for those whose mothers had suffered from bipolar disorder; in the latter group, children were more likely to engage in conflict with their mothers (Hay, Vespo, & Zahn-Waxler, 1998).

These findings suggest that the expression of anger in the context of family relationships is likely to reflect individual tendencies to be angry as well as family dynamics. This network of angry relationships soon becomes complicated in the case of families with more than two children. In such families, hostility between siblings is linked to the mother's symptoms of low mood as well as her own level of hostility (Jenkins, Rasbash, Leckie, Gass, & Dunn, 2012).

Temper tantrums

Beginning in the second year of life and continuing over early childhood, the expression of anger may take on dramatic features:

> There are children who grunt and growl and those whose shrieks reportedly sound to their parents like the cries of 'a prehistoric bird.' Parents have told us about children who scream so loudly and so long that capillaries in their cheeks burst and their eyes become bloodshot. Others scream until they vomit or become rigid as statues with tension, even to the point of toppling over if unsupported.
>
> *(Potegal & Davidson, 2003, p. 140)*

This dramatic phenomenon is familiarly known as a *temper tantrum*.

Temper tantrums are commonly observed but only rarely have been studied. In a telephone survey of 1219 families (Potegal & Davidson, 2003), over 80% of children were reported to have at least one tantrum per month, although the frequency of tantrums declined from 18 months to 5 years of age. Parents' detailed narratives about their children's tantrums revealed that expressions of anger were at their height at the beginning of the tantrum, followed by the emotionally upset children's attempts to seek comfort from the parents (Potegal, Kosorok, & Davidson, 2003). This suggests that extreme manifestations of anger soon merge into more global distress and perhaps fear and sadness.

When in development do infants first show signs of temper tantrums? In our longitudinal study of a community sample of firstborn infants (Hay et al., 2010), up to three informants (mothers, fathers and a third person who knew the infant well) reported on infants' display of tantrums as well as angry moods (these two items being significantly correlated). As would be expected, only 5% of parents reported that their 6-month-old infants experienced temper tantrums; however, over one-quarter of infants were reported to show tantrums sometimes, which suggests that some early precursors to true tantrums are evident in the first year of life (see Figure 5.2). This in turn suggests that it would be possible to study the gradual emergence of full tantrums, beginning in early infancy, and possible to predict which infants are most likely to throw frequent tantrums.

Potegal and his colleagues (2003) have pointed out that temper tantrums encompass two different patterns of behaviour: distress (e.g., crying, screaming and seeking

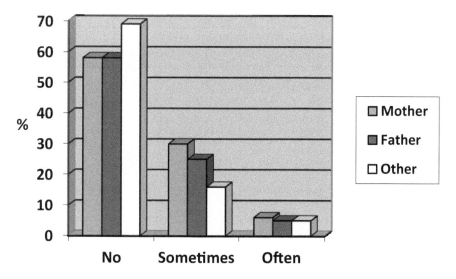

FIGURE 5.2   Percentage of mothers, fathers and other family members reports of infants'
temper tantrums at 6 months of age

Source: Hay et al. (2010)

comfort even in the middle of the tantrum) and physical expressions of anger
(which might take the form of hitting and kicking and grabbing things, as well as
showing overt distress). The two different patterns of tantrum behaviour appear to
have different correlates. In a study designed to test the two-factor model of temper tantrums in a community sample of preschool children (Giesbrecht, Miller, &
Müller, 2010), the children were assessed with respect to their knowledge about
emotion and their emotional regulation in response to experimental challenges.
Their parents had reported on their tendencies to engage in different behaviours
during tantrums. The two patterns of distress and anger emerged as separate but
overlapping factors, which were both related to the children's tendencies to react
emotionally to their experiences.

Verbal expressions of anger

Possession claims

In addition to the dramatic physical features of temper tantrums, purely verbal
expressions of anger are also evident in the toddler years, particularly in the context
of conflicts with siblings and peers. Initially, infants' protests take the form of fret-
ting or full-blown crying, but, as they learn words, they may say 'No!' or 'Don't!' to
their peers; they may also assert their ownership of particular possessions by saying
'Mine! (Hay, Hurst et al., 2011). Thus by the second or third year of life, anger is

often expressed as a means of asserting possession rights and may be seen as a constructive verbal alternative to seizing objects from other children. In a short-term longitudinal study of toddlers with familiar peers, those toddlers who were most likely to say 'Mine!' were significantly more likely to share and less likely to display aggression six months later (Hay, 2006).

Toddlers do not simply say 'Mine!' in response to every attempt on their possessions. Rather, they are more likely to make such claims when they actually own the toy in question and when their mothers support them in asserting their rights to its possession (Ross, 2013).

Insults, taunts and swearing

Children's speech during conflicts often escalates beyond possession claims, being used to insult, taunt or otherwise hurt other people emotionally, a form of behaviour that is associated with more physical forms of aggression and likely to lead to negative reactions from other children (Olson, 1992). The distinction between serious taunts and playful teasing gradually emerges in later childhood (Keltner, Capps, Kring, Young, & Heerey, 2001), but may still provoke angry retaliation from peers. More research is needed to determine how often teasing is used in anger and when it is used deliberately to provoke anger in another child.

Angry children also resort to swearing. Angry adults often use forbidden language to express their feelings, and the fact that swearing is associated with limbic system function and often retained in the context of brain injury and language impairment suggests that it constitutes a very basic way of expressing verbal anger, analogous to angry vocalisations in other primate species (Spinney, 2007). However, children's swearing differs across cultures; for example, in one study, Thai children were more likely to swear than American children of the same age (Weisz et al., 1989). Children themselves do not condone swearing and, at younger ages, are likely to confuse it with another type of forbidden speech, telling lies (Peterson, Peterson, & Seeto, 1983). In recent online discussions of the Finnish Children's Parliaments, the children agreed that both swearing and lying were 'stupid' and tended to lead to undesirable consequences (Tuukkanen, Kankaanranta, & Wilska, 2013).

Verbal quarrels and arguments

An argument is a purely verbal form of social conflict, characterised by an initial event, an opposition and a reaction to being opposed (Maynard, 1985); this set of events is equivalent to the initial action, opposition and further reactions that characterise young children's largely nonverbal conflicts with other people (e.g., Hay & Ross, 1982). Thus when children begin to acquire language, they express their opposition to other people's behaviour or requests with words, without necessarily resorting to overt expressions of anger or use of force. An example of two previously unacquainted toddlers arguing about whether to hold a tea party or put the play food items away is shown in Table 5.1.

TABLE 5.1 A verbal argument between two 3-year-old boys

Child A: 'Hey, where's the fire? Where's the fire?'
Child B: 'The fire's over there . . . that fire's out.'
Child B: (speaking to everyone) 'Look, my water's tipped . . .'
Child A: 'Your water's tipped?'
Child B: 'In there, let's put the cups away now . . . let's put the cups away now . . . let's put the cups away now.'
Child A: 'Cups are for tea party, cups are for tea party.'
Child B: 'I just need to put the cups away.'
Child A: 'No, I just want a tea party.'
Child B: 'No, I just want to put the cups away.'
Child A: 'Can I have some, I want a tea party?'

This example suggests that even quite young children may engage in conflict over ideas, asserting their needs and desires without becoming angry; however, for many children and indeed adults, there is always the possibility that purely verbal arguments will descend into more physical conflict. However, in preschool class-rooms, the early use of verbal objections, as opposed to more physical means of expressing anger or pure venting of emotion, was associated with the development of positive social skills and inversely related to behavioural problems (Eisenberg et al., 1999). It is therefore of interest to examine the biological aspects of anger that may constrain children's abilities to use verbal skills to make their protests.

Biological underpinnings of children's anger

Some researchers have tried to study what young infants feel on the inside when they are frustrated or expressing anger. One approach to this question is to take physiological measures as well as using direct observation when infants find that their goals are blocked (e.g., Lewis, Ramsay, & Sullivan, 2006). Frustrating situations that arise when infants can't pursue their goals may evoke sadness as well as anger (see Chapter 6 for an extended consideration of children's sadness in response to frustration). However, the physiological correlates of the two reactions may be different. In one study, infants who expressed sadness in response to a frustration task showed an increase in levels of the stress hormone cortisol, whereas those who expressed anger showed higher heart rate (Lewis et al., 2006). However, other researchers have reported that angry infants are likely to show higher levels of cor-tisol in response to a stressful situation, being confronted with a strange robot (van Bakel & Riksen-Walraven, 2004).

In later childhood, children's reactions to frustration may be manifested in a number of different channels, and behavioural and physiological reactions may not always be correlated. Furthermore, children's phenomenological experiences of anger, as communicated in self-report measures, may not always be corrobo-rated by other informants or behavioural observation (e.g., Casey, 1993). Measuring physiological reactions may be particularly helpful in understanding the multifaceted expression of anger. For example, in a study of 8-year-old children in primary school classrooms, teachers and children reported on the children's angry aggressiveness, and the children were directly observed in the context of a competitive game in which confederates acted in a way that might provoke angry reactions (Hubbard et al., 2004). Children's overt angry facial expressions and behavioural signs of frustration were significantly related to their own self-reports of angry aggression. Furthermore, the directly observed signs of anger were significantly related to skin conductance reactivity. However, some of the results were puzzling: Skin conductance was itself associated with heart rate reactivity, which was negatively related to children's self-reports of anger. These findings suggest that anger is expressed in the body, but there may be subtle relationships amongst physiological reactions, overt behaviour and more cognitive understanding of one's own anger, as revealed in self-reports. Most importantly, individual differences in any of these features of anger are clearly apparent.

Individual differences in infants' proneness to anger

Irritability and anger-proneness as dimensions of temperament

Several different theories of infant temperament incorporate a dimension related to the expression of general irritability, anger and/or intolerance of frustration. For example, McDevitt and Carey (1978) described infants' expression of negative mood as 'fussy-difficult.' By the toddler years, 'anger-proneness' is considered to be a feature of individual temperament (Goldsmith, 1996). However defined and measured, infants' tendencies to be angry are stable over time (Gartstein & Rothbart, 2003; Komsi et al., 2006). These individual differences emerge almost as soon as infants develop the capacity to express anger. For example, in our study, parents' and family members' ratings of infants' angry moods at 6 months of age (as depicted in Figure 5.1) significantly predicted their ratings of the child's tendency to experience angry moods two years later (Hay et al., 2014).

Emotion regulation and inhibitory control

Some temperament theorists have focussed not just on the overall tendency for some infants to express anger but also their emotion regulation abilities, in particular their abilities to regulate anger in response to frustration and other emotional challenges. Thus, the children who express the most anger may be both more likely to experience negative reactions to challenges and less able to cope with those negative emotions. However, the conceptual distinction between the expression of emotion and the regulation of emotion is not always clear; the fact that emotion is so difficult to define (see Chapter 1) makes this problem even worse (Cole, Martin, & Dennis, 2004). In a conceptual analysis of emotion regulation, Cole and her colleagues provide a very general definition – emotion regulation implies that emotions undergo change – and also make a distinction between the act of attempting to regulate emotion and the outcome indicating that emotion has been regulated. In the latter case, there is not always an obvious distinction between the expression of positive and/or neutral emotion and evidence for successful emotion regulation. It is also useful to make distinctions between self-regulation and the experience of having one's emotions regulated by another person, especially a parent or other caregiver (Cole et al., 2004).

Although developmental theorists sometimes speak of emotion regulation as a general process, it appears to be somewhat easier for infants to regulate their anger than their fear. In a study of 148 infants who were able to look at but not touch attractive toys behind an impenetrable plastic barrier or, in a separate task, infants who distracted themselves by looking away from the toys expressed less anger; however, this distraction technique did not work when they were challenged by fear-provoking toy dogs and spiders (Buss & Goldsmith, 1998).

The successful regulation of anger is thought to be related to broader self-regulatory abilities, which develop rapidly during early childhood (e.g., Jones, Rothbart, & Posner, 2003). Children's abilities to control their anger are likely to be related to more general inhibitory control, which cognitive and neuropsychological theorists view in the context of executive function (EF) abilities. When studying anger, it may prove useful to distinguish between 'hot' and 'cool' EF tasks, i.e., emotionally arousing tasks like delay of gratification or gambling tasks versus those that demand cooler heads and cognitive flexibility, such as card-sorting tasks (e.g., Hongwanishkul, Happeney, Lee, & Zelazo, 2005). Young children who are able to engage in 'effortful control' of their own behaviour, particularly when asked to wait for a treat or refrain from touching forbidden objects, are less likely to show anger (e.g., Kochanska & Knaack, 2003).

Inhibitory control abilities may be fostered in early parent-infant interaction but may also be influenced by genetic factors. For example, a genetically informative longitudinal study of twins who were observed between the first and third birthdays showed that 3-year-olds who had better inhibitory control abilities were less likely to express anger (Gagne & Goldsmith, 2011). However, in that sample, 1-year-olds who expressed anger during laboratory frustration tasks were significantly more likely to show better inhibitory control as 3-year-olds. Comparison of two types of twins – monozygous (MZ) twins who were genetically identical and dizygous (DZ) twins who on average shared half their genes like any other pairs of siblings – revealed genetic influence on both anger and inhibitory control. However, environmental effects were also apparent. Such evidence for environmental influence draws further attention to the socialisation processes in families and the broader social world that influence children's anger.

The socialisation of emotion

Emotion socialisation by parents

Nancy Eisenberg and her colleagues proposed a tripartite model of the processes in family life that promote children's learning about and understanding of emotion (Eisenberg, Cumberland, & Spinrad, 1998). They drew attention to parents' reactions to children's emotional displays, parents' discussions about emotion with their children and parents' own expression of emotion. Each of these socialisation processes influences the development of anger. It should be noted, however, that whilst these processes can be differentiated in the conceptual model, they co-occur when parents and infants both display emotion and talk about what they're feeling to each other. It is perhaps helpful to distinguish what happens in the heat of the moment when both parents and children are angry from the parent's role as an 'emotion coach' helping children deal with their anger (e.g., DeBaryshe & Fryxell, 1998).

Expressing and reacting to anger

We have already seen in Chapter 2 that parents react in variable ways when their infants cry (e.g., Wood & Gustafson, 2001), and that their reactions may differ if they perceive their infants as angry or frustrated as opposed to hungry or in pain. Parents also respond to infants' facial expressions of emotion; one observation suggested that parents responded immediately to about one-quarter of 3- and 6-month-olds' expressions of anger (Malatesta & Haviland, 1982), but were less likely to respond contingently to signs of pain. In that sample, infants' own expressions of anger were significantly more likely to lead to mothers' expressed anger or concern than to their expressions of interest or pleasure. Thus, even in the first half of the first year of life, infants' anger was contagious, provoking parents' anger in return.

This pattern of parents' differential reactions to emotional displays continues in the childhood years. For example, when parents were asked to respond to scenarios in which their children might show distress, some parents advocated comforting their children, whereas others minimised the distress and others recommended more punitive approaches (Eisenberg & Fabes, 1994; Eisenberg, Fabes, & Murphy, 1996). In general, those children whose parents minimised expressions of distress were more likely to vent their emotions than discover constructive ways of approaching problems that might make them upset. The overall pattern of findings suggested that moderate sensitivity to distress coupled with a focus on how to solve the problem was optimal.

Discussions about anger

Parents and children often discuss the child's emotional experiences when reminiscing about past events in family life. For example, in a study of 70 preschool-aged children (Fivush, Berlin, Sales, Menutti-Washburn, & Cassidy, 2003), mothers were asked to discuss past occasions when the child had experienced anger, sadness or fear. Events that might provoke anger concerned conflict between the parent and the child or between the child and other children, peers or siblings. In general, mothers tended to talk in a less elaborate way about anger as opposed to fear, and they were also more likely to suggest ways in which children's fearful reactions could be resolved, compared to ways in which the children could deal with anger. In general, however, mothers had more elaborate conversations about emotion with their daughters than with their sons.

Discussions about anger may also take place in real time in more emotionally charged situations, when the child is reacting to a disappointing or frustrating event. For example, in an experimental study of 4- to 9-year-old children, carried out in the children's own homes, the children were given a disappointing prize, such as a pair of old socks or broken sunglasses (Morris et al., 2011). Children's expression of emotion and mothers' behaviour were assessed. Mothers might attempt to distract or comfort the child but also might try to reframe the disappointment, suggesting useful things that might be done with the disappointing objects. Distraction was more effective than comforting was in reducing the child's anger. The reframing discussions were successful in reducing the child's anger only if child and mother participated jointly in the discussions of how best to use such unattractive objects.

As we have seen in the previous chapter, psychologists have begun to employ a sports metaphor, emotion coaching, to describe discussions about emotion between children and parents, in which parents and their children talk through ways to regulate anger and other negative emotions in particular situations (e.g., Hooven et al., 1995). These researchers suggest that parents have 'meta-emotion structures,' that is, their own feelings and attitudes about emotion that influence the way they respond to their children's anger and other negative emotional displays (Hooven et al., 1995). Depending on their own feelings and beliefs about emotion, parents might coach their children to express anger, mask it, or suppress it entirely. Parents' own awareness of emotion tends to promote better regulation of anger in their children (e.g., Katz & Windeker-Nelson, 2004; Shortt, Stoolmiller, Smith-Shine, Eddy, & Sheeber, 2010).

Parents' own displays of anger

Parents' own beliefs and feelings about emotion will of course be related to the overt emotional reactions that they model, such as their own angry reactions to their children and other family members. A study of emotional expression during mother-child interaction (Denham & Grout, 1993) revealed that the more often mothers expressed anger while interacting with their children, the less emotionally positive the children were in the preschool setting. Longitudinal analyses show that mothers' expression of negative emotions predicts later anger and related behavioural problems in children (Newland & Crnic, 2011).

However, links between mothers' tendencies to express anger and their children's own displays of anger may emerge much earlier in development. In a study of young mothers, angry, punitive mothers tended to have infants who are themselves angry and noncompliant (Crockenberg, 1987). Our own study of a community sample demonstrated that mothers' anger during and prior to their pregnancies predicts infants' early signs of anger and aggressiveness at 6 months of age (Phillips, 2013).

Genetic as well as socialisation processes may foster links between parents' angry tendencies and their children's own expressions of anger and associated behavioural problems. A genetically informative adoption study showed that adoptive parents' expression of anger in their couple relationships and their use of harsh punishment fostered anger in their children, but that association was enhanced if the child's biological mother had also been angry and aggressive (Rhoades et al., 2011). Thus, parents' expression of anger is a facet of emotion socialisation but also reflects biological transmission of angry temperament from one generation to the next.

Emotional socialisation in the context of sibling relationships

For many children, discussions with their parents about their angry feelings may occur when siblings are present, and indeed the child's anger may have been induced during sibling conflict. In a detailed observational study of first- and second-born children's conversations with their mothers and siblings, the majority of mothers and about one-quarter of children talked about anger; in that sample, children were more likely to talk about their own feelings whilst mothers talked about different people's feelings in a given situation (Dunn, Brown, & Beardsall, 1991).

Siblings talk about emotion in the context of their play together; firstborn children's talk about emotions to their younger siblings appears to promote the younger child's abilities to take on the perspectives of others and generally more friendly interaction (Howe & Ross, 1990). However, it is not just discussion about emotion but each child's expression of emotion that influences the quality of sibling relationships. Younger siblings' angry temperaments foster competitive relationships between siblings (Stocker, Dunn, & Plomin, 1989). Children report that in the context of sibling relationships, in contrast to relationships with friends and classmates, anger more often leads to physical harming of other children, which in turn leads to high levels of guilt and remorse (Recchia, Wainryb, & Pasupathi, 2013). In general, then, the sibling relationship is a domain in which anger and aggression are frequently displayed in the context of emotionally arousing conflict, and thus it is an important arena for learning about the nature and consequences of anger. A meta-analysis of relevant studies suggests that the quality of sibling conflict has stronger effects on children's feelings and behaviour than does more positive features of the relationship such as sibling warmth (Buist, Dekovic, & Prinzie, 2013).

Another dimension of children's experiences in family life affects the quality of sibling relationships and the expression and understanding of anger: differential treatment of siblings by the parents. Any discussion of this issue must begin with the observation that apparent differential treatment may reflect the ages of the siblings; what may appear to the younger child to be highly inconsistent treatment may actually be the way the elder child was treated at the same age. The actual age and the quality of the behaviours shown by each child may influence parents' differential approaches to the siblings; for example, when older siblings are showing high levels of negative emotion, parents may try to distract the younger child whilst disciplining the older one (Kojima, 2000). Furthermore, differential treatment of siblings is influenced by other sources of adversity in the family environment (Meunier, Boyle, O'Connor, & Jenkins, 2013), and children's anger and aggressiveness may foster parents' differential treatment, rather than the other way around (Richmond & Stocker, 2008). Nonetheless, despite these caveats, children's perception of differential treatment by the parents may heighten the rate of conflict between the siblings and thereby increase their levels of anger.

Differential treatment can take different forms, not all of which are present in a given family: parents' differential enjoyment of their relationships with each sibling, favouring one child over the other, and differential types of discipline used with each sibling (Volling & Elins, 1998). Each form of differential treatment may reflect different family processes; for example, conflict in the couple relationship may induce favouritism (Volling & Elins, 1998). Analyses of a relatively large sample of Canadian families revealed that children are not just sensitive to differential treatment but to differences in the extent to which both parents show differential treatment; the two parents do not always favour the same child, particularly in the context of their own problems in the couple relationship (Meunier, Bisceglia, & Jenkins, 2012). In that sample, the impact of differential treatment on children's protests and oppositional behaviour also depended on age gap between the children. With a larger age gap, some favouritism toward younger siblings reduced their oppositional behaviour; with a smaller age gap, a more balanced treatment of the siblings led to less opposition. However, differential treatment is associated with parents' own levels of hostility and anger, which may have direct effects on children's own anger, regardless of what they perceive is happening to their siblings (Jenkins et al., 2012).

Cultural influences on emotion socialisation

Do the dimensions of emotion socialisation identified by Eisenberg and her colleagues apply across cultures? Parents in different cultures may react to their children's anger in different ways, depending on the norms regarding appropriate behaviour for children in those cultures. These culturally influenced reactions may lead to different amounts of discussion of children's feelings, and the discussions that do take place may focus on different issues. Furthermore, to the extent that parents have been socialised within their own cultures, they may be more or less likely to express anger and other primary emotions.

For example, mothers' conversations about children's emotions differed in two samples, each using the same experimental protocol, in Boston, Massachusetts,

USA and Beijing, China (Wang, 2001). In both samples, 3-year-old children and their mothers were asked to talk about past emotional events in which the child experienced happiness, sadness, fear and anger. In their conversations the American mothers were more likely than the Chinese mothers to offer explanations for the child's experience of these emotions, including anger. However, in both cultures the mothers provided more explanations of emotion to their daughters than their sons. The Chinese mothers were more likely than the American mothers to be didactic, telling their children how to react emotionally and drawing a moral lesson from the experience; such didactic talk was especially frequent when the mothers and the children were talking about anger.

It is important not to draw sweeping conclusions about cultural differences in relatively small and perhaps not representative samples. It is also important to note that there may be marked differences in emotional socialisation within as well as between cultures. For example, in a comparison of a suburban sample with an old city sample from the Indian state of Gujarat (Raval & Martini, 2009), mothers from the old city were less likely than suburban mothers to find their toddlers' expression of anger (as opposed to the expression of physical pain) to be acceptable. Indeed, the old city mothers reported that their child's expression of anger would make them feel angry, and they were more likely than the suburban mothers to punish children's expressions of anger. In general, however, both samples of mothers were less likely to support children's problem-focussed coping with anger than with other negative emotions.

Is a child's excessive anger a clinical condition?

Parents' negative reactions to children's expressions of anger may be subject to cultural influence, but mutual anger between parents and children may be seen in any culture. Although some degree of parent-child conflict is inevitable, in extreme cases angry, defiant children are seen as suffering from a clinical disorder. Much past research on this topic drew upon the diagnostic definitions set out by the American Psychiatric Association in the fourth edition of the *Diagnostic and Statistical Manual* (DSM-IV), which set out diagnostic criteria for Oppositional-Defiant Disorder (ODD), which in the latest version of the manual (DSM-5; American Psychiatric Association, 2013) is subsumed into a broader category along with Conduct Disorder (CD) and other problems of impulse control. However, the research on the former category of ODD reveals the central importance of anger in the development of these problems.

Representative epidemiological samples in which children's psychological problems were systematically assessed suggested that about one in ten children experienced ODD (e.g., Nock, Kazdin, Hiripi, & Kessler, 2007). Very angry, oppositional children are likely to have other psychological problems. The disruptive behaviour disorders (ODD, CD, ADHD) commonly co-occur, and in clinical practice they are not infrequently confused with each other. Furthermore, children with symptoms of ODD may also experience anxiety disorders and are at risk for later depression

(Rowe, Costello, Angold, Copeland, & Maughan, 2010). Therefore, the pathways from fear to anxiety disorders discussed in the last chapter and from anger to ODD discussed in this chapter may actually overlap. Furthermore, both fear and anger pathways may overlap with a pathway from sadness to depression, which we will examine in the next chapter.

6

SADNESS

As we have seen in the previous chapter, some children make angry protests when their goals are blocked or they are otherwise frustrated. Other children may respond to frustration with sadness rather than anger. Such children may perceive no realistic way of pursuing their goals in the present circumstances and give up their efforts to reach those goals. In other words, expressions of sadness as opposed to anger might reflect acceptance of the status quo, a kind of mental flight-versus-fight response. Developmental psychologists have attempted to define characteristic facial expressions that suggest children are feeling sad, such as lowered eyebrows, downcast eyes, turned-down corners of the mouth and possible tears (Figure 6.1).

FIGURE 6.1 The characteristic facial expression associated with sadness

To the extent that sadness reflects reality testing, it is not always maladaptive (Cole, Luby, & Sullivan, 2008). However, at extreme levels, children's pervasive sadness may affect many other dimensions of their psychological functioning. In this chapter we ask when children first begin to express sadness, explore the evidence for factors that promote children's sadness and examine the relationship between the ordinary experience of sadness and children's clinically significant depression.

The first signs of sadness in infancy

Expressions of sadness are the least common of infants' expressions of emotion (Izard et al., 1995) and, perhaps because they are relatively rare, it is not always easy for observers to distinguish sadness from other negative emotions (Oster et al., 1992). Observers may be good at recognising that the infant is distressed but less good at identifying a particular negative emotion like sadness (Camras & Shutter, 2010). Computer modelling suggests that observers recognise pain more accurately than sadness (Pal, Iyer, & Yantorno, 2006).

Infants may communicate their sadness vocally as well as through their facial expressions. Studies of children's temper tantrums suggest that sadness is signalled by whining and fussing, whereas shouting and squealing indicate more intense anger (Green, Whitney, & Potegal, 2011). Different patterns of brain activation are found when infants' facial expressions of sadness are accompanied by full crying; sad expressions without crying are linked to activation of the left frontal lobe, but sadness that is accompanied by crying is associated with right frontal activation (Fox & Davidson, 1988). These findings suggest that infants' and young children's experiences of negative emotion result in expressions of discomfort across different channels of communication. Closing and widening of the eyes seems to be a mechanism whereby infants communicate the intensity of their negative emotions to other people (Messinger, Whitney, Mahoor, & Cohn, 2012).

Infants' responses to the withdrawal of their caregivers' attention

It may be easier to determine whether infants are feeling sad, fearful or angry when the context is one that might be expected to provoke sadness, e.g., physical or psychological separation from their caregivers. This possibility has been explored through use of an experimental procedure known as the 'still face paradigm,' which was first designed as a way of simulating the behaviour of depressed mothers (Cohn & Tronick, 1983). In the still face procedure, mothers are asked to interact with their infants as they normally might do, and then freeze their faces for a minute, not responding to the infant's signals. This procedure often puzzles infants, and some become extremely distressed. Six-month-old infants' reactions to the still face procedure – whether they smiled or cried while their mothers were presenting a still face – predict later psychological problems at 12 months old (Moore, Cohn, & Campbell, 2001). Infants who failed to cry were less likely to experience emotional problems than other infants, whereas those who smiled were more likely to develop behavioural problems.

Infants' sad responses to frustration

Infants' expressions of sadness may also be seen under frustrating conditions, such as the extinction phase of the operant learning experiment already discussed in Chapter 5 (Lewis et al., 1992). In this experiment, infants learned to pull on a string to get a contingent event, a three-second presentation of a photo of a smiling baby accompanied by the theme song from the television programme *Sesame Street*. Each infant was given the opportunity to learn to obtain the contingent event, followed by a two-minute period in which pulling on the string did not lead to that event (the extinction period) and finally a three-minute period in which the contingency was reinstated and the infants could relearn the contingent behaviour. Their facial expressions were coded during the extinction period. Half of the infants tested showed both anger and sadness expressions during extinction; 31% expressed only anger and 17% only sadness, with one infant not bothered by the withdrawal of the contingency. Infants who showed anger (unmixed with sadness) during the extinction period showed more overt joy when the contingency was reinstated. These individual differences were not predicted by behaviour during the original learning phase. These findings suggest that angry as opposed to sad responses to frustrating circumstances may influence later emotions and behaviour, even in infancy.

Sadness in childhood

The experience of sadness

At a somewhat older age, children express sadness in response to disappointment, i.e., when they have been led to expect a positive experience or event that does not materialise. For example, in an experimental study, 4- to 5-year-old children were asked by a researcher to select possible prizes from a range of possibilities (Cole, Zahn-Waxler, & Smith, 1994). A second researcher then asked each child to perform a task and awarded a prize; the prize given was the child's lowest ranked choice. The children's facial expressions and emotion regulation strategies were assessed, both when the child was left alone and when the second researcher was present, to see if children who expressed their negative emotions when they were alone masked their disappointment in the researcher's presence. The children were more likely to express joy after receiving an undesirable prize when the researcher was present. Their reactions were more honest when the researcher was not in the room. These negative reactions included anger as well as sadness, which was particularly true for boys who were at risk for behavioural problems.

Interview studies allow researchers to move beyond the direct observation of facial expressions and assess children's own interpretations of their negative emotions. Such studies suggest that older children report an increased understanding of sadness as part of one's personal experience; when shown drawings of children along a continuum of sadness from slightly downhearted expressions to full-blown crying, 7-year-olds were more likely than 5-year-olds to attribute such feelings to themselves (Glasberg & Aboud, 1982).

During that period in development, children also show a change in their understanding of the events that might provoke sadness as opposed to other negative emotions. In a longitudinal study of British children interviewed at 4 and 7 years of age, the children were asked to look at faces (allegedly gender-neutral) showing the typical facial expressions of happiness, anger, sadness or fear (Hughes & Dunn, 2002). The interviewers pointed to each face and asked the children to say what kinds of things might make them feel the same way. Their answers were coded for references to particular agents that might have provoked the emotion in question and for general themes. Analysis of the themes revealed that at 4 years of age, in response to the picture of the sad face, the children reported that they might feel that way in response to aggression, conflict or frustration, or loss of a person or a pet. By 7 years of age, children predominantly said that they would feel that way in response to loss.

Managing sadness

As is the case with other negative emotions, children gradually become aware of the rules in their cultures and families that govern the display of sad feelings. They learn that some ways of expressing sadness are more socially acceptable than others. For example, in an interview study of primary school-aged North American children, the children reported that verbal expressions of sadness were the most acceptable, sulking and physically aggressive behaviour the least (Shipman, Zeman, Nesin, & Fitzgerald, 2003).

Within families, mothers and fathers may respond differently to children's expressions of sadness, but that may also depend on the child's age and whether the child in question is a boy or a girl. For example, when reminiscing about the child's past, parents tend to mention sadness more often with their daughters than their sons (Adams, Kuebli, Boyle, & Fivush, 1995). In a study of parents' reports of ways in which they would manage their children's negative emotion (Cassano, Perry-Parrish, & Zeman, 2007), fathers were more likely than mothers to report that they would tend to minimise the intensity of their children's expressions of sadness, for example, suggesting that the child not see the event as a 'big deal.' However, mothers of older children used more minimising strategies, whereas fathers used fewer. Mothers were more likely than fathers to report they would encourage their children to use problem-solving strategies to cope with their sad feelings.

These differences between mothers' and fathers' reactions to children's expressions of sadness appear to transcend culture. For example, in a study of two communities in Gujarat, India (Raval, Martini, & Raval, 2007), children reported that in general their parents believed that expressions of physical pain were more acceptable than expressions of anger or sadness. However, the children reported that expressions of sadness were more acceptable in the presence of mothers than fathers, and indeed more acceptable in front of peers than in front of their fathers.

As children grow older, the expression of sadness in the presence of peers may grow less acceptable, particularly for boys. In a study of North American 13-year-olds, boys were more likely than girls to report that they would be likely to inhibit their expressions of sadness in front of peers (Perry-Parrish & Zeman, 2011). In that sample, reports from classmates on a peer nomination task revealed that those boys who did not inhibit their expressions of sadness were less likely to be accepted by their peers.

Sadness, dysphoria and depressive illness in childhood

As we have seen, individual differences in the expression of sadness versus anger in response to frustrating circumstances are already evident in infancy (Lewis et al., 1992). But does children's sadness in response to frustration lead to a sense of learned helplessness, which is itself a risk factor for clinical depression?

Rates of depression in childhood and adolescence

For many years, clinicians thought it inappropriate to diagnose depression in childhood, believing that children were too cognitively immature to experience such a complex emotion (Angold, 1988). However, in the last few decades, it has been increasingly recognised that a minority of children do experience depressive illness and that it is possible to apply diagnostic criteria developed for adults in the childhood and adolescent years.

Clinical depression is diagnosed on the basis of a complex set of symptoms that extend beyond the experience and expression of sadness. However, in the *Diagnostic and Statistical Manual* (DSM) used by many clinicians and researchers in psychiatry and psychology, dysphoria and/or loss of interest in one's usual activities is the key symptom that must occur before a diagnosis of depressive illness can be made. At least one of these features – feelings of extreme sadness/dysphoria or loss of interest in things that one enjoys – must be present, with at least five other symptoms, to meet these diagnostic criteria (American Psychiatric Association, 2013). When the criteria are applied, it has been estimated that 2% of preschool children experience clinically significant depression, with over one in ten adolescents experiencing depression (Hankin, 2015).

These prevalence rates differ somewhat from sample to sample. For example, in a longitudinal study of a largely working-class sample of British children who were born in South London, parents and children were both interviewed when the child was 11 and 16 years of age (Pawlby, Hay, Sharp, Waters, & O'Keane, 2009). The prevalence of Major Depressive Disorder (MDD) was 4.2% at age 11 and 14.3% at age 16. In our own longitudinal study of firstborn children born in Cardiff, Wales, 7% of 6- to 7-year-olds met the diagnostic criteria for at least one episode of depressive illness.

There is much debate about whether or not contemporary children and adolescents are experiencing higher levels of depression, compared to past generations. A meta-analysis of studies drawing on different birth cohorts found no evidence for a current epidemic of depressive illness (Costello, Erkanli, & Angold, 2006). However, more recent analyses of large cohort studies undertaken in the last few decades do suggest that the rate of adolescents' emotional problems, including depression, is on the increase, with the strongest evidence coming from high-income countries; evidence for a rise in emotional problems in younger children is less compelling (Collishaw, 2015).

Features of depression in childhood

As we have seen, depression occurs at lower rates in childhood than in adolescence. Does childhood depression also differ in its qualitative features from depressive illness that occurs at older ages?

In a clinical study of 3- to 6-year-old North American children who had been recruited from primary care and specialist mental health clinics, three groups of children were compared: (1) those with at least two symptoms of depression, (2) those with at least two symptoms of either Attention-Deficit Hyperactivity Disorder (ADHD) or Oppositional-Defiant Disorder (ODD) and (3) those who showed no clinical symptoms (Luby et al., 2003). The children showing depressive symptoms were more likely to come from families with lower incomes, to have parents who were not legally married and to have been exposed to more stressful life events. Compared to the other two groups, they were more likely to show a range of symptoms of depressive illness, including appetite problems, sleep problems, low energy, problems concentrating, low self-esteem and preoccupation with thoughts about death. They were more likely than children in the other groups to have a range of health problems. Furthermore, they showed very distinctive emotional responses to frustration.

As we have seen in the previous chapter, in the preschool years, children may experience temper tantrums. However, the tantrums shown by children who are experiencing depressive symptoms differ qualitatively from 'ordinary' tantrums. Depressed children's tantrums are more violent and more often involve self-harm. Depressed children take longer to recover from their tantrums, and afterwards they are more likely to be very distressed about having had a tantrum, sometimes showing signs of shame and guilt (Cole et al., 2008).

Precursors and predictors of sadness and depression in childhood

Individual differences in sadness and in clinically significant depression may both originate in infancy. Irritability in infancy, as described in Chapter 2, is a predictor of sadness in childhood, as shown in a longitudinal study of Finnish children (Komsi et al., 2006). Fearful temperament interacts with family life events and mothers' negative feedback to their children to predict a depressogenic cognitive style in middle childhood (Mezulis, Hyde, & Abramson, 2006). In such studies, it is important to consider the parents' own mental health and the possibility of transmission of sadness and depression from one generation to the next. Parents' own experience of depressive illness may lead to a parenting style that fosters sadness and depression in their children.

Even brief experimental manipulations of parents' emotions may influence infants' behaviour. For example, in a study of 9-month-olds, mood-induction procedures were used to influence the affect displayed by mothers (either joy or sadness). When mothers had been induced to feel sad, their infants were less likely to express joy and somewhat more likely to express sadness (Termine & Izard, 1988).

Parents' own experience of depression leads to changed behaviour with their infants. Infants who have been exposed to mothers' postpartum depression tend to experience interaction with their mothers that is somewhat less infant-focussed and more likely to feature expressions of negative emotion from both mother and infant (Cooper, Tomlinson, Swarz, & Woolgar, 1999; Murray, Kempton, Woolgar, & Hooper, 1993). Those infants who are exposed to mothers' depression are at elevated risk for depression themselves as adolescents (Halligan, Murray, Martins, & Cooper, 2007). However, this may be due to genetic risk as well as to the exposure to their depressed mothers' displays of sadness and other negative emotions. It is also possible that infants who are at genetic risk for depression are particularly affected by the emotions displayed by their parents and other caregivers.

Taken together, findings from studies of childhood depression suggest that there is a developmental pathway from irritable and fearful temperament in infancy to sadness in childhood that, in some individuals, consolidates into a lifelong vulnerability to depression. To the extent that depression is known to run in families, the child's genetic heritage intertwines with patterns of family interaction that may foster sadness and depressive thinking.

7
HAPPINESS, JOY AND ELATION

Bridges' theory of the early differentiation of emotion claimed that the infant's initial capacity for delight began to transform into signs of elation and joy over the first two years of life (see Figure 1.1). Furthermore, as infants grow older, they begin to find certain events funny; they also learn how to make other people laugh. Older children gradually come to a broader understanding of what it means to be happy. However, just as we know much more about infants' crying than about their laughter, we know more about older children's and adolescents' capacities for fear, anger and sadness than about their experiences of joy and happiness.

Compared to negative emotions, the feeling of happiness is associated with a distinct pattern of brain activation (e.g., Reiman et al., 1997). However, there are several different types of positive emotion, beyond general happiness. Some investigators have attempted to identify specific facial expressions associated with different positive emotions. For example, in an experiment in which young adults were asked to remember occasions when they felt particular emotions and try to make expressions that reflected those feelings, distinct patterns of facial expression were identified for three positive emotions: awe, pride and amusement (Shiota, Campos, & Keltner, 2003). Attempts to express awe were associated with raised eyes and somewhat raised eyebrows, suggesting that this form of positive emotion incorporated an element of surprise. Pride and amusement were both associated with smiling, but more tight-lipped smiling in the case of pride and more exaggerated 'play face' smiling in the case of amusement. The origins of these various shades of happiness lie in infancy and early childhood.

Pleasure in one's achievements

Even in the first two years of life, infants' successful accomplishment of tasks is often accompanied by signs of pleasure, sometimes referred to as 'mastery smiles'

(Kagan, 1981). Acquiring new skills may also induce infants' signs of happiness. For example, infants who have just learned to crawl show an increase in signs of happiness, although it declines after the infants have grown used to crawling (Zachry et al., 2015).

Children appear to be especially pleased when they succeed in tasks that pose some difficulty. For example, when toddlers are presented with puzzles that vary from easy to moderately difficult to very difficult, they are likely to persist longer at the moderately difficult puzzles; in general, 36-month-olds showed significantly more signs of pleasure than did younger toddlers, but they were least likely to show pleasure when faced with puzzles that were too easy (Redding, Morgan, & Harmon, 1988). Toddlers' sense of pride in their own achievements can be expressed in different ways, beyond their 'mastery smiles,' for example, by their posture, by breaking into applause at their own behaviour, or by making verbal remarks such as 'I did it!' (Kelley, Brownell, & Campbell, 2000). However, in one sample of 3-year-old British children, smiling was more common than overt self-congratulation (Reissland, 1994). In another sample of 3-year-olds, the children were more likely to show signs of pride on difficult as compared to easy tasks (Lewis et al., 1992).

By around 4 years of age, children can recognise other people's expressions of pride, although their ability to recognise this positive emotion and discriminate it from surprise and general happiness improves further with age (Tracy, Robins, & Lagattuta, 2005). However, even in middle childhood, children sometimes confuse body postures that are associated with pride with those that signify anger (Nelson & Russell, 2012).

Amusement

The development of humour

We have already seen that infants laugh at things they find amusing. Infants not only laugh at things they find amusing, but they also try to make their companions laugh (see Chapter 2). However, the development of a sense of humour rests on both social and cognitive foundations. During early childhood, children become increasingly aware of incongruities in their environments, and they notice events that violate people's prior expectations. Such unexpected events might provoke surprise or disgust or fear; under what circumstances do unusual events make children laugh?

Mutual laughter and silliness is an important component of parent-infant relationships. Parents of young infants often do deliberately silly things, in an attempt to get their infants to smile or laugh; absurd nonverbal behaviour shown by parents is often referred to as 'clowning' (Reddy, 2001). In a study of a small sample of parents who were asked to try to make their 3- to 6-month-old infants smile or laugh (Mireault et al., 2012), clowning was a favoured technique, being shown more commonly than tickling or singing or book-reading. The older infants in the sample were more likely to laugh and in some cases try to imitate the absurd actions, which in turn made the parents laugh.

Sharing an understanding that some things are funny is an important component of our personal relationships. Infants develop a sense of humour in the context of experiences with the adults who care for them. In this way, infants learn to make distinctions between jokes – deliberate attempts to be funny – and unintentional mistakes (Hoicka & Gattis, 2008). Three-year-olds are more likely to laugh at events that are intended to be funny; 2- to 3-year-olds begin to make their own jokes (Hoicka & Akhtar, 2012).

Play and laughter with siblings and peers

Laughter and humour are important components of children's interactions with other children, including their siblings as well as peers. Across various cultures, children play around with language to produce humour and engagement, telling jokes, making puns and engaging in rhythmic chants and silly songs. When children are conversing with other children, forms of humorous speech may also include nonsense words, 'wise guy' comments and scatological remarks (Ely & McCabe, 1994).

These playful interactions provide opportunities for learning but also may induce some conflict. Younger children may attempt to imitate their elder siblings' word play, not always accurately. For example, in a study of Canadian sibling pairs, the older child's proclamation of 'Boop a Doop!' was repeated by the younger sibling imperfectly as 'Froop a Doop!' to which the elder child responded, 'You can't say it very well!' (Howe, Rosciszewska, & Persram, 2017). Children's play with language is often combined with motor play: for example, Thai children were observed to

FIGURE 7.1   Shared amusement in childhood

ask each other humorous riddles about crabs and ghosts whilst spinning around a room (Howard, 2009).

These playful interactions that children have with other children make important contributions to their cognitive and emotional development. By playing and engaging in humour in this way, they construct 'shared meanings' (e.g., Dunn, 1988; Howe, Petrakos, Rinaldi, & LeFebvre, 2005); over time, sibling relationships and friendships are built on the bedrock of a network of shared meanings unique to that pair of siblings or friends. Children's conversations during these playful interactions provide an opportunity to acquire social understanding, as they make references to each other's mental states and motivations (e.g., Leach, Howe, & Dehart, 2015).

Children's reflections on their general happiness

As children grow older, they become able to reflect on their own happiness (e.g., Huebner, 1991) and the happiness of other people whom they know. For example, Canadian children were interviewed about their mothers' emotions, being asked how they could tell if their mothers were sad, angry or happy; they were also asked what might cause their own sadness, anger or happiness (Covell & Abramovitch, 1987). Younger children tended to see themselves as the cause of their mothers' happiness; older children drew attention to other people and abstract situations that might induce happiness.

In middle childhood, children can reflect on various sources of happiness in their lives. For example, in an interview study of 7- to 9-year-old Argentinian children, the children attributed their happiness to experiences with family members, friends and the pleasure of playing with their pets (Greco & Ison, 2014). Children's self-perceived happiness can serve as a protective factor in development, even when the children are facing very difficult circumstances, such as life within war zones. For example, the experience of positive emotion and a sense of well-being helped Palestinian children cope with the effects of political violence on their lives (Veronese & Castiglioni, 2015).

Exhilaration and elation

Can there be such a thing as too much happiness? Social psychologists have long drawn attention to the phenomenon of emotional contagion (e.g., Hatfield, Cacioppo, & Rapson, 1993), and generations of children who find themselves falling about with laughter have been warned that 'There will be tears before sunset.' Exhilaration combines positive emotion with excitement, being expressed by laughter as well as smiling and various changes in posture (Ruch, 1993). Are such extreme displays of positive emotion a sign of dysregulated emotion that poses problems for children?

Signs of mania in adults who suffer from bipolar illness may begin with happy excitement but end up in a psychotic state, often accompanied by self-destructive behaviour. Bipolar illness is heritable and can manifest itself in childhood (Hunt,

Schwarz, Nye, & Frazier, 2016). Does this imply that high levels of elation and exhilaration in childhood are signs of bipolar illness? Current work on bipolar illness suggests that its manifestations in childhood tend to take the form of general irritability and depressed mood, with episodes of mania only emerging later in adolescence (Hunt et al., 2016). However, the way mania manifests itself in childhood may differ both qualitatively and quantitatively from its manifestations in later adolescence or adulthood (Geller et al., 2001), and so there would be value in studying the phenomena of elation and exhilaration in middle childhood more closely, in both high-risk and community samples.

8

AFFECTION, LOVE AND JEALOUSY

As we have already seen, infants come into the world biased in favour of other human beings. They are drawn to the sight of human faces and sensitive to the properties of human voices, and, from the moment of birth onward, can express emotion in a way that has direct effects on their companions. In the next months, however, infants' general abilities to express positive emotion transform into displays of affection for particular people, both adults and other children (Bridges, 1932). Infants begin to establish particular, emotionally significant relationships with their caregivers – they develop attachments to the people who care for them. Although John Bowlby (1969) argued that infants have an inbuilt tendency to be *monotropic*, i.e., to form a particular attachment to the primary caregiver (usually, though not always, the biological mother), infants do show affection and develop attachments with other family members (Schaffer & Emerson, 1964), including their siblings (Teti & Ablard, 1989). In humans, a species where child-bearing is associated with considerable risk for maternal death, the ability to form attachments to people other than the biological mother is unquestionably adaptive (Nash, 1995; Smith, 1980).

However, infants who are cared for by a shifting number of impersonal or inadequate caregivers may not develop optimally. Even within institutional environments, focussed care by a single, dedicated caregiver can facilitate infants' social responsiveness (Rheingold, 1956). Nonetheless, the longer children stay in inadequate institutional care, the more likely it is that their cognitive and socioemotional development will be compromised (Rutter, Kreppner, & O'Connor, 2001).

In view of these considerations, in this chapter, we shall focus on the infant's emerging capacity to feel and express affection to other people and the further development of focussed attachment relationships. We shall then examine the claims made about the consequences of these attachment relationships for the child's later emotional development.

Infants' preferences for familiar companions

In early human development, familiarity does not breed contempt. Rather, the capacity to love begins with the ability to recognise familiar people, and that ability emerges soon after, if indeed not before, a child is born.

Newborn infants' recognition of their mothers

Voice recognition

Human newborns are biased in favour of their own species, showing particular interest in human faces and voices, as opposed to other stimuli. Their general affinity for other human beings can be thought of as *species recognition*, which fosters their interactions with other people who may care for their needs. Against that background of general interest in people, there is evidence that newborn infants already may recognise the distinctive voices of the women who gave birth to them. Even when they are still in the womb, infants' hearts beat faster when listening to a passage read by their mothers than by unfamiliar women (Kisilevsky et al., 2003). Shortly after they are born, infants will work to hear their mothers' voices, by sucking on a plastic nipple that does not deliver milk (DeCasper & Fifer, 1980), particularly if the mother is not whispering (Spence & Freeman, 1996). A study of newborns whose brain activity was measured by electroencephalography (see Figure 8.1) showed that the infants processed their mothers' and unfamiliar women's voices in different ways; the authors describe this process as tuning the brain for specialised recognition of familiar voices (Beauchemin et al., 2011).

FIGURE 8.1   An infant wearing the cap that measures EEG

Odour recognition

In the days after birth, infants begin to recognise other things about their mothers. For example, breast-feeding infants recognise their mothers' distinctive smell (Cernoch & Porter, 1985).

Displays of affection

But when does preference turn into love? One way to address that question is to examine infants' own displays of affection for familiar people, showing that the presence of the parent or other familiar person brings comfort and pleasure.

Bridges' original observations of the progression of emotional development (Figure 1.1) showed that, even in the institutionalised population that she was studying, infants began to show affection to other people around 12 months of age (Bridges, 1932). However, a longitudinal study of affection between infants and parents suggests that infants' expressions of affection become more common after the second year of life, with children's expression of affection to their mothers and fathers occurring at comparable rates (Barry & Kochanska, 2010). Toddlers express affection to familiar people with cries of joy, hugs and cuddles (Banham, 1950). Such displays of affection to others are common in 18-month-olds, both those who are showing neurotypical development and those with autism spectrum disorders (Barbaro & Dissanayake, 2013).

Young children's considerable knowledge about how to provide affection to others is evident in their imaginative play, in which they show affection to their dolls and teddies, and often imitate the role of a loving caregiver; in one study, naturalistic observations of young children at home revealed affectionate treatment of dolls, infant siblings and pets, and very little in the way of punitive behaviours (Rheingold & Emery, 1986). Many children report feeling great affection for their family pets (Triebenbacher, 1998).

Longitudinal analyses suggest that individual differences in displaying affection to parents emerge in the childhood years. Children's own displays of affectionate behaviour are likely to be a reflection of their own receipt of affection from their parents, with reciprocal levels of affection being observed over time (Barry & Kochanska, 2010). Parents' provision of affection may reflect the parents' memories of affectionate behaviour from their own parents (Bronson, Katten, & Livson, 1959). Children's attachments to parents are often formed in the context of affectionate, caring relationships across generations of family members (Main, Kaplan, & Cassidy, 1985).

Jealousy

Jealousy has been defined as 'a normal response to actual, supposed or threatened loss of affection' (Vollmer, 1946, p. 660). In the context of Bridges' (1932) differentiation theory, jealousy is one of the negative emotions that emerges from general distress (see Figure 1.1). Within children's early development, one of the first sources of jealousy may be caregivers' interactions with other people, particularly siblings.

Some investigators have argued that, under some conditions, signs of distress in infancy could be interpreted as early forms of jealousy. For example, in one study, mothers were instructed to divert their attention from their 6-month-old infants, instead focussing on either a book or a lifelike doll that made characteristic infant vocalisations when touched (Hart & Carrington, 2002). The infants looked at the mother and showed positive affect at equal rates across the two conditions; however, they were significantly more likely to show negative affect when their mothers were paying attention to the lifelike doll.

In a follow-up experiment (Hart, Carrington, Tronick, & Carroll, 2004), 6-month-old infants' facial expressions were coded for different emotions when their mothers interacted with them and when they interacted with the lifelike doll, as well as when the mother engaged in the still face procedure (see Chapter 6). In contrast to periods where the mother and infant were interacting normally, the infants showed more sadness and anger and less positive affect and interest when the mother was interacting with the doll. Furthermore, the infants reacted as negatively to the interaction with the doll as they did to the stress-provoking still face procedure. These findings also suggest that the phenomenon of jealousy entails a blend of different negative emotions and cannot be reduced to pure sadness or anger.

Such jealous reactions are also observed when children watch their mothers interacting with other children, not just lifelike dolls. In a cross-sectional study, where mothers were instructed to pay attention to other children rather than their own, signs of jealousy specific to that procedure were seen from the second year of life onwards (Masciuch & Kienapple, 1993). In that study, attention-seeking behaviour as well as negative affect indicated feelings of jealousy when mothers paid attention to someone other than their own children.

At later ages, children express jealousy not just of someone else's affection but their attainments; this form of jealousy reflects the children's comparison of themselves with others and potential resentment of other children's achievements. For example, children between 6 and 11 years of age were interviewed about their views on stories about a child protagonist's failures (Bers & Rodin, 1984). The stories about the protagonist's failures either did or did not involve comparison with another character. The children were asked to state what the protagonist might think or feel, and what they might do, in response to the events of each story. The children's responses to the interviewers' questions revealed a profile of jealous reactions, in which social comparison was bound up with anger; this was particularly true for the younger children in the sample.

As children form close personal relationships, they may experience jealousy; they may also need to understand the manifestations of jealousy in others. In a study that compared typically developing young adolescents with those who had been given diagnoses of autism spectrum disorders (Bauminger, 2004), the investigators sought evidence for the young people's understanding of jealousy as depicted in pictures, self-reports of situations in which they felt jealous, or reports of ways to cope with feelings of jealousy. In comparison with the typically developing sample, the participants with diagnoses of autism, who were matched on cognitive ability, reported qualitatively different ways of showing jealousy; they were also less likely to recognise manifestations of jealousy in pictures. The use of a case-comparison design, however, does not allow us to draw conclusions about the range of individual differences in the understanding of jealousy in more broadly representative community samples.

Attachment relationships

Within psychology, the development of love has primarily been discussed in the context of the enduring influence of infants' attachments to those adults who care for them. Attachment is not a simple emotion or an individual trait; rather, it is a *developmental process* whereby two people form a relationship with each other over time. Both infants and their caregivers bring their own individual characteristics and developmental histories to the formation of their mutual relationships.

The Bowlby-Ainsworth attachment theory

In the second half of the first year of life, when many infants develop strong preferences for their caregivers, individual differences in the quality of infants' relationships with their caregivers become apparent. These different patterns of attachment relationships have been most often discussed in the context of attachment theory (Bowlby, 1969; Ainsworth, 1969; Ainsworth, Blehar, Waters, & Wall, 2015). The intellectual roots of attachment theory lie in John Bowlby's experiences as a psychoanalytic psychiatrist, faced with the major humanitarian crisis of the displacement of children after the second World War, coupled with his theoretical interest in both ethology and cognitive science. Attachment theory was also advanced theoretically by Mary Ainsworth's observations of infants with their parents in Uganda and Baltimore, Maryland, which drew an emphasis on the construct of *security*, as set forth by her mentor, the Canadian personality theorist William Blatz (1966).

The collaboration between Bowlby and Ainsworth at the Tavistock Clinic in London led to a focus on the articulation of attachment theory and the development of methods for its study. Whilst Ainsworth carried out studies of the normative development of attachment, her focus soon turned to individual differences in the quality of attachment relationships, which she characterised in terms of Blatz's key concept of security. In Ainsworth's view, children did not fail to become attached to their caregivers, but rather their experiences of those attachment relationships felt more or less secure.

Exploration from a secure base

As we have seen in Chapter 3, human infants are interested in exploring their environments, but they may also become frightened by the novel places and events they encounter. Bowlby (1969) suggested that infants in attachment relationships must balance their tendencies toward exploration with their tendencies to seek comfort from caregivers, who provide a secure base from which to explore. After some naturalistic observation of infants in the first year of life, Ainsworth developed a standardised procedure for measuring individual differences in the security of attachment, which she called the Strange Situation (Ainsworth et al., 2015). In a laboratory procedure that takes less than 15 minutes, infants experience the opportunity to explore a new environment in the presence of their caregivers but also meet unfamiliar people and experience two brief periods of separation from their caregivers. Qualitative analyses of infants' behaviour led to an initial distinction between infants' secure behaviour in the face of these challenges versus their manifestations of insecurity, which might take the form either of extreme independence from and avoidance of their caregivers (subsequently referred to as *avoidant attachment*), or more negative or ambivalent reactions when the caregivers returned after separation (subsequently referred to as *resistant attachment*). Other procedures for the measurement of attachment security have been developed, such as the Attachment Q Set (Waters & Deane, 1985), but in the decades following Ainsworth's initial work, the Strange Situation became the primary paradigm in developmental psychology for the study of attachment relationships and their predictive power with respect to the child's later development.

Is attachment security simply a reflection of the infant's temperament?

We have already seen in Chapter 2 that infants differ in their emotional expressiveness. Do those individual differences in temperament account for differences in attachment relationships? Many studies have shown that secure attachment relationships, as measured by Ainsworth's Strange Situation procedure, are often predated by sensitive caregiver-infant interactions in early infancy (e.g., De Wolff & van IJzendoorn, 1997) and followed by positive outcomes in development (Ainsworth et al., 2015). Some features of infant temperament, which can be measured by the Brazelton Neonatal Assessment shortly after birth, predicted later security of attachment (Waters, Vaughn, & Egeland, 1980). This finding raised the possibility that some infants are more temperamentally suited to become securely attached than others, and therefore individual differences in attachment security might reflect more fundamental differences in temperament.

If the security of infant-parent attachment were merely a reflection of an individual infant's temperament, then it would seem likely that the infant's relationships with both their parents would be equally secure or insecure, as the case might be. If, on the other hand, the security of attachment reflected the infant's experiences within a particular relationship, the infant might show security with the father but not the mother, or vice versa. Some initial studies suggested that this was the case (e.g., Main & Weston, 1981), which was taken as proof that attachment reflected interpersonal relationships, not just temperament. However, in a meta-analysis of studies that measured infants' attachment to both their parents, there was substantial concordance in attachment classifications across parents (Fox, Kimmerly, &

Schafer, 1991), which strengthened the case for a link between temperament and attachment.

More recently, a meta-analysis of 131 different samples of infants (Groh et al., 2017) identified a specific association between the infant's temperament and the form of insecurity known as *resistant attachment*, which is characterised by an ambivalent response in the Strange Situation when the mother returns after a brief separation. In contrast, there was less evidence for a link between the infant's temperament and the *avoidant* pattern of attachment, where the infant shows more independent play and is less upset by meeting a stranger or the brief separations from the mother. In general, the development of an attachment relationship may be affected by the infant's temperament, but the concept of attachment does not simply reduce to that of individual temperament. As is the case in all love relationships, infant-parent attachment refers to a dynamic two-person relationship, not just one person's temperament.

Furthermore, the security of infants' relationships with their caregivers is not necessarily stable over time, which is what might be expected if security were simply due to individual differences in temperament. Rather, attachment relationships may change over time, in relation to their circumstances. Although there is a tendency to think that a secure attachment relationship in infancy somehow inoculates the child against subsequent adversity in life, the security of attachment relationships can increase or decrease over time. In the face of change in family circumstances, some children become less secure and others become more secure (e.g., Hamilton, 2000; Weinfield, Sroufe, & Egeland, 2000). The quality of attachment relationships seems most likely to remain stable when children remain in the same environment. However, as children grow older and, especially, seek to define themselves over later childhood and adolescence, their attachments to their parents may take a different shape over time. Does the teenager's level of attachment security simply change over the years of adolescence? Or does some fundamental quality of the original attachment relationship established in infancy remain stable over those years of growth and change?

These issues of change and continuity in adolescents' attachment relationships were investigated via an age-appropriate self-report questionnaire about *attachment style*, which was given repeatedly over a five-year period, beginning when the teenagers were 14 years of age (Jones et al., 2018). The participants showed considerable stability in their attachment styles over the five years of adolescence, but their attachment styles were influenced by their ethnicity and by turmoil in their parents' own love relationships.

Love and cognition: representations of attachment relationships

Infants' and toddlers' signs of affection are often nonverbal, and their nonverbal behaviour in the Strange Situation is used to characterise the security of their attachment relationships. However, by the second year of life, the word 'love' has entered their vocabularies (Bretherton, McNew, & Beeghly-Smith, 1981). Over the years, John Bowlby's influential theory of infant-parent attachment moved from a consideration of 'component instinctual responses' to the concept of the 'internal working model,' which drew attention to cognitive as well as affective and behavioural aspects of infants' relationships with their attachment figures (Bowlby, 1969). In other words, the child's experience of love for a caregiver is representational, not simply emotional. Bowlby's concept of the working model was influenced by contemporary information-processing theory of adult memory and cognition (Craik, 1943), as well as his background in psychoanalysis (see Bretherton, 1985, for a discussion of the development of Bowlby's ideas about the working model of attachment).

Other attachment theorists have attempted to link the concept of a working model to other cognitive processes. For example, Inge Bretherton (1985) proposed that the child's development of expectations of the caregiver's behaviour could be analysed in terms of script theory and the child's acquisition of social knowledge. In other words, as children grow older, they come to understand how close relationships are supposed to work, almost like the script of a play where they needed to learn the lines. Bretherton's use of script theory to explain the cognitive dimensions of attachment relationships has been extended by empirical studies in which children are prompted to talk about their everyday experiences with caregivers. These studies have demonstrated that children in different cultures have complex representations of their security in their relationships with their parents (Vaughn et al., 2007; Waters et al., 2015).

Children's working models of their relationships with their caregivers endure into young adulthood, and the nature of individuals' working models are influenced by the quality of their early relationships. For example, in a large sample from a longitudinal study of children's experiences in early child care settings, young adults' script knowledge about attachment relationships was predicted by their own experiences of caregiving from both their mothers and fathers (Steele et al., 2014).

Taken together, these findings suggest that children's love for those who care for them is a complex social emotion that has both affective and cognitive dimensions that consolidate over time.

Disorganised attachment relationships

In recent years, attachment researchers using Ainsworth's Strange Situation paradigm began to observe children whose reactions did not fit into the original coding scheme. These children showed unexpected and sometimes mutually incompatible reactions, such as 'a) the complete absence of an apparent attachment strategy; b) contradictory behaviours or affects occurring virtually simultaneously; c) freezing, stilling, apparent dissociation; d) abnormal movements; or e) direct indices of apprehension of the parent' (Green & Goldwyn, 2002, p. 836). The rate of such 'disorganised' attachment classifications is especially high in clinical samples and is particularly high when children have been exposed to maltreatment (e.g., Carlson, 1998; Cicchetti & Doyle, 2016). As discussed in Chapter 4, some of the behaviours associated with disorganised attachment are shown in fear-provoking contexts, which suggests that the child's disorganised behaviour is a response to frightening behaviour shown by caregivers (Lyons-Ruth, Bronfman, & Parsons, 1999). However, factors within the child, including birth weight and genetic factors, may interact with the parents' treatment of the child to produce disorganised attachments (Wazana et al., 2015).

Attachment disorders in childhood

In some cases, children's attachment patterns are so aberrant that they have been classified as childhood psychological disorders. Two different types of attachment disorders are recognised in the DSM-5 diagnostic system: Reactive Attachment Disorder and Disinhibited Social Engagement Disorder. Both tend to be seen in the context of children's adverse experiences, such as maltreatment or having been brought up in institutions, but they differ in their symptoms and implications for clinical interventions.

Reactive Attachment Disorder is diagnosed when children appear not to have focussed attachments to their caregivers, coupled with other social and emotional difficulties (Zeanah & Gleason, 2015). The diagnosis requires that the child have a developmental age of at least 9 months, to rule out other maturational problems that might make it impossible to form attachments.

In contrast, Disinhibited Social Engagement Disorder is diagnosed when a child behaves toward unfamiliar people with inappropriate friendliness, a pattern of behaviour that is particularly common for children who have spent their early lives in group care in an institutional setting. The longer the time spent in the institutional environment, the more likely it is that children will show such inappropriate friendly behaviour (Rutter et al., 2010). These children can form focussed attachments with adoptive parents, but their disinhibited behaviour often poses a problem of keeping them safe in the outside world. This form of attachment behaviour is sometimes correlated with other clinical conditions, such as Attention-Deficit and Hyperactivity Disorder (ADHD) and autism spectrum disorders.

Although all children who have experienced adversity in infancy do not develop these disorders, it is important to provide support for those who do. In particular, it is important to support foster carers and adoptive parents who look after children who have experienced trauma and chaotic circumstances in their past and may find it difficult to learn how to love new people.

9

EMPATHY

So far we have discussed the developmental progression from infants' early feelings of distress and delight to the experience of different primary emotions, including surprise, fear, disgust, anger and sadness. We now consider more complex emotional experiences, sometimes referred to as social or moral emotions – emotions that are bound up with children's understanding of the social world. In this chapter we shall examine the development of empathy, i.e., feeling and understanding what another person feels. In common with the primary emotions described in the earlier chapters, the developmental origins of empathy lie in the early months of life, although cognitive dimensions of empathy develop over childhood. Empathy theorists make a distinction between *affective* and *cognitive empathy* (e.g., Preston & de Waal, 2002). Mature empathy entails both feeling for another person and understanding the reasons why that person feels that way (Decety & Meyer, 2008). An accurate understanding of another person's emotions rests on the ability to recognise emotional signals and also comprehend the context in which the emotional signal is produced. In other words, children come to understand why a person is laughing, crying, or showing anger in a given situation.

The roots of empathy

At what point in development do we begin to feel what another person feels? And at what point can it be said that we feel concern for that person? Some scholars have pointed out that even young infants seem attuned to emotion, smiling when another smiles (Field, Guy, & Umbel, 1985), crying when another cries (Sagi & Hoffman, 1976). But is this form of emotional contagion the first step in the development of true empathy?

It has been argued that infants cry when they hear the cry of another infant because they are confused – because they cannot really tell the difference between themselves and other people (Darwin, 1877; Preyer, 1889). This idea of a blurred boundary between self and other was set forth in psychoanalytic writings, both in terms of Freud's (1949) initial ideas about the 'primary process' of infancy and Winnicott's (1960) object relations theory, which held that there was 'no such thing as an infant' – meaning that the infant did not perceive any boundary between itself and its mother. Within this framework, infants might cry when other people cried because they did not understand that they were not already crying.

Hoffman (1975) argued that, over the course of infancy, this early form of vicarious distress would gradually transmute into a more mature form of sympathetic behaviour, where infants would not just get distressed themselves but would try to comfort the person who was distressed. Thus, in Hoffman's theory, contagion of distress would be replaced by a more mature concern for others that was underpinned by cognitive understanding. Younger infants' emotional reactions would not yet qualify as true empathy.

More recently, the notion that infants are not able to tell the difference between themselves and other people has been challenged. Infants can in fact tell the difference between their own previously recorded cries and the cries of another infant (Dondi, Simion, & Caltran, 1999) and between videos of themselves and other infants (Legerstee, Anderson, & Schaffer, 1998). Therefore, if crying when another infant cries is not simply the consequence of confusion between self and other, it can be examined as an early step on the pathway toward empathy and compassion (Davidov, Zahn-Waxler, Roth-Hanania, & Knafo, 2013).

An observational study of 6-month-olds' responses to peers showed that the longer the time one infant spent fussing or crying, the more likely it was that a peer would break down and cry as well; in that sample, the infants responded to the peer's distress not just by becoming distressed themselves but by watching, gesturing to and touching the other infant and turning their heads to look at the peer's own mother (Hay, Nash, & Pedersen, 1981). When 8- to 10-month-olds observed distressed peers, they showed facial expressions and gestures that signified concern for the upset peers (Roth-Hanania, Davidov, & Zahn-Waxler, 2011). Thus, these early reactions to another's distress are not limited to contagious crying.

The 'baby biographers' – early scholars who kept diaries about their children's development – have provided many anecdotal reports of young children becoming distressed at the sight of the uncooked holiday turkey. For example, Wilhelm Stern's (1924) son wept and cried out 'Poor turkey has no clothes!' In general, children's earliest emotional reactions to overt and possible distress are not accompanied by signs of confusion between themselves and others but rather by attempts to comprehend what might be the matter.

FIGURE 9.1   The early origins of empathy

Very young children's reactions to people's distress

Providing comfort in the face of distress

Many toddlers are sensitive to the occurrence of distress and sometimes try to help or comfort the people who are distressed (Zahn-Waxler, Radke-Yarrow, Wagner, & Chapman, 1992). The comfort offered may not always be appropriate for the recipient, as when a small child offers an adult her own teddy. Such instrumental attempts to provide comfort to people who are distressed emerge by the second year of life, around the time that toddlers often provide help to adults who are experiencing practical difficulties (Warneken & Tomasello, 2006). Very young children have been observed to behave prosocially in response to the distress of their parents (Zahn-Waxler et al., 1992), siblings (Dunn & Munn, 1986) and peers (Lamb & Zakhireh, 1997; Murphy, 1937). Young children's prosocial responses to distress may go beyond providing comfort; they may try to distract or share with or provide other sorts of assistance (Demetriou & Hay, 2004).

When examining young children's abilities to respond to distress with comfort or other prosocial actions, it is important to take into account the difference between competence and performance. For example, in an observational study of toddlers attending day care centres, 22% of the sample responded prosocially to distress on at least one occasion, but only 3% of episodes of distress evoked such prosocial responding (Lamb & Zakhireh, 1997). When 3- and 4-year-olds were shown a video of a distressed classmate (Caplan & Hay, 1989), virtually all made relevant suggestions about how the child could be comforted, thus showing appropriate knowledge about how to provide help in the response to distress; when asked who should provide the help, they overwhelming suggested the teacher. In that sample, most of the children had responded prosocially to a classmate's distress at least once, but did not do so often, a pattern of behaviour that reflected their views that providing comfort to a distressed child was the responsibility of adults, not other small children.

On some occasions young children react negatively to another person's distress, responding to the distress with amusement or physical aggression. Such negative responses are not uncommonly seen between siblings (Dunn & Munn, 1986; Dunn & Brown, 1994) and also amongst familiar peers (Demetriou & Hay, 2004). The likelihood of a negative response to another's distress is heightened when the child was the perpetrator of that distress (Zahn-Waxler et al., 1992).

Biological processes and empathy: physiology, hormones and neural networks

Some investigators have tried to identify bodily responses that accompany expressed concern for other people in distress. The absence of such physiological reactions may correlate with a lack of concern or negative responses in the face of another person's distress.

Heart rate and empathy

One physiological process thought to be relevant to children's responses to distress is heart rate (e.g., Eisenberg et al., 1989; Zahn-Waxler, Cole, Welsh, & Fox, 1995). These theorists suggested that increases in heart rate (HR) might represent one's own emotional arousal as a function of exposure to someone's distress, which might interfere with the production of empathic concern, whereas HR deceleration might accompany expressions of concern for the distressed person.

These ideas were tested in a longitudinal study of a large sample of 7-year-old children, whose responses to people in distress were measured by observed responses to parents' and experimenters' simulations of distress and by parents' reports during an interview (Van Hulle et al., 2013). The children's HR was measured during mood-induction procedures. In this study, empathic concern was contrasted with two different types of non-empathic behaviour: *active disregard*, which reflected negative attitudes and behaviour toward the distressed person, and *passive disregard*, which simply showed the absence of concern for that person's welfare. The researchers also distinguished *empathic concern* toward the distressed person from *personal distress* that was focussed on the self rather than the other person.

On average, the children's mean HR in response to the sadness-inducing mood inductions was lowest for the group who showed active disregard of other people's distress. The other two groups – those who showed empathic concern and those who showed passive disregard – did not differ in HR. This was true when the groups were identified via maternal interview as when they were identified through the experimental probes. All three groups (empathic concern, active disregard and passive disregard) showed HR deceleration in response to the sadness-inducing scenarios, compared to baseline. Rather than serving as a physiological indicator of empathic concern, HR deceleration might simply reflect increased attention to the mood-inducing scenario. However, the fact that children showing active disregard to the distress of another person were physiologically less aroused by the distress reveals a basic difference between those who simply don't respond to distress and those who respond negatively to distressed people.

Oxytocin: the empathy hormone?

Recent research on empathy in adults and children has focussed on the neuropeptide oxytocin, which can be studied as both a hormone and a neurotransmitter (Rodrigues, Saslow, Garcia, John, & Keltner, 2009). Oxytocin is associated with caregiving behaviour in mammals, including humans. The relationships between oxytocin levels and mother-infant interaction reveal a pattern of reciprocal influence between mother and child (see Chapter 7). Mothers' oxytocin levels in pregnancy predict later patterns of their interactions with their infants (Feldman, Weller, Zagoory-Sharon, & Levine, 2007). Newborn infants' behaviour (e.g., touching or sucking on the mother's breast) stimulates the mother's production of oxytocin (e.g., Matthiesen, Ransjo-Arvidson, Nissen, & Uvnas-Moberg, 2001). Oxytocin also contributes to mothers' empathic responses to their infants' cries (Riem et al., 2011). It has therefore been argued that oxytocin may contribute to humans' caring and empathic responses to other people, beyond their own children.

This speculation has led to experimental studies where oxytocin is directly administered. One question raised is how oxytocin might affect brain regions that underpin empathy.

In a randomly controlled trial, women either received a dose of oxytocin (administered through the nose) or a placebo (Riem et al., 2011). Neuroimaging analyses of the two groups of women showed that their brains responded differently to recordings of infants' cries. Those women who had received the dose of oxytocin showed fewer responses in the amygdala (a key component of the 'empathy circuit' identified by Decety, 2015). The authors suggested that higher levels of oxytocin may have reduced the women's emotional response to the aversive sound of an infant's cry and enabled their response to the needs of the infant. In other words, oxytocin levels may have reduced the likelihood that affective empathy would get in the way of cognitive empathy.

Children's own oxytocin levels, which are quite stable over the course of development, are affected by genetic factors and their early caregiving experiences; they are also associated with the children's behaviour toward others (Feldman, Gordon, Influs, Gutbir, & Ebstein, 2013). Thus, there is a complex pathway from the biological factors that regulate parents' empathy and the biological and social supports for children's empathy in their own social relationships.

Cognitive empathy: understanding other people's emotions

Providing the right sort of comfort to a person in distress depends on some degree of *cognitive empathy* (understanding that the other person feels a certain way for a particular reason). This understanding requires an ability to *detect emotional signals* from another person and also *understand the context* in which those signals have been made. Even if infants respond when another person cries, would they necessarily detect subtler emotional signals, such as sad or fearful facial expressions? And when in development do children become sensitive to the fact that different contexts may elicit quite different emotional responses?

Identification of other people's emotional signals

In the previous chapters, we have seen that children gradually come to recognise other people's expressions of emotion and draw upon those facial and vocal signals for important information, for example, when infants use social referencing to guide their own actions, such as when infants react to their caregivers' smiles or fearful expressions when placed on the visual cliff (Sorce, Emde, Campos, & Klinnert, 1985). We have also seen that children become aware of a basic distinction between other people's positive and negative emotions before being able to differentiate negative emotions (e.g., Widen & Russell, 2013). Taken together, these lines of research suggest that very young infants must first learn to identify different signs of emotion and discriminate between positive and negative emotions before learning to tell different types of negative emotion apart.

Across the first year of life, infants gradually acquire the ability to recognise the distinct features of emotional signals (e.g., a smile or an angry scowl), no matter who is showing that facial expression (e.g., Nelson & Dolgin, 1985). They also come to recognise some perceptual features of emotional expressions in photographs, no matter whether the face is right side up or not (Kestenbaum & Nelson, 1990). But it is not until later in childhood that children acquire the emotion recognition skills shown by adults.

By 5 years of age, children can clearly recognise people's expressions of happiness (e.g., Gao & Maurer, 2010). However, they are not nearly so successful at recognising different expressions of negative emotion (e.g., de Sonneville et al., 2002). They may not be able to tell the difference between neutral and negative facial expressions, or may mix up different expressions of negative emotion (Gao & Maurer, 2010). Recognition of anger in particular seems to pose problems throughout middle childhood (Gao & Maurer, 2010; Herba, Landau, Russell, Ecker, & Phillips, 2006). The recognition of emotion is influenced by children's understanding of emotion words, not just their perceptual abilities; it also depends on exactly how the children's abilities are being assessed (Vicari et al., 2000).

The gradual development of the ability to discriminate amongst different expressions of emotion has implications for children's social lives. Not being able to tell when someone is feeling unhappy will make it difficult for the child to respond empathically to that person's distress, especially if the emotions are not being shown at peak intensity. This may lead to some misinterpretation of the children's motivation to help or hurt other people. Many parents may assume that their children's recognition of other people's emotions are as good as the parents' own abilities, which may lead to misunderstandings in real-life situations, such as when the child is engaged in conflict with siblings, peers or the parents.

Decoding the contexts in which emotions are expressed

The child's interpretation of another's emotional signal, which might have implications for that child's own safety, may partly depend upon deciphering information about the context in which that signal was produced. Understanding of context may also facilitate any empathy that the child feels in response to the emotional signals being made by another. For example, younger children may not be able to tell apart easily the facial expressions signifying sadness, fear and anger; however, they may be able to draw on situational cues to understand what might be wrong.

Some classic experiments on children's empathy showed children pictures of different situations (e.g., a birthday party; a lost dog) and asked the participants to identify what the story protagonist might be feeling (Borke, 1971). In common with the experimental studies of children's responses to facial expressions, 3-year-old Chinese and American children who were told such stories also tended to make a basic distinction between happiness and negative emotions; older children performing the task were more likely to make distinctions amongst the negative emotions (Borke, 1973).

One variation on this method is shown by studies that presented children with congruent or incongruent facial expressions and contexts; in such a task, younger children are sometimes more likely to rely on the facial expression than the context (Gnepp, 1983). In other cases, children who are told stories that explain why a character might feel a certain way correctly identify the child's incongruent emotion, but note that they would feel differently in that situation (Denham, 1986).

Children are able to judge emotions from the tone of people's voices as well as their facial expressions, but in this case context is still important; if there is a conflict between the tone of the voice and the words people say, children tend to judge emotion from words, not the acoustic properties of their voices (Waxer & Morton, 2011).

Older children become more sensitive to the nuances of expressions of emotions and the social contexts in which they are expressed. They become increasingly aware of the fact that the same context can evoke mixed emotions and also that there are social norms governing the display of emotion in different contexts (Gross & Ballif, 1991). Thus, it seems likely that both discrimination of different sorts of negative emotions and awareness of the nuances of emotion-evoking contexts improve across the years of childhood.

Biological contributions to cognitive empathy

We have already seen that biological processes contribute to a person's ability to respond emotionally to another person's distress, i.e., affective empathy. It is also possible to identify the biological underpinnings of cognitive empathy.

For example, Decety (2011) has proposed a theoretical model of empathy that involves three components, each supported by different brain regions: *affective arousal*, *emotion understanding* and *self-regulation*. In other words, an effective empathic response would entail (1) a heightened emotional response to distress; (2) an understanding of the nature of the distress, in terms of emotion signals and context; and (3) self-regulation of one's own emotions, to remain capable of providing help. In this model, emotional understanding – which may also be referred to as *cognitive empathy* – is supported by the ventromedial prefrontal cortex. Links with the amygdala and other cortical areas would help the individual regulate the affective response to pain and distress and therefore deploy appropriate prosocial responses to the distressed person. Neuroimaging work following from this model has shown different regions of grey matter density associated with cognitive vs. affective empathy (Figure 9.2; Eres, Decety, Louis, & Molenberghs, 2015).

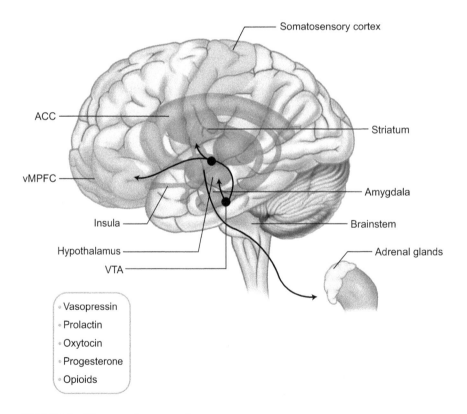

FIGURE 9.2 The empathy network

Source: Decety (2015)

Some investigators have also sought neuroimaging evidence for links between empathy and the mirror neuron network of the brain, which supports our abilities to understand other people's actions and imitate what other people are doing (Gazzola, Aziz-Zadeh, & Keysers, 2006). For example, a small sample of 10-year-olds participated in a functional magnetic resonance imaging (fMRI) study of responses to facial displays of emotion (Pfeifer, Iacoboni, Mazziotta, & Dapretto, 2008). In one condition, the children were asked to imitate the expressions shown; in the other condition, they were instructed simply to observe without imitating the emotion. Activation in the brain regions associated with mirror neurons was found during imitation of the facial expressions and to a somewhat lesser extent during mere observation of the faces, and was significantly correlated with the children's scores on a test of empathic concern. Both lines of research demonstrate that the capacity for empathy is a fundamental social talent supported by the human brain.

Gender differences in empathy

Over 30 years ago, in an influential review of the literature on gender differences, Eisenberg and Lennon (1983) concluded that, although women have traditionally been seen as more empathic than men are, the direct evidence for gender differences in empathy was less clear. In particular, while self-reports were in line with the stereotype, direct observations or physiological measurement revealed fewer gender differences. Thus, the extent of difference between male and female responses to other people's emotions may depend on the techniques used to measure empathy and the dimensions of empathy being measured. Different types of designs also yield studies with different sample sizes: Questionnaire studies typically have larger samples than experimental or observational studies of infants. Therefore, different methods convey different levels of power to test against the null hypothesis.

Evidence for gender differences in empathy

Infants' early responses to distress

Some marginal evidence for gender differences was reported in early studies of contagious crying, with girl infants reported to be more sensitive to the cries of other infants than were their male peers (Sagi & Hoffman, 1976; Simner, 1971). However, other studies of infants' responses to other infants' cries have not found significant differences (Martin & Clark, 1982) or have not reported testing for associations with gender (Dondi et al., 1999; Hay et al., 1981).

In any case, these small samples of infants are not representative of the larger population. In our larger, nationally representative sample of British infants, their mothers, fathers and a third person who knew the infant well were asked to complete a developmental milestones questionnaire when the infant was 6 months of age (Hay et al., 2010). One of the items on the milestones questionnaire asked, 'Does the infant get distressed when another baby cries?' Crying in response to another infant's cries was reported for about half the infants in the sample, with significant agreement between all pairs of informants. Boys were slightly more likely to show responsive crying than girls were, but the difference was very small and non-significant. Thus, at the beginning of the developmental progression toward empathy, there is little evidence of gender differences.

Emergence of gender differences in empathy in childhood

In contrast to the early manifestations of empathy in infancy, assessments of empathy in early childhood already reveal gender differences. In contrast to Eisenberg and Lennon's (1983) earlier review of the literature, these differences are identified using directly observed assessments as well as informants' reports. Girls already show higher scores on empathy tasks in the preschool years (e.g., Ball, Smetana, & Sturge-Apple, 2017). In a large community sample of twins, gender differences in empathic concern were discernible by the second year of life (Knafo, Zahn-Waxler, Van Hulle, Robinson, & Rhee, 2008).

In the early years of life, it is useful to remember that gender differences often are confounded with maturational differences; in general, girls have a maturational advantage in acquiring language (Bornstein, Hahn, & Haynes, 2004). Some gender differences in empathic concern as opposed to disregard of another's distress are explained by girls' advantage in language skills (Rhee et al., 2013). Nevertheless, gender differences on a variety of measures of empathy are still apparent in middle childhood and adolescence, especially with respect to cognitive empathy (e.g., Schwenck et al., 2013). In some cases, the gender differences in late childhood appear to derive from a decline in empathy for boys at that point in development (Van der Graff et al., 2014). These persistent gender differences have often been attributed to biological factors, coupled with gender socialisation.

Empathy and the female brain

In recent years, some investigators have studied gender differences in empathy in the context of overarching biological theories about the male and female brains. As we have seen, advances in neuroimaging tasks have made it possible to examine gender differences in the activation of different brain regions during psychological tasks that assess empathy (e.g., Derntl et al., 2010; Schulte-Ruther, Markowitsch, Shah, Fink, & Piefke, 2008). For example, in a small sample of men and women (who were further classified in terms of the stage of the menstrual cycle they were in when tested), the participants were assessed on several different measures of empathy (Derntl et al., 2010). In line with the earlier review of the evidence for gender differences in empathy, the women and men differed in their self-reports, but not in their directly measured empathy. However, gender differences were observed in the activation of brain regions associated with empathy, including the amygdala; activation of the latter structure was also influenced by the women's stage in their menstrual cycle, suggesting that hormonal influences might be involved.

Although the neuroimaging data provides interesting insights into the brain circuits that support empathic behaviour, these findings primarily derive from studies of small, selected samples of adults who have been exposed to different social influences during their development. Thus, it is also important to examine how girls' and boys' empathic behaviour is encouraged or discouraged during childhood.

Gender differences in emotional socialisation

Adults do not always encourage children to respond empathically to other people's distress. For example, in a study of 3- and 4-year-olds in preschool classrooms, teachers tended to discourage the children from responding to each other's distress; during an interview in which they were shown a video of a classmate's distress, the children revealed that they knew how to help but also suggested that responding to distress was a job that was more suitable for adults (Caplan & Hay, 1989). In that sample, neither girls nor boys were encouraged to help others, although they were praised for pretending to comfort dolls and stuffed toys.

Parents are more likely to stress the overall importance of emotional experience with girls than with boys, although that may depend on the parent's gender. For example, in a study of mothers' and fathers' conversations with their 3-year-old sons and daughters (Fivush, Brotman, Buckner, & Goodman, 2000), the parents were asked to talk about past events in their children's experience that had evoked the primary emotions of happiness, fear, anger and sadness. Mothers and fathers were observed conversing with their children in separate sessions, in counterbalanced order. In general, the conversations with mothers lasted longer than conversations with fathers. Mothers were also more likely than fathers were to use emotion words during the conversations. However, gender differences in either parents' or children's talk about emotions also depended on the particular emotion being discussed, suggesting that girls and boys may have different opportunities to learn about different types of positive and negative emotions.

In subsequent research on parents' talk about emotions, in a sample of families from The Netherlands, the investigators developed an 'Emotions Picture Book' to standardise the topic of conversations held by mothers and fathers with their sons and daughters (van der Pol et al., 2015). The wordless picture book contained gender-neutral illustrations of children in situations that might evoke different emotions. The attributions parents made about the gender of the children in the illustrations depended on the emotions being portrayed. If the situation evoked sadness, the parents were more likely to refer to the child as a girl. If, instead, the situation evoked anger, the parents were more likely to refer to the child in the drawing as a boy.

During interactions with their parents, young children may also learn which emotions are most appropriate for them to display, in line with gender norms. For example, in a longitudinal study of mothers' and fathers' interactions with their young children at 4 and 6 years of age (Chaplin, Cole, & Zahn-Waxler, 2005), the parents and children were observed playing a competitive game. Because the overall purpose of the research was to study the development of children with behavioural problems, children who were seen as 'hard-to-manage' were over-represented in the sample. The children's facial emotions were coded, and blends of different emotions were classified in terms of the interpersonal context as 'harmonious,' 'disharmonious' and 'submissive.' In comparison to boys, girls' expressions of emotion were more likely to be classified as 'submissive,' but the two genders were not significantly different in the display of 'disharmonious' emotions. Both mothers and fathers were more likely to pay attention to submissive emotions shown by girls as opposed to boys. Thus, expectations about gender norms may influence parental behaviour when children express emotion, which may eventually channel girls and boys into different preferences for emotional expression, bound up with gender-differentiated social strategies.

Individual differences in empathy

The previous section on gender differences underscores the fact that, although a capacity for empathy is present in the human species, there are nonetheless individual differences. It is important to go beyond the study of gender differences and examine individual variation in empathy. Are some children more empathic than others? And, if so, do their empathic tendencies appear to be inborn – is there evidence for genetically determined differences in empathy?

Early individual differences in concern for others

Toddlers do not always respond in the same way to other people's distress; some react not with empathic concern but rather with amusement or aggression (Demetriou & Hay, 2004; Zahn-Waxler et al., 1992). Those toddlers who respond positively to their peers' distress are also more likely to share in response to their peers' requests (Hay, Castle, Davies, Demetriou, & Stimson, 1999). But do these early individual differences originate from genetic factors, or experiences in the social environment, or the interplay between the two?

Individual differences in early empathic concern have been studied systematically in a large, genetically informative study of young twins (Knafo et al., 2008). In this study, over 400 twin pairs were studied longitudinally at intervals from the first to the third birthday. As part of the study protocol, experimenters simulated distress. Mothers were asked to simulate distress as well, for example, by pretending to hurt their knees or catch their fingers in a clipboard. The twins' empathic concern in the face of mothers' and experimenters' simulated distress was examined in relation to whether or not they were genetically identical or non-identical twins. In the logic of behavioural geneticists' use of twin studies, the concordance between twins – the extent to which they both show empathic concern – should be greater if the twins are genetically identical. Non-identical twins on average would share half their genes, like any other pairs of siblings, but identical twins would share all their genes. This fact was used in statistical analyses designed to assess the extent of genetic influence on empathic concern, as well as the effects of their shared family environment.

At the earliest age that was assessed (14 months), there was significant concordance between identical twins but not between non-identical twins, particularly with respect to empathic concern toward the experimenter. Genetic influence on empathy across the two people simulating distress – mother and experimenter – was evident by 24 months, although the environment also influenced the level of empathic concern that individual toddlers showed across this time period. Thus, individual differences in very young children's responses to people in distress reflect differences in both their genes and their social environments.

Empathy and other forms of prosocial behaviour

In both childhood and adulthood, individual differences in measures of empathy may also be associated with individual differences in other forms of prosocial behaviour. Neuroscientists who study empathy have argued that empathy has been selected for in the course of evolution, is underpinned by distinct neural networks and is therefore the 'driver' of all other forms of prosocial behaviour (Decety, Bartal, Uzefovsky, & Knafo-Noam, 2016). These authors note that the biological substrate that supports human empathy is identifiable in species other than our own; they argue for the importance of processing distress cues in supporting social affiliation and nurturance across different species.

The question of links between empathy and other forms of prosocial behaviour has been addressed in a developmental as well as an evolutionary framework, by looking at patterns of individual differences across different types of prosocial actions. It is noteworthy that different types of prosocial actions do not always correlate with each other (Hay & Cook, 2007; Radke-Yarrow, Zahn-Waxler, & Chapman, 1983). Particularly when the capacity for prosocial action is first emerging in the human repertoire, there are dissociations as well as associations across prosocial behaviours. Paulus (2014) has drawn distinctions between different theoretical models of early prosocial development, noting that different types of prosocial behaviour (e.g., instrumental helping versus comforting a person in distress) are supported by different neurobiological mechanisms and draw upon different sets of cognitive skills.

In an analysis of the development of prosocial behaviour in the toddler years (Hay & Cook, 2007), we proposed that three different abilities developed between infancy and early childhood: (1) *feeling for others* (i.e., affective empathy); (2) *working with others* (e.g., sharing resources, cooperating with another person, and instrumental helping); and (3) *ministering to others' needs* (e.g., comforting and caregiving a person in distress, which might reflect cognitive empathy that was not bound up with affective arousal). The strongest correlations amongst prosocial behaviours in early childhood are within domains, such as sharing and cooperating as two forms of working with others (Hay, 1979) or sensitivity to distress and sharing in response to another person's stated needs (Hay et al., 1999). Over the course of development, however, these strands may come together and a more trait-like disposition to be prosocial will be observed. Is this general disposition to be kind to others underpinned by empathy? And, if so, do genetic as well as environmental factors contribute to the development of a 'prosocial personality'?

In a genetically informative longitudinal study of twins living in Israel (Knafo-Noam, Uzefovsky, Israel, Davidov, & Zahn-Waxler, 2015), parents reported on the twins' prosocial behaviour at the age of 7 years. The dimensions of prosocial behaviour that were assessed (sharing, social concern, helping, kindness, and empathic concern) were all significantly correlated at that age, and their shared variance could be explained by a single factor with a high degree of heritability. This finding could partly be explained by relying on the report from a parent who might have a global perception of the child's prosocial skills. Nonetheless, the study does suggest that different strands of prosocial behaviour, including empathy, consolidate by middle childhood.

Empathy and callousness

In recent years, investigators have been interested in studying what might be seen as the opposite of empathy: callousness. Increased interest in callousness arose in the context of attempts to study children's conduct problems in relation to the phenomenon of psychopathy in adulthood (Hare, 1996). Studies of children who had been diagnosed with severe conduct problems revealed a subgroup who showed a range of what was labelled *callous-unemotional (CU) traits*, which included the absence of the moral emotions of empathy and guilt (Frick, Ray, Thornton, & Kahn, 2014). Boys with conduct problems accompanied by high levels of CU traits were observed to be less responsive to other people's distress, and in particular less able to process other people's fearful facial expressions as conveyed by the eyes (Dadds, El Masry, Wimalaweera, & Guastella, 2008). Girls with conduct problems also find other people's expressions of disgust and anger difficult to understand, although they show no problem in recognising people's faces (Fairchild, Stobbe, van Goozen, Calder, & Goodyer, 2010). At the biological level, callousness has been linked to a lower responsiveness to stress, which may also interfere with the recognition of stress in others (Shirtcliff et al., 2009). Neuroimaging analyses also show that, within the population of children with conduct problems, those children with high levels of CU traits also show a lowered response to other people's pain (Lockwood et al., 2013).

These studies demonstrate that both affective and cognitive empathy rely on perception, and in particular, sensitivity to the emotional signals of others. Indeed, children with better emotional understanding in early childhood are less likely to go on to develop CU traits (Centifanti, Meins, & Fernyhough, 2016). Children's callousness is often related to other predictors of conduct problems, including fearlessness (Waller, Shaw, & Hyde, 2017) and impulsivity (Centifanti et al., 2016). Indeed, very young children with fearless temperament are at high risk for the development of CU traits (Goffin, Boldt, Kim, & Kochanska, 2018).

Thus, children who show callousness in response to the distress of others may also show a broader pattern of interacting with the physical and social world that leads to a general disregard of social rules and the needs of other members of society.

It is important to note that the strengths of the associations between fearlessness, impulsivity and callousness are reduced by the experience of positive interactions with parents (Centifanti et al., 2016; Waller et al., 2017). In other words, more pleasant experiences in our social worlds reduce callousness and promote more positive, empathic responses to other people.

10

SHAME AND GUILT

In this chapter, we focus on another domain of social and moral emotions: shame and guilt. In the last chapter, we noted that children with callous-unemotional traits not only show low rates of empathy, but they also tend to show less guilt (Frick et al., 2014). Guilt is closely related to the self-conscious emotion of shame; both emotions reflect our ability to reflect on ourselves in the context of the expectations other people have for us in our social worlds. Therefore, both shame and guilt draw on a more basic developmental attainment: self-consciousness.

Early signs of self-consciousness

As we have seen in the previous chapter, despite some theoretical claims, it is unlikely that infants cannot differentiate between themselves and others. Nonetheless, one of the major attainments of the first years of life is the development of a representation of the self, which incorporates the ability to *recognise* oneself, to *recall* things about oneself (what is sometimes known *as autobiographical memory*) and, eventually, to *evaluate* oneself with reference to other people's expectations and one's own goals and desires. This latter capacity for self-evaluation makes possible the emotional experiences of shame and guilt.

Self-recognition

Studies of the self-concept in adults and older children have traditionally relied on self-reports, i.e., people's introspection about the self. Such methods are clearly inappropriate for studies of the developmental origins of the self-concept in pre-verbal infants. Experimental methods were therefore developed to ask a very basic question about the development of self: When are infants able to recognise them-selves (e.g., Amsterdam & Greenberg, 1977; Bertanthal & Fischer, 1978)? If they are placed in front of a reflective surface, at what age do they understand they are seeing themselves, not another infant? Similar studies have also been conducted with non-human primates.

Taken together, the mirror studies have demonstrated that only humans and the great apes (in particular, chimpanzees and orangutans) show signs of recognising themselves in mirrors; there is anecdotal evidence that some gorillas also are capable of self-recognition (Anderson & Gallup, 2015). In our own species, the ability to recognise oneself in a mirror has been thought to emerge between 18 and 21 months of age (e.g., Anderson, 1984; Nielsen & Dissanayake, 2004), and is associated with other forms of social cognition that develop around the same time (Wade, Moore, Astington, Frampton, & Jenkins, 2015).

There are some suggestions that rudiments of self-recognition begin to emerge earlier in development. For example, in one study of 4- and 9-month-old infants' behaviour, the infants were shown live video images of themselves and another person, an adult experimenter who mimicked what the infant was doing (Rochat & Striano, 2002). When the video was stopped (a form of the still face procedure described in Chapter 5), the infants' reactions were recorded. Even at 4 months of age, the infants' behaviour differed, depending on whether they were watching another person or themselves. The infants were more likely to smile at the adult experimenter, but more likely to 'talk' to themselves, vocalising more when looking at their own videos.

Neuroimaging studies have also provided evidence for the development of self-recognition over the first 2 years of life. For example, EEG analyses have attempted to identify neural body maps in infants' brains (Marshall & Meltzoff, 2015). A different neuroimaging technique, functional multi-channel near-infrared spectroscopy (fNIRS), demonstrated that, when 6-month-old infants heard their names, their brains showed activation in the frontal cortex (Imafuku, Hakuno, Uchida-Ota, Yamamoto, & Minagawa, 2014). The activation was especially likely to occur if the infants heard their names spoken by their mothers.

Autobiographical memory in infancy

In order to experience either shame or guilt, we need to remember what it was that we did. At what point in development do we become able to recall past events in our lives? Again, when asking whether infants are capable of such recall of the past, methods need to be developed that do not depend on verbal abilities. One such method, *deferred imitation*, was first noted by Jean Piaget (1962), who reported that his toddler daughter had witnessed another child experience a florid temper tantrum and later replicated the peer's tantrum with considerable fidelity.

Subsequent experimental studies have documented infants' abilities to replicate actions they had seen modelled after a delay, even in the first years of life (e.g., Bauer, 2015). Infants who experience unusual events (such as being able to make a mobile move by kicking their foot) can show that they recall the event nonverbally, even months later – by kicking their feet to make a similar mobile move around

(Rovee-Collier, Hartshorn, & DiRubbo, 1999). Infants' long-term memory for such behavioural contingencies is particularly relevant for the development of self-conscious emotions, because to experience either shame or pride, children must become aware that certain outcomes are contingent on their own actions (Stipek, 1983).

However, these nonverbal memories of past experiences do not always translate into verbal accounts of the experience (Tustin & Hayne, 2016). Younger infants are also more prone to forgetting (Bauer, 2015). Nonetheless, the studies of infants' memory abilities show that, over the first years of life, children are gradually acquiring a sense of what has happened to them in the past and, once they acquire language, begin to put their memories into words.

Taken together, these findings show that the development of the ability to recognise the self, recall past experiences and understand contingent action emerges over the first two years, underpinned by infants' developing brains and shaped further by their social experiences. Once this rudimentary sense of self has emerged, very young children become able to recall their past actions and evaluate themselves, in relation to the standards expected of them by their parents and other important people in their social environments.

The manifestations of shame in childhood

Shame and awareness of social norms

Shame is defined in the Oxford English Dictionary as 'a painful feeling of humiliation or distress caused by the consciousness of wrong or foolish behaviour.' It is noteworthy that, in this definition, shame is defined as a particular form of psychological distress, based on what the person has done to make himself or herself feel that way. Furthermore, the fact that the concept of humiliation is embedded in this definition implies that the experience of shame goes beyond internal distress and is felt in relation to one's evaluation in the eyes of others. Shame is truly a social emotion.

This fact draws attention to a fundamental paradox in the development of our sense of self: the more we become aware of ourselves, the more we are evaluating ourselves in the light of other people's needs and opinions. Shame can be seen as the opposite of pride (see Chapter 7), but whereas pride can be felt in relation to one's own standards of achievement, shame is more often a response to social norms, even if those norms have already been internalised into our own self-concepts.

Behavioural signs of shame in early childhood

Distinct facial expressions associated with shame in adults include a lowered head and eye gaze directed toward the ground (Keltner & Buswell, 1996). Feelings of shame are also sometimes accompanied by physiological reactions such as blushing (Stipek, 1983). Such expressions of shame can be identified in children by 3 years of age. In a laboratory study, 3-year-olds were observed playing freely with their parents and also asked to complete six tasks: an easy and a difficult jigsaw puzzle, an easy and a difficult copying task, and an easy and a difficult ball-tossing game (Lewis, Alessandri, & Sullivan, 1992). In this study, the expression of shame was operationally defined as follows: 'body collapsed, corners of the mouth are downward/lower lip tucked between teeth, eyes lowered with gaze downward or askance' (p. 632). The child's withdrawing from the tasks and negative self-evaluation were also coded as signs of shame.

In that study, signs of shame were more likely to be observed when the 3-year-olds failed easy tasks, rather than difficult ones. In contrast, the children were more likely to show signs of pride when they completed the difficult tasks. However, there was also a significant difference between girls and boys: Girls were equally likely to show pride when completing the difficult tasks but more likely to show shame than boys were (Lewis et al., 1992).

Other research groups have similarly found that some signs of shame are apparent by very early childhood (Barrett, Zahn-Waxler, & Cole, 1993; Belsky, Domitrovich, & Crnic, 1997). For example, in a community sample of 3-year-old boys, the investigators tested whether expressions of shame were linked to a boy's temperament (in terms of a general tendency to show negative emotion) and/or to the parent's behaviour. Again, expressions of shame were more likely to be seen when the boys failed at easy tasks. The expression of shame in the context of failure at an easy task was not related to a boy's general tendency to experience negative emotion. Furthermore, in that sample, more negative styles of parenting were associated with significantly fewer signs of shame. Put the other way around, boys who had experienced more positive treatment from their parents were more likely to experience shame when they failed at easy tasks.

Using a different paradigm to explore the developmental origins of shame and guilt, Barrett and her colleagues (1993) conducted a study in which they staged a mishap that apparently had been caused by the 2-year-olds themselves. The toddlers' reactions were characterised as 'avoiders' or 'amenders' on the basis of whether they subsequently avoided the experimenters or tried to make some kind of amends. The researchers considered the avoidance approach to be relevant to the emotion of shame, whereas they saw the amending approach to be more relevant to feelings of guilt (see the following discussion). The pattern of reactions shown in the laboratory were corroborated by mothers' independent reports of their toddlers' tendencies to express shame versus guilt in everyday situations.

These findings have been replicated in a study in which 2-year-olds were made to believe that they had broken an adult's toy (Drummond, Hammond, Satlof-Bendrick, Waugh, & Brownell, 2017). Once again, a shame-relevant pattern of behaviour was identified, with the 2-year-old toddlers avoiding further interaction with the adult whose toy they had broken. Furthermore, they were less likely than other toddlers to confess to what had happened or to attempt to make reparations.

These findings are in line with patterns of behaviour shown by adults who are prone to expressing shame as opposed to guilt. Adult participants were given questionnaires that tapped into their approach vs. avoidance tendencies in their daily lives (Sheikh & Janof-Bulman, 2010). They were also asked to report how they would feel in a number of everyday situations, including ones where they had made some kind of mistake; their answers were analysed in terms of whether the participants were prone to feelings of shame or guilt in those situations. The tendency to feel shame was related to a general tendency to avoid difficult situations, in line with the 2-year-old children's avoidance of the experimenter whom they may have displeased in Barrett and colleagues' study.

Understanding other people's feelings of shame

As children grow older, they become more sensitive to other people's feelings of shame in particular situations. For example, in a study of Dutch children between 10 and 12 years of age (Ferguson, Stegge, & Damhuis, 1991), the children were asked about a set of stories that portrayed either violations of moral principles or what the investigators referred to as 'social blunders.' The children were told to respond as if they were the protagonists of all the stories. They were then asked if they would feel guilty and/or ashamed, in the context of each story. The children reported that they would feel guilty if they had committed a moral transgression. They would feel ashamed as well, and would also feel ashamed if they had merely committed a social blunder. This implies that by this point in middle childhood, children are well aware of social norms governing behaviour and the appropriateness of feeling ashamed when violating those norms.

The socialisation of shame

As we have seen, shame is a self-conscious emotion, but it is also a social emotion, insofar that it reflects how we see ourselves in relation to other people in our social worlds. Thus, shame depends on social learning, in the context of our families and the broader culture. Belsky and colleagues' (1997) finding that 3-year-old boys were more likely to express shame if they had experienced positive parenting reminds us that a reasonable sense of shame is socially valued. The extent to which this is true is affected by culture.

The anthropologist Ruth Benedict (1946), drawing upon her field work in Japan, proposed that cultures could be categorised as 'shame' or 'guilt' cultures, in terms of an emphasis on social responses to transgressions versus an internalised sense of guilt. But does Benedict's notion of a 'shame-culture' have any relevance for the ways in which children are socialised in different cultural contexts? Or, as many of Benedict's critics have stated, is this a false dichotomy? Studies of cultural differences in relation to the development of shame have often compared the socialisation environments in Western individualistic cultures with Eastern collectivist cultural practices.

For example, in an essay on the socialisation of shame in Chinese culture, Fung (1999) criticised the dichotomy between shame- and guilt-cultures and examined the development of a sense of shame in the context of general social competence and the development of the self as an interdependent being. She then undertook a qualitative study of nine middle-class families in Taiwan, drawing on interviews with the parents and observations of the children. These parents saw shame as a moral emotion and believed that it was important that their children felt shame when they had engaged in a moral transgression. Observations of the children's behaviour demonstrated that, in common with the Western samples described earlier in this chapter, the children's sense of shame was evident by 3 years of age.

Although Fung's interview data indicated that the parents felt the development of the capacity for shame was important, and in the course of family life they engaged in both serious and playful shaming of their children, they did not agree with excessive shaming of children, particularly in the school context.

In a more recent quantitative survey of a large sample of 10- to 11-year-old children from Japan, South Korea and the United States, the children's responses to fictional scenarios were recorded (Furukawa, Tangney, & Higashibara, 2012). The children were encouraged to think of themselves as protagonists in these scenarios. They also reported on their tendencies to become angry, and their teachers reported on their behaviour. The findings revealed cultural differences but not a simple dichotomy between Eastern and Western cultures. In this three-way comparison, the Japanese children scored higher on shame responses than did the Korean or American children. These findings draw attention to the complexity of the socialisation of moral emotions in different cultures, which goes well beyond Benedict's (1946) dichotomy.

The development of the capacity to feel guilt

In contrast to shame, guilt is less likely to be associated with a distinct pattern of facial expression (Keltner & Buswell, 1996). Rather, the experience of guilt entails evaluation of the self against some moral standard, not a transient emotional expression (Malti, 2016). In other words, the experience of guilt depends on having acquired a moral framework in which to evaluate one's own actions. However, guilt is not purely cognitive; it is affectively charged, being associated with the basic emotion of sadness and more complex emotions of regret and empathy for people who have been wronged (Hoffman, 2001; Malti et al., 2016). In practical terms, this means that guilt cannot be detected simply from a photograph of someone's face. More information about the context is needed. Furthermore, guilt is often discussed as an internalised phenomenon, not overt behaviour. Therefore, the study of guilt (as opposed to shame, which can be inferred from facial expressions) relies more on self-reports. These in turn depend on individuals' language skills.

The earliest manifestations of guilt

Findings from several research groups suggest that the first signs of guilt begin to manifest around 3 years of age, at the time when many children acquire language and have begun to develop a concept of self. At that age, however, children's experience of guilt is primarily inferred from their emotional reactions or behaviour, in particular, their tendencies to try to repair mistakes or make amends for their actions. The studies that have attempted to measure guilt in this way rest on the assumption that the participating children have sufficient causal understanding to realise that their actions have consequences.

We have already seen in Chapter 9 that very young children are sometimes observed to respond sensitively to other people's distress. When their own actions have caused the distress, they may respond more positively, although they occasionally respond with amusement or aggression (e.g., Demetriou & Hay, 2004). Such findings suggest that toddlers are aware of their own agency in provoking distress, and their actions are affected by that awareness. But do children's prosocial actions in response to distress they have caused necessarily imply they feel guilt for those actions?

For example, in an experimental study, toddlers were asked to play with a doll whose leg fell off (Garner, 2003); following this accident, the experimenter, pretending to be the doll, expressed pain and distress. The children's expressed concern about the doll's wellbeing were interpreted as 'empathy-based guilt responses' but, again, the presence of sympathetic behaviour does not necessarily imply that the sympathy was motivated by feelings of guilt. It is necessary to distinguish general feelings of sympathy that are evoked by another person's overt distress from guilt-induced responses that reflect children's understanding of their own responsibility.

For example, in an experimental study, 2- and 3-year-old children were tested in an experimental setting that featured a large, colourful tower of blocks (Vaish, Carpenter, & Tomasello, 2016). An experimenter either admired the tower, saying how unhappy she would be if it were destroyed, or just commented on it in a more neutral way. Later, in the course of the experiment, the tower was in fact knocked down by marbles, which was either due to the child's or a second experimenter's actions. The first experimenter returned, expressing either sadness or a more neutral reaction, in line with her comments at the beginning of the experiment, when the tower was still standing. The children were then given the opportunity to help repair the tower and to share stickers with the first experimenter. The extent to which children expressed guilt in their speech was also measured; however, only one 2-year-old was able to do so. The 2-year-olds tended to show prosocial behaviour toward the sad experimenter, even if they had not caused the tower to collapse; the 3-year-olds' behaviour was more affected by their own role in its destruction. The investigators interpreted the findings to mean that guilt for causing another person harm could be distinguished from general sympathy in 3- but not 2-year-olds.

In another experiment in which toddlers had apparently broken an adult's toy (Drummond et al., 2017), an attempt was made to distinguish between shame and guilt responses in children who were around 2.5 years of age. As in the study of children's responses to a mishap by Barrett and colleagues discussed earlier (1993), avoidant behaviour was considered shame-related, whereas confessing the misdeed to parents or trying to make repairs were considered possible indicators of guilt.

Several tasks designed to measure prosocial behaviour were also administered. The children who had shown more guilt-prone responses to the mishap were also more likely to show empathic helping, although the frequency of instrumental helping was not significantly related to the patterns of shame versus guilt. These findings suggest that the origins of guilt-related responses lie in the third year of life, although the ability to confess one's transgressions obviously depends upon verbal fluency as well as causal understanding.

The development of guilt in later childhood

Toddlers' earliest manifestations of guilt will eventually consolidate into a broader understanding of the moral framework of their society and their own sense of right and wrong. Developmental theorists such as Jean Piaget and Lawrence Kohlberg have drawn attention to different stages of moral development (Piaget, 1965; Kohlberg, 1969). However, individual differences in moral understanding are also evident, and these originate after the toddler years; this process has been described as the development of a conscience (Kochanska, 1993). Therefore, those children who are most sensitive to issues of right and wrong may be more likely than others to experience feelings of guilt about their own behaviour.

Kochanska (1991) has argued that the development of a conscience has both an affective dimension – which includes feelings of guilt – and the capacity for self-regulation, which helps children control their own behaviour to avoid making transgressions. The affective dimension incorporates the expressions of distress in response to mishaps recorded in the experimental studies of toddlers' reactions to staged accidents, as described above. In older children, the intensity of feelings of guilt can be measured by responses to stories about transgressions in which the children are encouraged to identify with the protagonist and report how they would feel, after having committed the fictional transgressions (Kochanska, 1991). This work points to the importance of both the children's temperament and their parents' socialisation strategies in the development of feelings of guilt for transgressions.

As children grow older, they acquire more sophisticated concepts of the emotions of shame and guilt and become sensitive to the contexts in which a person might be likely to feel guilt versus shame. For example, in one study, 10- to 12-year-old Dutch children were presented with stories in which they were encouraged to identify with the protagonist (Ferguson et al., 1991). Some stories featured different sorts of moral transgression, ranging from not keeping a promise to meet a friend to personal injury. A second group of stories featured social blunders that were embarrassing but not moral transgressions; the latter stories were presumed to evoke shame, not guilt. The children were asked whether they felt any guilt or shame and, if so, why. They did indeed report more feelings of guilt with respect to moral transgressions; their feelings of shame were bound up with a fear of the social consequences of the embarrassing blunders. Subsequent work in another Dutch sample suggested that this differentiation of shame and guilt was seen only in children over the age of 9 years old (Olthof, Schouten, Kuiper, Stegge, & Jennekins-Schinkel, 2000).

In middle childhood, as children in many cultures engage in increasingly complicated relationships with their peers, they will experience occasions where they might be bullied, or witness bullying, or bully other children. These occasions may elicit feelings of both shame and guilt. The roles children play in their peer groups may determine whether they are more prone to shameful or guilty feelings. For example, the extent to which the experience of shame and guilt was affected by children's peer experiences was assessed in a study of Italian children between 9 and 11 years of age (Meneseni & Camodeca, 2008). The children were asked to nominate classmates whom they thought to be either bullies or victims, in line with definitions provided by the experimenters. Bullying was defined through a series of specific examples which incorporated physical harm, mean words, and restrictions on children's actions. The children were also asked to nominate classmates who were especially prosocial. The peer nomination procedure enabled the investigators to identify bullies, victims, prosocial children and other children who did not involve themselves in these fraught interactions in their peer groups. All of the children were asked to say how they might feel in several hypothetical situations, some of which were thought to provoke shame only and others which might provoke either shame or guilt. Some of the hypothetical situations involved intentional harm. The children reported that they would feel more guilt if they had intentionally harmed someone, as opposed to accidentally doing so (e.g., tripping over something and thereby harming another child). Prosocial children were most likely to report that they would show guilt in scenarios that might evoke either shame or guilt; children with a history of being victimised were likely to report they would feel shame, particularly in the shame-only scenarios. Bullies were least likely to show guilt, but that only differed significantly from the highly prosocial children.

These findings suggest that children's understanding of guilt develops across middle childhood and are affected by their social experiences, with caregivers but also with peers. It is likely, however, that the impact of children's social experiences on the development of feelings of guilt are also influenced by culture.

Cultural differences

The studies on children's moral understanding that have just been discussed rest on the assumption that children will gradually see shame and guilt as very different moral emotions. This may only be true within individualistic cultures, such as the European samples just described. The distinction between shame and guilt may be less pronounced in collectivist cultures, and indeed some collectivist cultures do not even have a word that is equivalent to the English word 'guilt' (Wong & Tsai, 2007). In contrast, in collectivist cultures, the concept of shame might be finely differentiated; Wong and Tsai (2007) noted that, in Chinese, there are more than 100 terms that refer to shame.

However, recent conceptualisations of shame and guilt suggest that a feeling of shame encompasses the entire self, whereas the feeling of guilt focuses on a particular regrettable action; using this definition, signs of both shame and guilt might be seen across individualistic and collectivist cultures (Furukawa et al., 2012). In such studies, it sometimes proves useful to include more than one example of each type of culture. For example, in a comparison of 10- to 11-year-old children in Japan, South Korea and the US, we have already seen that Japanese children were the most likely to report experiences of shame; however, this should not necessarily be interpreted as a difference between collectivist and individualistic cultures. The Korean children were most likely to report feelings of guilt (Furukawa et al., 2012). These findings suggest that, while cultural influences are likely to play a role in the development of moral emotions, Benedict's (1946) distinction between 'shame-cultures' and 'guilt-cultures' is oversimplified.

Guilt in relation to children's psychological disorders

Fear, anxiety and guilt

As we have seen, children's expressions of guilt often take the form of emotionally distressed behaviour after a mishap (e.g., Kochanska, 1991). Thus, guilt has been associated theoretically with emotional vulnerability. We have also seen in Chapter 4 that some individuals are more prone to fear, whereas other people are fearless in the face of potential danger. At extreme levels, fearfulness is associated with anxiety disorders. In contrast, fearlessness is sometimes associated with conduct problems (e.g., Colder, Mott, & Berman, 2002), which are sometimes also marked by lower levels of guilt. Investigators of children's psychopathology have therefore sought to identify links between fearfulness and the ability to experience guilt.

Evidence for a link between fearfulness and guilt can be discerned by the third year of life. For example, in a longitudinal study of infants observed at 12, 24 and 36 months of age, the infants were invited to a university and, amongst other challenges, presented with a fear-provoking robot at each time point (Baker, Baibazarova, Ktistaki, Shelton, & van Goozen, 2012). The children's expressions of fear were assessed by observation and physiological measurement of heart rate and skin conductance. Parents also rated the infants' fearful temperament. At 24 and 36 months, the investigators used a mishap procedure in which children thought they had broken something to assess the children's expressions of guilt.

By 36 months, more fearful children were more likely to express distress in response to the mishap. Analysis of the physiological measures revealed that the children who showed more arousal in response to the frightening robot were also more aroused in the mishap procedure. These findings suggest that, from a very young age, those children who are prone to fear may also be prone to feelings of guilt when they have made mistakes or violated social norms.

The absence of guilt in conduct disorder

Other studies of young children's reactions to mishaps show a negative correlation between empathy-based guilt, i.e., distress at having caused some unpleasantness to another person, and conduct problems (e.g., Garner, 2003). This association between guilt and conduct problems emerges over the first year of life. For example, in a longitudinal study of 112 families (Kochanska, Gross, Lin, & Nichols, 2002), toddlers were observed at home and in the laboratory; in the latter context, both mishap procedures and fear-invoking procedures were used. Their interactions with their mothers were observed, and the mothers also reported on their children's usual temperament and expressions of guilt. The toddlers' expressions of guilt were already apparent by the second year of life. A follow-up study showed that those toddlers who were most likely to express guilt were still likely to do so when they were nearing their fourth birthdays.

When the children in that sample were nearly 5 years of age, their risk for later conduct problems was assessed, through measurement of their antisocial approaches to interpersonal problems, their tendencies to break rules and their general moral understanding. Those children who had expressed more signs of guilt were less likely to engage in rule-breaking or antisocial behaviours.

Links between a child's capacity to feel guilt and later conduct problems can still be detected in adolescence. For example, in a longitudinal sample, when the participants were assessed as 18- to 21-year-olds, those children who had shown higher levels of guilt in childhood were less likely to experience arrests and convictions by young adulthood, even when controlling for parents' education and income and the children's own conduct problems whilst still in primary school (Stuewig et al., 2015).

However, only some children who show conduct problems will be free from feelings of guilt. As we have seen in Chapter 9, a subset of children who show conduct problems possess what is known as *callous-unemotional (CU)* traits (Frick et al., 2014). Such children tend not to show empathy in response to other people's feelings; they also tend to show less guilt about their own harmful actions. Follow-up analyses of the longitudinal sample studied by Kochanska and her colleagues (2002), in which both guilt in response to mishaps and fearfulness had been observed in early childhood, showed that those toddlers who had less concern about mishaps were significantly more likely to show CU traits in early adolescence (Goffin et al., 2018). Early fearlessness also predicted CU traits in that sample. Thus, very young children's lack of concern about the consequences of their mistakes may consolidate into a pattern of callous behaviour that endures over childhood.

Guilt and childhood depression

While children with conduct problems may be less prone to feeling guilty, children with other types of psychological problems may feel unreasonable levels of guilt; this is a pattern well known to be associated with childhood depression (Cole et al., 2008). As we have seen in Chapter 6, it is only in the last few decades that it has been recognised that even quite young children can experience clinically significant depression. Although depression becomes more prevalent during the transition from childhood to adolescence (Patterson et al., 2018), it can be detected at earlier ages. For example, in our own longitudinal study of a nationally representative sample, the Cardiff Child Development Study (CCDS), 7% of 6- to 7-year-olds (3.4% of girls and 10% of boys) met the diagnostic criteria for a depressive illness. The clinical interview also revealed that a larger number of children (27% of this community sample) were prone to expressing a strong sense of worthlessness or guilt, even though they did not meet the full criteria for a diagnosis of depression.

Children who are experiencing clinically significant depression have been observed to show high levels of both guilt and shame, coupled with a lower tendency to make reparations for their mistakes, similar to that shown by children with conduct problems (Luby et al., 2009). This finding suggests that depressed children may feel more guilt after their transgressions, but they have a difficult time resolving the interpersonal problems that may have followed on from their initial mistakes. They may also feel guilt that is out of proportion with what they have done.

The aforementioned patterns of lower levels of guilt associated with conduct problems and higher levels associated with childhood depression need to be examined further, because in childhood, higher levels of depression are *positively* associated with higher levels of conduct problems. Our analyses of the CCDS longitudinal data show that feelings of worthlessness and guilt are present in about 80% of children who are experiencing clinically significant depression, regardless of whether or not the children also have conduct disorder. These strong feelings of guilt and worthlessness may affect children's social and emotional development, even if their other symptoms of depression are alleviated.

11
AFTERWORD

The value of a developmental perspective on emotion

The purpose of this book was to review evidence and draw some conclusions about the course of emotional development from infancy to adolescence. In order to provide a framework for all the disparate findings presented in the foregoing chapters, I resurrected Katherine Bridges' (1932) theoretical model of the gradual differentiation of children's emotional experience over time (Figure 11.1).

My focus on Bridges' explicitly *developmental* theory of emotional development in this book does not negate the importance of our evolutionary heritage, nor

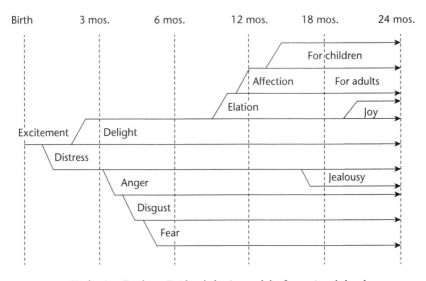

FIGURE 11.1 Katherine Banham Bridges' classic model of emotional development

downplay our species-typical ways of communicating our inner feelings through our faces and voices, as so extensively studied by the differential emotions theorists, Paul Ekman (1993) and Carroll Izard (1994), as described in Chapter 1. Furthermore, the key proposal that emotions develop over infancy is not incompatible with new evidence for the neural basis of emotion. Although Bridges' differentiation theory is sometimes presented in contrast to the differential emotions theory set forth by the evolutionary theorists (e.g., Widen & Russell, 2008), the two theories are in fact complementary, operating at two different levels of analysis.

What Bridges' theory offers to the modern developmental scientist is a conceptual framework in which to study change as well as stability in children's experience of emotion over the first years of life. The sample she drew upon was not representative, and so her specific hypotheses about timing are not likely to be corroborated by later empirical evidence. Furthermore, by focussing solely on the first two years, her theory did not address the emergence of the sociomoral emotions, which consolidate over the next few years of childhood. However, her theory succeeded in drawing attention to the fact that emotions do develop, and as such Bridges' theory of emotional development remains very compatible with other theoretical perspectives in developmental science.

In particular, Bridges' theory predates but is compatible with the perspective of *developmental psychobiology*, as set forth by theorists such as Theodore Schneirla (1959) and Gilbert Gottlieb (2007). Bridges' starting point – her focus on infants' distress and delight – is compatible with Schneirla's emphasis on the importance of approach-withdrawal processes in development and evolution. Furthermore, her developmental perspective on emotion is compatible with the focus of developmental psychobiology. In Gottlieb's view, development must be studied at different levels of analysis, with a focus on learning and self-generated change, as well as biological maturation. Within this perspective, all of the forces that influence the young organism also influence each other, leading to a complex set of changes and continuities over time, partly depending on chance (Figure 11.2).

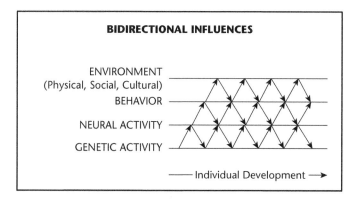

FIGURE 11.2   A schematic portrayal of Gilbert Gottlieb's developmental theory of *probabilistic epigenesis*; all of these influences impinge upon emotional development

As we have seen in the previous chapters of this book, the sources of influence identified by Gottlieb (2007) – genes, the nervous system, the child's behaviour, and the physical, social and cultural environment – all contribute to a person's emotional development. However, we still know less than we should about the ways in which those forces interact with each other to shape that child's capacity for emotional expression and emotion regulation. The developmental perspective on emotion set forth in this book highlights the differences amongst individual children as well as all they hold in common with other members of our species.

Expanding upon Bridges' model of emotional development

In sketching out the course of emotional development, we expanded on Bridges' original framework in several ways. We began, as she did, with an analysis of very young infants' capacities to feel distress and delight, but then moved on to consider two early-appearing emotions that reflect infants' abilities to compare their sensory experiences with their expectations: surprise and disgust. We then went on to consider all of the other positive and negative emotions identified in Bridges' original scheme.

Although some psychologists make a distinction between cognition and emotion, it soon became clear that as infants developed, their growing cognitive abilities as well as their social experiences contributed to the emergence of more complex emotions such as sadness (which did not appear in Bridges' scheme) and the sociomoral emotions of empathy, shame and guilt. Bridges' framework was a starting point, not a complete blueprint for the development of emotion in childhood. Chapters 3–10 summarise what we currently know about the development of both basic and more complex emotions, including the genetic and neural substrates that contribute to all of these different facets of emotional experience.

Emotion and emotional problems

The view of emotional development set forth in this book has also drawn upon the perspective of *developmental psychopathology*, which holds that the clinical study of children's psychological problems should be undertaken with reference to what we know about child development (Sroufe & Rutter, 1984). Within this perspective, investigators have tried to identify early pathways toward serious psychological problems, partly because such knowledge might help prevent or provide appropriate treatment for troubled children. Therefore, in each of the preceding chapters on different emotions, we also consider some of the clinical literature on comparable emotional disorders that emerge in childhood and feature some dysregulation of the emotion being considered in that chapter.

Although this approach – pairing the study of a particular emotion with a comparable emotional disorder – helps us understand the continuum from individual differences in emotional experience to mental health problems, it does obscure an important point. Children's emotional and behavioural disorders often co-occur. Anxiety often accompanies depression; depressed children may also have conduct problems (Angold, Costello, & Erkanli, 1999).

Although traditional psychiatric thinking about children's mental health problems has tried to create operational definitions that would distinguish different disorders (American Psychiatric Association, 2013), some investigators argue for a focus on dimensions of children's functioning, not discrete diagnoses (Insel et al., 2010). This new approach advocates for the use of research diagnostic criteria (RDoC) to specify the strengths and difficulties in children's psychological lives.

One of the domains identified in the RDoC criteria is an emotional one, described as *negative* versus *positive hedonia* – or, as Bridges (1932) once put it, in simpler terms, distress versus delight. From a developmental perspective, it seems possible that the co-occurrence of different childhood disorders partly derives from a kind of *emotional entanglement*, in which different negative emotions intertwine with each other and with the more complex sociomoral emotions that follow. Thus, the dimensional approach to mental illness set forth in RDoC is unexpectedly compatible with Bridges' ideas about emotional development, which still provide a helpful framework for the study of emotional development.

REFERENCES

Adams, S., Kuebli, J., Boyle, P. A., & Fivush, R. (1995). Gender differences in parent-child conversations about past emotions: A longitudinal investigation. *Sex Roles, 33*, 309–323.

Ainsworth, M. D. S. (1969). Object relations, dependency, and attachment: A theoretical view of the infant-mother relationship. *Child Development, 40*, 969–1025.

Ainsworth, M. D. S. (1979). Infant-mother attachment. *American Psychologist, 34*, 932–937.

Ainsworth, M. D. S., Blehar, M., Waters, E., & Wall, S. N. (2015). *Patterns of attachment.* New York, NY: Psychology Press.

Allport, F. H. (1924). *Social psychology.* Cambridge, MA: Riverside Press.

American Psychiatric Association. (2013). *Diagnostic and statistical manual of mental disorders* (5th ed.). London: APA.

Amsterdam, B., & Greenberg, L. M. (1977). Self-conscious behaviour of infants: A videotape study. *Developmental Psychobiology, 10*, 1–6.

Anderson, J. R. (1984). The development of self-recognition: A review. *Developmental Psychobiology, 17*, 35–49.

Anderson, J. R., & Gallup, G. G., Jr. (2015). Mirror self-recognition: A review and critique of attempts to promote and engineer self-recognition in primates. *Primates, 56*, 317–326.

Angold, A. (1988). Childhood and adolescent depression: Aetiological and epidemiological aspects. *British Journal of Psychiatry, 152*, 601–617.

Angold, A., Costello, E. J., & Erkanli, A. (1999). Comorbidity. *Journal of Child Psychology and Psychiatry, 40*, 57–87.

Arcus, D., & Kagan, J. (1995). Temperament and craniofacial variation in the first two years. *Child Development, 66*, 1529–1540.

Baibazarova, E., van de Beek, C., Cohen-Kettenis, P. T., Buitelaar, J., Shelton, K. H., & van Goozen, S. H. M. (2013). Influence of prenatal maternal stress, maternal plasma cortisol and cortisol in the amniotic fluid on birth outcomes and child temperament at 3 months. *Psychoneuroendocrinology, 38*, 907–915.

Bakeman, R., & Adamson, L. B. (1986). Infants' conventionalized acts: Gestures and words with mothers and peers. *Infant Behavior and Development, 9*, 215–230.

Baker, E., Baibazarova, E., Ktistaki, G., Shelton, K. H., & van Goozen, S. H. M. (2012). Development of fear and guilt in young children: Stability over time and relations with psychopathology. *Development and Psychopathology, 24*, 833–845.

Baldwin, J. M. (1895). *Mental development in the child and the race: Methods and processes*. New York: MacMillan.

Ball, C. L., Smetana, J. G., & Sturge-Apple, M. L. (2017). Following my head and my heart: Integrating preschoolers' empathy, theory of mind, and moral judgments. *Child Development, 88*, 597–611.

Banham, K. M. (1950). The development of affectionate behaviour in infancy. *Pedagogical Seminar and Journal of Genetic Psychology, 76*, 283–289.

Barbaro, J., & Dissanayake, C. (2013). Early markers of autism spectrum disorders in infants and toddlers prospectively identified in the Social Attention and Communication Study. *Autism, 17*, 64–86.

Barr, C. S., Newman, T. K., Shannon, C., Parker, C., Dvoskin, R. L., Becker, M. L., . . . Higley, J. D. (2004). Rearing condition and rh5-HTTLPR interact to influence limbic-hypothalamic-pituitary-adrenal axis response to stress in infant macaques. *Biological Psychiatry, 55*, 733–738.

Barrett, K. C., Zahn-Waxler, C., & Cole, P. M. (1993). Avoiders vs. amenders: Implications for the investigation of guilt and shame during toddlerhood. *Cognition and Emotion, 7*, 481–505.

Barry, R. A., & Kochanska, G. (2010). A longitudinal investigation of the affective environment in families with young children: From infancy to early school age. *Emotion, 10*, 237–249.

Bates, J. E., & Bayles, K. (1984). Objective and subjective components in mothers' perceptions of their children from age 6 months to 3 years. *Merrill-Palmer Quarterly, 30*, 111–130.

Bauer, D. H. (1976). An exploratory study of developmental changes in children's fears. *Journal of Child Psychology and Psychiatry, 17*, 69–74.

Bauer, P. J. (2015). Development of episodic and autobiographical memory: The importance of remembering forgetting. *Developmental Review, 38*, 146–166.

Bauminger, N. (2004). The expression and understanding of jealousy in children with autism. *Development and Psychopathology, 16*, 157–177.

Bayet, L., Quinn, P. C., Tanaka, J. W., Lee, K., Gentaz, E., & Pascalis, O. (2015). Face gender influences the looking preference for smiling expressions in 3.5-month-old human infants. *PLOS One, 10*, e0129812.

Beauchemin, M., Gonzalez-Frankenburger, B., Tremblay, J., Vannasing, P., Martinez-Montes, E., Belin, P., . . . Lassonde, M. (2011). Mother and stranger: An electrophysiological study of voice processing in newborns. *Cerebral Cortex, 21*, 1705–1711.

Beebe, B., Messinger, D., Bahrick, L. E., Margolis, A., Buck, K. A., & Chen, H. (2016). A systems view of mother-infant face-to-face communication. *Developmental Psychology, 52*, 556–571.

Beeghly, M., Frank, D. A., Rose-Jacobs, R., Cabral, H., & Tronick, E. (2003). Level of prenatal cocaine exposure and infant-caregiver attachment behaviour. *Neurotoxicology and Teratology, 25*, 23–38.

Bell, R. Q. (1968). A reinterpretation of the direction of effects in studies of socialization. *Psychological Review, 75*, 81–95.

Bell, S. M., & Ainsworth, M. D. S. (1972). Infant crying and maternal responsiveness. *Child Development, 43*, 1171–1190.

Belsky, J., Domitrovich, C., & Crnic, K. (1997). Temperament and parenting antecedents of individual differences in three-year-old boys' pride and shame reactions. *Child Development, 68*, 456–466.

Benedict, R. (1946). *The chrysanthemum and the sword: Patterns of Japanese culture*. Boston, MA: Houghton Mifflin.

Bergmann, K., Sarkar, P., O'Connor, T., Modi, N., & Glover, V. (2007). Maternal stress during pregnancy predicts cognitive ability and fearfulness in infancy. *Journal of the American Academy of Child and Adolescent Psychiatry, 46*, 1454–1463.

Berlyne, D. E. (1960). *Conflict, arousal, and curiosity.* New York, NY: McGraw Hill.

Berntson, G. G., & Cacioppo, J. T. (2009). *Handbook of neuroscience for the behavioural sciences.* Chichester: Wiley.

Bers, S. A., & Rodin, J. (1984). Self-comparison jealousy: A developmental and motivational study. *Journal of Personality and Social Psychology, 47*, 766–779.

Bertanthal, B. I., & Fischer, K. W. (1978). Development of self-recognition in the infant. *Developmental Psychology, 14*, 44–50.

Biederman, J., Hirshfeld-Becker, D. R., Rosenbaum, J. F., Hérot, C., Friedman, D., Snidman, N., . . . Faraone, S. V. (2001). Further evidence of association between behavioural inhibition and social anxiety in children. *American Journal of Psychiatry, 158*, 1673–1679.

Bigelow, A. E. (1998). Infants' sensitivity to familiar imperfect contingencies in social interaction. *Infant Behavior and Development, 21*, 149–162.

Birns, B. (1965). Individual differences in human neonates' responses to stimulation. *Child Development, 36*, 249–256.

Blandon, A. Y., Calkins, S. D., Keane, S. P., & O'Brien, M. (2010). Contribution of child's physiology and maternal behaviour to children's trajectories of temperamental reactivity. *Developmental Psychology, 46*, 1089–1102.

Blatz, W. E. (1966). *Human security: Some reflections.* Toronto: University of Toronto Press.

Borke, H. (1971). Interpersonal perception of young children: Egocentrism or empathy? *Developmental Psychology, 5*, 263–269.

Borke, H. (1973). The development of empathy in Chinese and American children between three and six years of age: A cross-cultural study. *Developmental Psychology, 9*, 102–108.

Bornstein, M. H., & Arterberry, M. E. (2003). Recognition, discrimination and categorization of smiling by 5-month-old infants. *Developmental Science, 6*, 585–599.

Bornstein, M. H., Hahn, C.-S., & Haynes, O. M. (2004). Specific and general language performance across early childhood: Stability and gender considerations. *First Language, 24*, 267–304.

Bowlby, J. (1969). *Attachment.* London: Hogarth.

Brackbill, Y. (1958). Extinction of the smiling response in infants as a function of reinforcement schedule. *Child Development, 29*, 113–124.

Braithwaite, E. C., Pickles, A., Sharp, H., Glover, V., O'Donnell, J. O., Tibu, F., & Hill, J. (2017). Maternal prenatal cortisol predicts infant negative emotionality in a sex-dependent manner. *Physiology and Behavior, 175*, 31–36.

Braungart-Rieker, J. M., Hill-Soderlund, A. L., & Karrass, J. (2010). Fear and anger reactivity trajectories from 4 to 16 months: The roles of temperament, regulation, and maternal sensitivity. *Developmental Psychology, 46*, 791–804.

Bretherton, I. (1985). Attachment theory: Retrospect and prospect. *Monographs of the Society for Research in Child Development, 50*(1/2).

Bretherton, I., McNew, S., & Beeghly-Smith, M. (1981). When do infants acquire a "theory of mind"? In M. E. Lamb & L. R. Sherrod (Eds.), *Infant social cognition: Empirical and theoretical considerations.* Hillsdale, NJ: Erlbaum.

Bridges, K. M. B. (1932). Emotional development in early infancy. *Child Development, 3*, 324–341.

Bronson, G. (1968). The fear of novelty. *Psychological Bulletin, 69*, 350–358.

Bronson, W. C., Katten, E. S., & Livson, N. (1959). Patterns of authority and affection in two generations. *Journal of Abnormal and Social Psychology, 58*, 143–152.

Brooker, R. J., & Buss, K. A. (2010). Dynamic measures of RSA predict distress and regulation in toddlers. *Developmental Psychobiology*, *52*, 372–382.

Brooker, R. J., Buss, K. A., Lemery-Chalfant, K., Aksan, N., Davidson, R. J., & Goldsmith, H. H. (2013). The development of stranger fear in infancy and toddlerhood: Normative development, individual differences, antecedents, and outcomes. *Developmental Science*, *16*, 864–878.

Brossard, L. M., & Decarie, T. G. (1968). Comparative reinforcing effect of eight stimulations on the smiling response of infants. *Journal of Child Psychology and Psychiatry*, *9*, 51–59.

Buist, K. L., Dekovic, M., & Prinzie, P. (2013). Sibling relationship quality and psychopathology of children and adolescents: A meta-analysis. *Clinical Psychology Review*, *33*, 97–106.

Buss, A. H., & Plomin, R. (1975). *A temperament theory of personality development*. Oxford: Wiley-Interscience.

Buss, K. (2011). Which fearful toddlers should we worry about? Context, fear regulation, and anxiety risk. *Developmental Psychology*, *47*, 804–819.

Buss, K., Davidson, R. J., Kalin, N. H., & Goldsmith, H. H. (2004). Context-specific freezing and associated physiological activity as a dysregulated fear response. *Developmental Psychology*, *40*, 583–594.

Buss, K., & Goldsmith, H. H. (1998). Fear and anger regulation in infancy: Effects on the temporal dynamics of affect expression. *Child Development*, *69*, 359–374.

Buss, K., & Kiel, E. J. (2004). Comparison of sadness, anger and fear expressions when toddlers look at their mothers. *Child Development*, *75*, 1761–1773.

Byrnes, J. P., Miller, D. C., & Schaefer, E. D. (1999). Gender differences in risk taking: A meta-analysis. *Psychological Bulletin*, *125*, 367–383.

Campos, J. J., Frankel, C., & Camras, L. (2004). On the nature of emotion regulation. *Child Development*, *75*, 377–394.

Campos, J. J., Thein, S., & Owen, D. (2003). A Darwinian legacy to understanding human infancy: Emotional expressions as behavioural regulators. *Annals of the New York Academy of Science*, *1000*, 110–134.

Camras, L. A., Oster, H., Bakeman, R., Meng, Z., Ujiie, T., & Campos, J. J. (2007). Do infants show distinct negative facial expressions for fear and anger? Emotional expression in 11-month-old European-American, Chinese, and Japanese infants. *Infancy*, *11*, 131–155.

Camras, L. A., Oster, H., Campos, J., Ujiie, R., Miyake, T., Wang, L., & Meng, Z. (1998). Production of emotional facial expressions in European American, Japanese, and Chinese infants. *Developmental Psychology*, *34*, 616–628.

Camras, L. A., & Shutter, J. M. (2010). Emotional facial expressions in infancy. *Emotion Review*, *2*, 120–129.

Cannon, P. R., Schnall, S., & White, M. (2011). Transgressions and expressions: Affective facial muscle activity predicts moral judgements. *Social Psychological and Personality Science*, *2*, 325–331.

Cannon, W. B. (1927). The James-Lange theory of emotion: A critical examination and an alternative theory. *The American Journal of Psychology*, *39*, 106–124.

Caplan, M. Z., & Hay, D. F. (1989). Preschoolers' responses to peers' distress and beliefs about bystander intervention. *Journal of Child Psychology and Psychiatry*, *30*, 231–242.

Carlson, E. A. (1998). A prospective longitudinal study of attachment disorganization/disorientation. *Child Development*, *69*, 1107–1128.

Carver, C. S., & Harmon-Jones, E. (2009). Anger is an approach-related affect: Evidence and implications. *Psychological Bulletin*, *135*, 183–204.

Casey, R. J. (1993). Children's emotional experience: Relations among expression, self-report, and understanding. *Developmental Psychology*, *29*, 119–129.

Caspi, A., Sugden, K., Moffitt, T. E., Taylor, A., Craig, I. W., Harrington, H., & McClay, J. (2003). Influence of life stress on depression: Moderation by a polymorphism in the 5HTT gene. *Science, 301,* 386–389.

Cassano, M., Perry-Parrish, C., & Zeman, J. (2007). Influence of gender on parental Socialisation of children's sadness regulation. *Social Development, 16,* 210–231.

Cecchini, M., Baroni, E., DiVito, C., Piccolo, F., Aceto, P., & Lai, C. (2013). Effects of different types of contingent stimulation on crying, smiling and sleep in newborns: An observational study. *Developmental Psychobiology, 55,* 508–517.

Centifanti, L. C. M., Meins, E., & Fernyhough, C. (2016). Callous-unemotional traits and impulsivity: Distinct longitudinal relations with mind-mindedness and understanding of others. *Journal of Child Psychology and Psychiatry, 57,* 84–92.

Cernoch, J. M., & Porter, R. H. (1985). Recognition of maternal axillary odors by infants. *Child Development, 56,* 1593–1598.

Chaplin, T. M., Cole, P. M., & Zahn-Waxler, C. (2005). Parental socialization of emotion expression: Gender differences and relation to child adjustment. *Emotion, 5,* 80–88.

Chapman, H. A., & Anderson, A. K. (2013). Things rank and gross in nature: A review and synthesis of moral disgust. *Psychological Bulletin, 139,* 300–327.

Cicchetti, D., & Doyle, C. (2016). Child maltreatment, attachment and psychopathology: Mediating relations. *World Psychiatry, 15,* 89–90.

Cicchetti, D., & Sroufe, L. A. (1976). The relationship between affective and cognitive development in Down's syndrome infants. *Child Development, 47,* 920–929.

Cohn, J. F., & Tronick, E. Z. (1983). Three-month-old infants' reactions to simulated maternal depression. *Child Development, 54,* 185–193.

Colder, C. R., Mott, J. A., & Berman, A. S. (2002). The interactive effects of infant activity level and fear on growth trajectories of early childhood behavior problems. *Development and Psychopathology, 14,* 1–23.

Cole, P. M. (1986). Children's spontaneous control of facial expressions. *Child Development, 57,* 1309–1321.

Cole, P. M., Luby, J., & Sullivan, M. W. (2008). Emotions and the development of childhood depression: Bridging the gap. *Child Development Perspectives, 2,* 141–148.

Cole, P. M., Martin, S. E., & Dennis, T. A. (2004). Emotion regulation as a scientific construct: Methodological challenges and directions for child development research. *Child Development, 75,* 317–333.

Cole, P. M., & Moore, G. A. (2015). About face! Infant expression of emotion. *Emotion Review, 7,* 116–120.

Cole, P. M., Zahn-Waxler, C., & Smith, K. D. (1994). Expressive control during a disappointment: Variations related to preschoolers' behaviour problems. *Developmental Psychology, 30,* 835–846.

Collishaw, S. (2015). Annual research review: Secular trends in child and adolescent mental health. *Journal of Child Psychology and Psychiatry, 56,* 370–393.

Cooper, P., Tomlinson, M., Swarz, L., & Woolgar, M. (1999). Post-partum depression and the mother-infant relationship in a South African peri-urban settlement. *British Journal of Psychiatry, 175,* 554–558.

Coplan, R., Caldwell, B., & Rubin, K. H. (1998). Shyness and little boy blue: Iris pigmentation, gender, and social wariness in preschoolers. *Developmental Psychobiology, 32,* 37–44.

Costello, E. J., Erkanli, A., & Angold, A. (2006). Is there an epidemic of child or adolescent depression? *Journal of Child Psychology and Psychiatry, 47,* 1263–1271.

Côté, S., Tremblay, R., E., Nagin, D. S., Zoccolillo, M., & Vitaro, F. (2002). Childhood behaviour profiles leading to adolescent conduct disorder: Risk trajectories for boys and girls. *Journal of the American Academy for Child and Adolescent Psychiatry, 41,* 1086–1094.

Covell, K., & Abramovitch, R. (1987). Understanding emotion in the family: Children's and parents' attributions of happiness, sadness and anger. *Child Development, 58,* 985–991.

Craik, K. J. W. (1943). *The nature of explanation.* Cambridge: Cambridge University Press.

Croake, J. W. (1969). Fears of children. *Human Development, 12,* 239–247.

Crockenberg, S. (1987). Predictors and correlates of anger toward and punitive control of toddlers by adolescent mothers. *Child Development, 58,* 964–975.

Curtis, V., de Barra, M., & Aunger, R. (2011). Disgust as an adaptive system for disease avoidance behaviour. *Philosophical Transactions of the Royal Society B: Biological Sciences, 366,* 389–401.

Dadds, M., El Masry, Y., Wimalaweera, S., & Guastella, A. J. (2008). Reduced eye gaze explains 'fear blindness' in childhood psychopathic traits. *Journal of the American Academy of Child and Adolescent Psychiatry, 47,* 455–463.

Dahl, A., Campos, J. J., Anderson, D. I., Uchiyama, I., Witherington, D. C., Ueno, M., . . . Barbu-Roth, M. (2013). The epigenesis of wariness of heights. *Psychological Science, 24,* 1361–1367.

Danovitch, J., & Bloom, P. (2009). Children's extension of disgust to physical and moral events. *Emotion, 9,* 107–112.

Darwin, C. (1872). *The expression of the emotions in man and animals.* London: Murray.

Darwin, C. (1877). A biographical sketch of an infant. *Mind, 2,* 285–294.

Davidov, M., Zahn-Waxler, C., Roth-Hanania, R., & Knafo, A. (2013). Concern for others in the first year of life: Theory, evidence, and avenues for Research. *Child Development Perspectives, 7,* 126–131.

Davis, E. P., Snidman, N., Wadhwa, P. D., Glynn, L. M., Schetter, C. D., & Sandman, C. A. (2004). Prenatal maternal anxiety and depression predict negative behavioural reactivity in infancy. *Infancy, 6,* 319–331.

Dawson, G., Klinger, L. G., Panagiotides, H., Hill, D., & Spieker, S. (1992). Frontal lobe activity and affective behaviour of infants with mothers with depressive symptoms. *Child Development, 63,* 725–737.

DeBaryshe, B. D., & Fryxell, D. (1998). A developmental perspective on anger: Family and peer contexts. *Psychology in the Schools, 35,* 205–216.

DeCasper, A. J., & Fifer, W. P. (1980). Of human bonding: Newborns prefer their mothers' voices. *Science, 208,* 1174–1176.

Decety, J. (2011). Dissecting the neural mechanisms mediating empathy. *Emotion Review, 3,* 92–108.

Decety, J. (2015). The neural pathways, development and functions of empathy. *Current Opinion in Behavioural Sciences, 3,* 1–6.

Decety, J., Bartal, I. B.-A., Uzefovsky, F., & Knafo-Noam, A. (2016). Empathy as a driver of prosocial behaviour: Highly conserved neurobehavioural mechanisms across species. *Philosophical Transactions of the Royal Society B. Biological Sciences, 371,* 20150077.

Decety, J., & Meyer, M. (2008). From emotion resonance to empathic understanding: A social developmental neuroscience account. *Development and Psychopathology, 20,* 1053–1080.

Degnan, K. A., & Fox, N. A. (2007). Behavioral inhibition and anxiety disorders: Multiple levels of a resilience process. *Development and Psychopathology, 19,* 729–746.

Degnan, K. A., Hane, A. A., Henderson, H. A., Moas, O. L., Reeb-Sutherland, B. C., & Fox, N. A. (2011). Longitudinal stability of temperamental exuberance and social-emotional outcomes in early childhood. *Developmental Psychology, 47,* 765–780.

Demetriou, H., & Hay, D. F. (2004). Toddlers' reactions to the distress of familiar peers: The importance of context. *Infancy, 6,* 299–318.

Denham, S. (1986). Social cognition, prosocial behaviour and emotion in preschoolers: Contextual validation. *Child Development, 57,* 194–201.

Denham, S., & Grout, L. (1993). Socialization of emotion: Pathway to preschoolers' emotional and social competence. *Journal of Nonverbal Behavior, 17,* 205–227.

Denham, S., Mitchell-Copeland, J., Strandberg, K., Auerbach, S., & Blair, K. (1997). Parental contributions to preschoolers' emotional competence: Direct and Indirect effects. *Motivation and Emotion, 21,* 65–86.

Derntl, B., Finkelmeyer, A., Eickhoff, S., Kellermann, T., Falkenberg, D. I., Schneider, F., & Habel, U. (2010). Multidimensional assessment of empathic abilities: Neural correlates and gender differences. *Psychoneuroendocrinology, 35,* 67–82.

De Sonneville, L. M. J., Verschoor, C. A., Njiokiktjien, C., Op het Veld, V., Toorenaar, N., & Vranken, M. (2002). Facial identity and facial emotions: Speed, accuracy, and processing strategies in children and adults. *Journal of Clinical and Experimental Neuropsychology, 24,* 200–213.

Dessereau, B. K., Kurowski, C. O., & Thompson, N. S. (1998). A reassessment of the role of pitch and duration in adults' responses to infants' crying. *Infant Behavior and Development, 21,* 367–371.

de Weerth, C., van Hees, Y., & Buitelaar, J. K. (2003). Prenatal maternal cortisol levels and infant behavior during the first 5 months. *Early Human Development, 74,* 139–151.

De Wolff, M. S., & van IJzendoorn, M. H. (1997). Sensitivity and attachment: A meta-analysis on parental antecedents of infant attachment. *Child Development, 68,* 571–591.

Dilalla, L. F., Kagan, J., & Reznick, J. S. (1994). Genetic etiology of behavioral inhibition among 2-year-old children. *Infant Behavior and Development, 17,* 405–412.

Dondi, M., Messinger, D., Colle, M., Tabasso, A., Simion, F., Dalla Barba, B., & Fogel, A. (2007). A new perspective on neonatal smiling: Differences between the judgments of expert coders and naïve observers. *Infancy, 12,* 235–255.

Dondi, M., Simion, F., & Caltran, G. (1999). Can newborns distinguish between their own cry and the cry of another newborn infant? *Developmental Psychology, 35,* 418–426.

Drummond, J. D. K., Hammond, S. I., Satlof-Bedrick, E., Waugh, W. E., & Brownell, C. (2017). Helping the one you hurt: Toddlers' rudimentary guilt, shame and prosocial behaviour after harming another. *Child Development, 88,* 1382–1397.

Dunn, J. (1988). *The beginnings of social understanding.* Cambridge, MA: Harvard.

Dunn, J., & Brown, J. (1994). Affect expression in the family, children's understanding of emotions, and their interactions with others. *Merrill-Palmer Quarterly, 40,* 120–137.

Dunn, J., Brown, J., & Beardsall, L. (1991). Family talk about feeling states and children's later understanding of others' emotions. *Developmental Psychology, 27,* 448–455.

Dunn, J., & Munn, P. (1986). Siblings and the development of prosocial behaviour. *International Journal of Behavioural Development, 9,* 265–284.

Durbin, E. (2010). Validity of young children's self-reports of their emotion in response to structured laboratory tasks. *Emotion, 4,* 519–535.

Egger, H., & Angold, A. (2006). Common behavioural and emotional disorders in preschool children: Presentation, nosology, and epidemiology. *Journal of Child Psychology and Psychiatry, 47,* 313–337.

Eisenberg, N., Cumberland, A., & Spinrad, T. L. (1998). Parental socialisation of emotion. *Psychological Inquiry, 9,* 241–273.

Eisenberg, N., & Fabes, R. A. (1994). Mothers' reactions to children's negative emotions: Relation to children's temperament and angry behaviour. *Merrill-Palmer Quarterly, 40,* 138–156.

Eisenberg, N., Fabes, R. A., Miller, P. A., Fultz, J., Shell, R., Mathy, R. M., & Reno, R. R. (1989). Relation of sympathy and personal distress to prosocial behaviour: A multimethod study. *Journal of Personality and Social Psychology, 57,* 55–66.

Eisenberg, N., Fabes, R. A., & Murphy, B. C. (1996). Parents' reactions to children's negative emotions: Relations to children's social competence and comforting behaviour. *Child Development*, 2227–2247.

Eisenberg, N., Fabes, R. A., Murphy, B. C., Shepard, S., Guthrie, I. K., Mazsk, P., . . . Jones, S. (1999). Prediction of elementary school children's socially appropriate and problem behaviour from anger reactions at age 4–6 years. *Journal of Applied Developmental Psychology*, *20*, 119–142.

Eisenberg, N., & Lennon, R. (1983). Sex differences in empathy and related capacities. *Psychological Bulletin*, *94*, 100–131.

Ekman, P. (1993). Facial expression and emotion. *American Psychologist*, *48*, 384–392.

Ekman, P., & Friesen, W. V. (1978). *Manual for the facial action coding system*. Bel Air, CA: Consulting Psychologists Press.

Ekman, P., Friesen, W. V., & Ellsworth, P. (1972). *Emotion in the human face: Guidelines for research and an integration of findings*. New York: Pergamon.

Ekman, P., Sorensen, E. R., & Friesen, W. V. (1969). Pan-cultural elements in facial displays of emotion. *Science*, *164*, 86–88.

Ely, R., & McCabe, A. (1994). The language play of kindergarten children. *First Language*, *14*, 19–35.

Eres, R., Decety, J., Louis, W. R., & Molenberghs, P. (2015). Individual differences in local gray matter density are associated with differences in affective and cognitive empathy. Neuroimage, *117*, 305–310.

Esposito, G., Nakazawa, J., Venuti, P., & Bornstein, M. (2012). Perceptions of distress in young children with autism compared to typically developing children: A cultural comparison between Japan and Italy. *Research in Developmental Disabilities*, *33*, 1059–1067.

Esposito, G., & Venuti, P. (2010). Developmental changes in the fundamental frequency (f0) of infants' cries: A study of children with Autism Spectrum Disorder. *Early Child Development and Care*, *180*, 1093–1102.

Fairchild, G., Stobbe, Y., van Goozen, S. H. M., Calder, A. J., & Goodyer, I. M. (2010). Facial expression recognition, fear conditioning, and startle modulation in female subjects with conduct disorder. *Biological Psychiatry*, *68*, 272–279.

Fairchild, G., van Goozen, S. H. M., Calder, A. J., Stollery, S. J., & Goodyer, I. M. (2009). Deficits in facial expression recognition in male adolescents with early-onset or adolescence-onset conduct disorder. *Journal of Child Psychology and Psychiatry*, *50*, 627–636.

Feldman, R. (2015). The adaptive human parental brain: Implications for children's social development. *Trends in Neuroscience*, *38*, 387–399.

Feldman, R., Gordon, I., Influs, M., Gutbir, T., & Ebstein, R. P. (2013). Parental oxytocin and early caregiving jointly shape children's oxytocin response and social reciprocity. *Neuropsychopharmacology*, *38*, 1154–1162.

Feldman, R., Weller, A., Zagoory-Sharon, O., & Levine, A. (2007). Evidence for a neuroendocrinological foundation of human affiliation: Plasma oxytocin levels across pregnancy and the postpartum period predict mother-infant bonding. *Psychological Science*, *18*, 965–970.

Ferguson, T. J., Stegge, H., & Damhuis, I. (1991). Children's understanding of guilt and shame. *Child Development*, *62*, 827–839.

Field, T. M., Guy, L., & Umbel, V. (1985). Infants' responses to mothers' imitative behaviors. *Infant Mental Health Journal*, *6*, 40–44.

Field, T. M., Woodson, R., Greenberg, R., & Cohen, D. (1982). Discrimination and imitation of facial expression by neonates. *Science*, *218*, 179–181.

Filliter, J. H., Longard, J., Lawrence, M. A., Zwaigenbaum, L., Brian, J., Garon, N., . . . Bryson, S. E. (2015). Positive affect in infant siblings of children diagnosed with autism spectrum disorder. *Journal of Abnormal Child Psychology*, *43*, 567–575.

Fivush, R., Berlin, L., Sales, J. M., Menutti-Washburn, J., & Cassidy, J. (2003). Functions of parent-child reminiscing about emotionally negative events. *Memory, 11*, 179–192.

Fivush, R., Brotman, M. A., Buckner, J. P., & Goodman, S. H. (2000). Gender differences in parent-child emotion narratives. *Sex Roles, 42*, 233–253.

Folkman, S., & Moskowitz, J. T. (2000). Positive affect and the other side of coping. *American Psychologist, 55*, 647–654.

Foote, R. C., & Holmes-Lonergan, H. A. (2003). Sibling conflict and theory of mind. *British Journal of Developmental Psychology, 21*, 45–58.

Fox, N. A., & Davidson, R. J. (1986). Taste-elicited changes in facial signs of emotion and the asymmetry of brain electrical activity in human newborns. *Neuropsychologia, 24*, 417–422.

Fox, N. A., & Davidson, R. J. (1988). Patterns of brain electrical activity during facial signs of emotion in 10-month-old infants. *Developmental Psychology, 24*, 230–236.

Fox, N. A., Henderson, H. A., Rubin, K. H., Calkins, S. D., & Schmidt, L. A. (2001). Continuity and discontinuity of behavioural inhibition and exuberance: Psychophysiological and behavioural influences over the first four years of life. *Child Development, 72*, 1–21.

Fox, N. A., Kimmerly, N. L., & Schafer, W. D. (1991). Attachment to mother/attachment to father: A meta-analysis. *Child Development, 62*, 210–225.

Fox, N. A., Nichols, K. E., Henderson, H. A., Rubin, K., Schmidt, L., Hamer, D., . . . Pine, D. S. (2005). Evidence for a gene-environment interaction in predicting behavioural inhibition in middle childhood. *Psychological Science, 16*, 921–926.

Freedman, D. G. (1964). Smiling in blind infants and the issue of innate vs. acquired. *Journal of Child Psychology and Psychiatry, 5*, 171–184.

Freud, S. (1949). *An outline of psychoanalysis* (J. Strachey, Ed. & Trans.). New York, NY: Norton.

Frick, P. J., Ray, J. V., Thornton, L. C., & Kahn, R. E. (2014). Can callous-unemotional traits enhance the understanding, diagnosis, and treatment of serious conduct problems in children and adolescents? A comprehensive review. *Psychological Bulletin, 140*, 1–57.

Frodi, A., & Lamb, M. L. (1980). Child abusers' responses to infants' smiles and cries. *Child Development, 51*, 238–241.

Fung, H. (1999). Becoming a moral child: The socialisation of shame among young Chinese children. *Ethos, 27*, 180–209.

Furukawa, E., Tangney, J., & Higashibara, F. (2012). Cross-cultural continuities and Discontinuities in shame, guilt, and pride: A study of children residing in Japan, Korea, & the USA. *Self and Identity, 11*, 90–113.

Gagne, H. R., & Goldsmith, H. H. (2011). A longitudinal analysis of anger and inhibitory control in twins from 12 to 36 months of age. *Developmental Science, 14*, 112–124.

Gagne, H. R., van Hulle, C. A., Aksan, N., Essex, M. J., & Goldsmith, H. H. (2011). Deriving childhood temperament measures from emotion-eliciting behavioural episodes: Scale construction and initial validation. *Psychological Assessment, 23*, 337–353.

Gagnon, M., Gosselin, P., Hudon-ven der Buhs, I., Larocque, K., & Milliard, K. (2010). Children's recognition and discrimination of fear and disgust facial expressions. *Journal of Nonverbal Behavior, 34*, 27–42.

Gao, X., & Maurer, D. (2010). A happy story: Developmental changes in children's sensitivity to facial expressions of different intensities. *Journal of Experimental Child Psychology, 107*, 67–86.

Garcia, M. M., Shaw, D. S., Winslow, E. B., & Yaggi, K. E. (2000). Destructive sibling conflict and the development of conduct problems in young boys. *Developmental Psychology, 36*, 44–53.

Garcia-Coll, C., Kagan, J., & Reznick, J. S. (1984). Behavioral inhibition in young children. *Child Development, 55*, 1005–1019.

Garner, P. W. (2003). Child and family correlates of toddlers' emotional and behavioural responses to a mishap. *Infant Mental Health Journal, 24,* 580–596.

Garside, R. B., & Klimes-Dougan, B. (2002). Socialization of discrete negative emotions: Gender differences and links with psychological distress. *Sex Roles, 47,* 115–128.

Gartstein, M. A., Bridgett, D. J., Rothbart, M. K., Robertson, C., Iddins, E., Ramsay, K., & Schlect, S. (2010). A latent growth examination of fear development in infancy: Contributions of maternal depression and the risk for toddler anxiety. *Developmental Psychology, 46,* 651–668.

Gartstein, M. A., & Rothbart, M. K. (2003). Studying infant temperament via the Revised Infant Behaviour Questionnaire. *Infant Behavior and Development, 26,* 64–86.

Gazzola, V., Aziz-Zadeh, L., & Keysers, C. (2006). Empathy and the somatotopic auditory mirror system in humans. *Current Biology, 18,* 1824–1829.

Geller, B., Craney, J. L., Bolhofner, K., DelBello, M. P., Williams, M., & Zimmerman, B. (2001). One-year recovery and relapse rates of children with a prepubertal and early adolescent bipolar disorder phenotype. *American Journal of Psychiatry, 158,* 303–305.

Gewirtz, J., & Boyd, E. (1977). Does maternal responding imply reduced infant crying? A critique of the 1972 Bell and Ainsworth report. *Child Development, 48,* 1200–1207.

Gibson, E. J., & Walk, R. D. (1960). The "visual cliff". *Scientific American, 202,* 64–71.

Giesbrecht, G. F., Miller, M. R., & Müller, U. (2010). The anger-distress model of temper tantrums: Associations with emotional reactivity and emotional competence. *Infant and Child Development, 19,* 478–497.

Glasberg, R., & Aboud, F. (1982). Keeping one's distance from sadness: Children's reports of emotional experience. *Developmental Psychology, 18,* 287–293.

Glynn, L., Poggi Davis, E., Dunkel Shetter, C., Chicz-Demet, A., Hobel, C. J., & Sandman, C. A. (2007). Postnatal maternal cortisol levels predict temperament in healthy breastfed infants. *Early Human Development, 83,* 675–681.

Gnepp, J. (1983). Children's social sensitivity: Inferring emotion from conflicting cues. *Developmental Psychology, 19,* 805–814.

Goberman, A. M., & Robb, M. P. (1999). Acoustic examination of preterm and full-term infant cries: The long-time average spectrum. *Journal of Speech, Language and Hearing, 42,* 850–861.

Goffin, K. C., Boldt, L. J., Kim, S., & Kochanska, G. (2018). A unique path to callous-unemotional traits for children who are temperamentally fearless and unconcerned about transgressions: A longitudinal study of typically developing children from age 2 to 12. *Journal of Abnormal Child Psychology, 46,* 769–780.

Goldsmith, H. H. (1996). Studying temperament via the construction of the Toddler Behavior Assessment Questionnaire. *Child Development, 67,* 218–235.

Goldsmith, H. H., & Campos, J. J. (1990). The structure of temperamental fear and pleasure in infants: A psychometric perspective. *Child Development, 61,* 1944–1964.

Goodwin, R. D., Fergusson, D. M., & Horwood, L. J. (2004). Early anxious/withdrawn behaviours predict later internalising disorders. *Journal of Child Psychology and Psychiatry, 45,* 874–883.

Gottlieb, G. (2007). Probabilistic epigenesis. *Developmental Science, 10,* 1–11.

Graham, A. M., Ablow, J. C., & Measelle, J. R. (2010). Interparental relationship dynamics and cardiac vagal functioning in infancy. *Infant Behavior and Development, 33,* 530–544.

Grauel, E. L., Hock, S., & Rothganger, H. (1990). Jitter-index of the fundamental frequency of infant cry as a possible diagnostic tool to predict future development problems. *Early Child Development and Care, 65,* 23–29.

Greco, C., & Ison, M. S. (2014). What makes you happy? Appreciating the reasons that bring happiness to Argentine children living in vulnerable social contexts. *Journal of Latino/Latin American Studies, 6*, 4–18.

Green, B. L., Grace, M. C., Vary, M. C., Kramer, T. L., Gleser, G. C., & Leonard, A. C. (1994). Children of disaster in the second decade: A 17-year follow-up of Buffalo Creek survivors. *Journal of the American Academy of Child and Adolescent Psychiatry, 33*, 71–79.

Green, J. A., & Goldwyn, R. (2002). Annotation: Attachment disorganisation and psychopathology: New findings in attachment research and their potential implications for developmental psychopathology in childhood. *Journal of Child Psychology and Psychiatry, 43*, 835–846.

Green, J. A., & Gustafson, G. E. (1983). Individual recognition of human infants on the basis of cries alone. *Developmental Psychobiology, 16*, 485–493.

Green, J. A., Gustafson, G. E., & McGhie, A. C. (1998). Changes in infants' cries as a function of time in a cry bout. *Child Development, 69*, 271–279.

Green, J. A., Whitney, P. G., & Potegal, M. (2011). Screaming, yelling, whining and crying: Categorical and intensity differences in vocal expressions of anger and sadness in children's tantrums. *Emotion, 11*, 1124–1133.

Grey, K. R., Poggi Davis, E., Sandman, C. A., & Glynn, L. M. (2011). Human milk cortisol is associated with infant temperament. *Psychoneuroendocrinology, 38*, 1178–1185.

Groh, A. M., Narayan, A. J., Bakermans-Kranenburg, M. J., Roisman, G. I., Vaughn, B. E., Fearon, R. M. P., & van IJzendoorn, M. H. (2017). Attachment and temperament in the early life course: A meta-analytic review. *Child Development, 88*, 770–795.

Gross, A. L., & Ballif, B. (1991). Children's understanding of emotion from facial expressions and situations: A review. *Developmental Review, 11*, 368–398.

Gunnar, M., & Nelson, C. A. (1994). Event-related potentials in year-old infants: Relations with emotionality and cortisol. *Child Development, 65*, 80–94.

Gunnar, M., & Vazquez, D. M. (2000). Low cortisol and a flattening of daytime rhythm: Potential indices of risk in human development. *Development and Psychopathology, 13*, 515–538.

Gunnar-von Gnechten, M. R. (1978). Changing a frightening toy into a pleasant toy by allowing the infant to control its actions. *Developmental Psychology, 14*, 157–162.

Gustafson, G. E., & Green, J. A. (1989). On the importance of fundamental frequency and other acoustic features in cry perception and infant development. *Child Development, 60*, 772–780.

Gustafson, G. E., Sanborn, S. M., Lin, H.-C., & Green, J. A. (2017). Newborns' cries are unique to individuals (but not language environment). *Infancy, 22*, 736–747.

Halligan, S. L., Murray, L., Martins, C., & Cooper, P. (2007). Maternal depression and psychiatric outcomes in adolescent offspring: A 13-year longitudinal study. *Journal of Affective Disorders, 97*, 145–154.

Hamilton, C. E. (2000). Continuity and discontinuity of attachment from infancy through adolescence. *Child Development, 71*, 690–694.

Hankin, B. L. (2015). Depression from childhood through adolescence: Risk mechanisms across multiple systems and levels of analysis. *Current Opinion in Psychology, 4*, 13–20.

Hare, R. D. (1996). Psychopathy: A clinical construct whose time has come. *Criminal Justice and Behaviour, 23*, 25–54.

Harris, P. L. (2000). *Understanding children's worlds: The work of the imagination*. Malden, MA: Blackwell.

Hart, S. L., & Carrington, H. A. (2002). Jealousy in 6-month-old infants. *Infancy, 3*, 395–402.

Hart, S. L., Carrington, H. A., Tronick, E. Z., & Carroll, S. R. (2004). When infants lose exclusive maternal attention: Is it jealousy? *Infancy, 6,* 57–78.

Hatfield, E., Cacioppo, J. T., & Rapson, R. L. (1993). Emotional contagion. *Current Directions in Psychological Science, 2,* 96–99.

Hay, D. F. (1979). Cooperative interactions and sharing between very young children and their parents. *Developmental Psychology, 15,* 647–653.

Hay, D. F. (2006). "Yours and mine": Toddlers' talk about possession with familiar peers. *British Journal of Developmental Psychology, 24,* 39–52.

Hay, D. F., Castle, J., Davies, L., Demetriou, H., & Stimson, C. A. (1999). Prosocial action in very early childhood. *Journal of Child Psychology and Psychiatry, 40,* 905–916.

Hay, D. F., & Cook, K. V. (2007). The transformation of prosocial behavior from infancy to childhood. In C. A. Brownell & C. B. Kopp (Eds.), *Socioemotional development in the toddler years: Transitions and transformations* (pp. 100–131). New York, NY: Guilford.

Hay, D. F., Hurst, S. L., Waters, C. S., & Chadwick, A. (2011). The developmental origins of intentional instrumental aggression. *Infancy, 16,* 471–489.

Hay, D. F., Nash, A., Caplan, M., Ishikawa, F., & Vespo, J. E. (2011). The emergence of gender differences in physical aggression in the context of conflict between young peers. *British Journal of Developmental Psychology, 29,* 158–175.

Hay, D. F., Nash, A., & Pedersen, J. (1981). Responses of six-month-olds to the distress of their peers. *Child Development, 52,* 1071–1075.

Hay, D. F., Perra, O., Hudson, K., Waters, C. S., Mundy, L., Goodyer, I., Harold, G. T., Thapar, A., & van Goozen, S. (2010). Identifying precursors to aggression: Psychometric properties of the Cardiff Infant Contentiousness Scale (CICS). *Aggressive Behaviour, 36,* 351–357.

Hay, D. F., & Ross, H. S. (1982). The social nature of early conflict. *Child Development, 53,* 105–113.

Hay, D. F., van Goozen, S. H., Mundy, L., Phillips, R., Roberts, S., Meeuwsen, M., . . . Perra, O. (2017). If you go down to the woods today: Infants' distress during a Teddy Bear's Picnic in relation to peer relations and later emotional problems. *Infancy, 22,* 552–570.

Hay, D. F., Vespo, J. E., & Zahn-Waxler, C. (1998). Young children's conflicts with their siblings and mothers: Links with maternal depression and bipolar illness. *British Journal of Developmental Psychology, 16,* 519–538.

Hay, D. F., Waters, C. S., Perra, O., Swift, N., Jones, R., Jones, I., . . . van Goozen, S. (2014). Precursors to aggressive conduct problems are evident by six months of age. *Developmental Science, 17,* 471–480.

He, J., Xu, Q., & Degnan, K. A. (2011). Anger expression and persistence in young children. *Social Development, 21,* 343–353.

Herba, C., Landau, S., Russell, T., Ecker, C., & Phillips, M. L. (2006). The development of emotion-processing in children: Effects of age, emotion, and intensity. *Journal of Child Psychology and Psychiatry, 47,* 1098–1106.

Herba, C., & Phillips, M. (2004). Annotation: Development of facial expression recognition from childhood to adolescence: Behavioural and neurological perspectives. *Journal of Child Psychology and Psychiatry, 45,* 1185–1198.

Hiatt, S., Campos, J., & Emde, R. N. (1979). Facial patterning and infant emotional expression: Happiness, surprise and fear. *Child Development, 50,* 1020–1035.

Hietanen, J. K., Glerean, E., Hari, R., & Nummenmaa, L. (2016). Bodily maps of emotions across child development. *Developmental Science, 19,* 1111–1116.

Hoffman, M. L. (1975). Developmental synthesis of affect and cognition and its implications for altruistic motivation. *Developmental Psychology, 11,* 607–622.

Hoffman, M. L. (2001). Toward a comprehensive empathy-based theory of prosocial moral development. In A. C. Bohart & D. J. Stipek (Eds.), *Constructive and destructive behaviour: Implications for family, school, and society*. Washington, DC: APA.

Hoicka, E., & Akhtar, N. (2012). Early humour production. *British Journal of Developmental Psychology, 30*, 586–603.

Hoicka, E., & Gattis, M. (2008). Do the wrong thing: How toddlers tell a joke from a mistake. *Cognitive Development, 23*, 180–190.

Hongwanishkul, D., Happeney, K. R., Lee, W. S. C., & Zelazo, P. D. (2005). Assessment of hot and cool executive function in young children: Age-related changes and individual differences. *Developmental Neuropsychology, 28*, 617–644.

Hooven, C., Gottman, J. M., & Katz, L. F. (1995). Parental meta-emotion structure predicts family and child outcomes. *Cognition and Emotion, 9*, 229–264.

Howard, K. M. (2009). Breaking in and spinning out: Repetition and decalibration in Thai children's play genres. *Language in Society, 38*, 339–363.

Howe, N., Petrakos, H., Rinaldi, C. N., & LeFebvre, R. (2005). "This is a bad dog, you know . . .": Constructing shared meaning during sibling pretend play. *Child Development, 76*, 783–794.

Howe, N., Rinaldi, C. N., Jennings, M., & Petrakos, H. (2002). 'No! The lambs can stay out because they got cozies" Constructive and destructive sibling conflict, pretend play, and social understanding. *Child Development, 73*, 1460–1473.

Howe, N., Rosciszewska, J., & Persram, R. J. (2017). "I'm an ogre so I'm very hungry!" "I'm assistant ogre": The social function of sibling imitation in early childhood. *Infant and Child Development*, e2040.

Howe, N., & Ross, H. S. (1990). Socialization, perspective-taking and the sibling relationship. *Developmental Psychology, 26*, 160–165.

Hubbard, F. O. A., & van IJzendoorn, M. H. (1991). Maternal unresponsiveness and infant crying across the first nine months: A naturalistic longitudinal study. *Infant Behavior and Development, 14*, 299–312.

Hubbard, J. A., Parker, E. H., Ramsden, S. R., Flanagan, K. D., Relyea, N., Dearing, K. F., . . . Hyde, C. T. (2004). The relations among observational, physiological and self-report measures of children's anger. *Social Development, 13*, 14–39.

Huebner, E. S. (1991). Correlates of life satisfaction in children. *School Psychology Quarterly, 6*, 103–111.

Hughes, C., & Dunn, J. (2002). "When I say a naughty word": A longitudinal study of young children's accounts of anger and sadness in themselves and close others. *British Journal of Developmental Psychology, 20*, 515–535.

Hughes, C., Jaffee, S. R., Happé, F., Taylor, A., Caspi, A., & Moffitt, T. E. (2005). Origins of individual differences in theory of mind: From nature to nurture? *Child Development, 76*, 356–370.

Hunt, J., Schwarz, C. M., Nye, P., & Frazier, E. (2016). Is there a bipolar prodrome among children and adolescents? *Current Psychiatry Reports, 18*, 35.

Imafuku, M., Hakuno, Y., Uchida-Ota, M., Yamamoto, J., & Minagawa, Y. (2014). "Mom called me!" Behavioural and prefrontal responses by infants to self-names spoken by their mothers. *Neuroimage, 103*, 476–484.

Insel, T., Cuthbert, B., Garvey, M., Heinssen, R., Pine, D. S., Quinn, K., . . . Wang, P. (2010). Research Domain Criteria (RDoC): Toward a new classification framework for research on mental disorders. *American Journal of Psychiatry, 167*, 748–751.

Irwin, J. R. (2003). Parent and nonparent perception of the multimodal infant cry. *Infancy, 4*, 504–516.

Izard, C. E. (1971). *The face of emotion*. East Norwalk, CT: Appleton-Century-Crofts.

Izard, C. E. (1983). *The maximally discriminative facial action coding system (MAX)*. Newark, DE: University of Delaware Press.

Izard, C. E. (1994). Innate and universal facial expressions: Evidence from developmental and cross-cultural research. *Psychological Bulletin, 115*, 288–299.

Izard, C. E., Fantauzzo, C. A., Castle, J. M., Haynes, O. M., Rayias, M. F., & Putnam, P. H. (1995). The ontogeny and significance of infants' facial expressions in the first 9 months of life. *Developmental Psychology, 31*, 97–1013.

Izard, C. E., Huebner, R. R., Risser, D., & Dougherty, L. M. (1980). The young infant's ability to produce discrete emotion expressions. *Developmental Psychology, 16*, 132–140.

James, W. (1894). Discussion: The physical basis of emotion. *Psychological Review, 1*, 516–529.

Jenkins, J., Rasbash, J., Leckie, G., Gass, K., & Dunn, J. (2012). The role of maternal factors in sibling relationship quality: A multilevel study of multiple dyads per family. *Journal of Child Psychology and Psychiatry, 53*, 622–629.

Jersild, A. T., Markey, F. V., & Jersild, C. L. (1933). Children's fears, dreams, wishes, daydreams, likes, dislikes, pleasant, and unpleasant memories. *Child Development Monographs, 12*, 144–159.

Jones, L. B., Rothbart, M. K., & Posner, M. I. (2003). Development of executive attention in preschool children. *Developmental Science, 6*, 498–504.

Jones, J. D., Fraley, R. C., Erlich, K. B., Stern, J. A., LeJuez, C. W., Shaver, P. R., & Cassidy, J. (2018). Stability of attachment style in adolescence: An empirical test of alternative developmental processes. *Child Development, 89*, 871–880.

Jones, S. S., Collins, K., & Hong, H.-W. (1991). An audience effect on smile production in 10-month-old infants. *Psychological Science, 2*, 45–49.

Jones, S. S., & Hong, H.-W. (2001). Onset of voluntary communication: Smiling looks to mother. *Infancy, 2*, 353–370.

Kagan, J. (1981). *The second year: The emergence of self-awareness*. Cambridge, MA: Harvard.

Kagan, J., & Moss, H. (1962). *Birth to maturity: A study in psychological development*. New York, NY: Wiley.

Kagan, J., Reznick, J. S., Clarke, C., & Snidman, N. (1984). Behavioral inhibition to the unfamiliar. *Child Development, 55*, 2212–2225.

Kagan, J., Reznick, J. S., & Gibbons, J. (1989). Inhibited and uninhibited children. *Child Development, 60*, 838–845.

Kagan, J., Reznick, J. S., & Snidman, N. (1987). The physiology and psychology of behavioural inhibition in children. *Child Development, 58*, 1459–1473.

Kajiurwa, H., Cowart, B. J., & Beauchamp, G. K. (1992). Early developmental change in bitter taste responses in human infants. *Developmental Psychobiology, 25*, 375–386.

Katz, L. F., & Windecker-Nelson, B. (2004). Parental meta-emotion philosophy in families with conduct problem children: Links with peer relations. *Journal of Abnormal Child Psychology, 32*, 385–398.

Kaye, K., & Wells, A. J. (1980). Mothers' jiggling and the burst-pause pattern in neonatal feeding. *Infant Behavior and Development, 3*, 29–46.

Kayed, N. S., & van der Meer, A. (2000). Timing strategies used in defensive blinking to optical collisions in 5- to 7-month-old infants. *Infant Behavior and Development, 23*, 253–270.

Kearney, J. A. (2004). Early reactions to frustration: Developmental trends in anger, individual response styles, and caregiving risk implications in infancy. *Journal of Child and Adolescent Psychiatric Nursing, 17*, 105–112.

Kelley, S. A., Brownell, C. A., & Campbell, S. B. (2000). Mastery motivation and Self-evaluative affect in toddlers: Longitudinal relation with maternal behaviour. *Child Development, 71*, 1061–1071.

Keltner, D., & Buswell, B. N. (1996). Evidence for the distinctness of embarrassment, shame, and guilt: A study of recalled antecedents and facial expressions of emotion. *Cognition and Emotion, 10,* 155–171.

Keltner, D., Capps, L., Kring, A. M., Young, R. C., & Heerey, E. A. (2001). Just teasing: A conceptual analysis and empirical review. *Psychological Bulletin, 127,* 229–248.

Keppel-Bensen, J. M., Ollendick, T. H., & Benson, M. J. (2002). Post-traumatic stress in children following motor vehicle accidents. *Journal of Child Psychology and Psychiatry, 43,* 203–212.

Kestenbaum, R., & Nelson, C. A. (1990). The recognition and categorization of upright and inverted emotional expressions by 7-month-old infants. *Infant Behavior and Development, 13,* 497–511.

Kisilevsky, B. S., Hains, S. M. J., Lee, K., Xie, X., Huang, H., Ye, H. H., . . . Wang, Z. (2003). Effects of experience on fetal voice recognition. *Psychological Science, 14,* 220–224.

Knafo, A., Zahn-Waxler, C., Van Hulle, C., Robinson, J. L., & Rhee, S. H. (2008). The developmental origins of a disposition toward empathy: Genetic and environmental contributions. *Emotion, 8,* 737–752.

Knafo-Noam, A., Uzefovsky, F., Israel, S., Davidov, M., & Zahn-Waxler, C. (2015). The prosocial personality and its facets: Genetic and environmental architecture of mother-reported behavior of 7-year-old twins. *Frontiers in Psychology, 6,* 112.

Kochanska, G. (1991). Socialisation and temperament in the development of guilt and conscience. *Child Development, 62,* 1379–1392.

Kochanska, G. (1993). Toward a synthesis of parental socialisation and child temperament in the early development of conscience. *Child Development, 64,* 325–347.

Kochanska, G., Gross, J. N., Lin, M.-H., & Nichols, K. E. (2002). Guilt in young children: Development, determinants and relations with a broader system of standards. *Child Development, 73,* 461–482.

Kochanska, G., & Knaack, A. (2003). Effortful control as a personality characteristic of young children: Antecedents, correlates, and consequences. *Journal of Personality, 71,* 1087–1112.

Kohlberg, L. (1969). *Stages in the development of moral thought and action.* New York, NY: Holt, Rinehart, & Winston.

Kojima, Y. (2000). Maternal regulation of sibling interaction in the preschool years: Observational study of Japanese families. *Child Development, 71,* 1640–1647.

Kollak, A. M., & Volling, B. L. (2011). Sibling jealousy in early childhood: Longitudinal Links to sibling relationship quality. *Infant and Child Development, 20,* 213–226.

Komsi, N., Räikkönen, K., Pesonen, A. K., Heinonen, K., Keskivaara, P., Järvenpää, A. L., & Strandberg, T. E. (2006). Continuity of temperament from infancy to middle childhood. *Infant Behavior and Development, 29,* 494–508.

Kopp, C. B., Baker, B. L., & Brown, K. W. (1992). Social skills and their correlates: Preschoolers with developmental delays. *American Journal on Mental Retardation, 96,* 357–366.

Kouider, S., Long, B., Le Stanc, L., Charron, S., Fievet, A.-C., Barbosa, L. S., & Gelskov, S. V. (2015). Neural dimensions of prediction and surprise in infants. *Nature Communications, 6,* 8537.

Koutseff, A., Reby, D., Martin, O., Levrero, F., Patural, H., & Mathevon, N. (2018). The acoustic space of pain: Cries as indicators of distress recovering dynamics in preverbal infants. *Bioacoustics, 27,* 313–325.

Kuchuk, A., Vibbert, M., & Bornstein, M. H. (1986.) The perception of smiling and its experiential correlates in three-month-old infants. *Child Development, 57,* 1054–1061.

Lahikainen, A. R., Kraav, I., Kirmanen, T., & Taimalu, M. (2006). Child-parent agreement in the assessment of children's fears. *Journal of Cross-Cultural Psychology, 37,* 100–119.

Lamb, S., & Zakhireh, B. (1997). Toddlers' attention to the distress of peers in a daycare setting. *Early Education and Development, 8*, 105–118.

Lazarus, R. S., & Folkman, S. (1984). *Stress, appraisal, and coping.* New York, NY: Springer.

Leach, J., Howe, N., & DeHart, G. (2015). "An earthquake shocked up the land!" Children's communication during play with siblings and friends. *Social Development, 24*, 95–112.

Leerkes, E. M., Blankson, A. N., & O'Brien, M. (2009). Differential effects of maternal sensitivity to infant distress and non-distress of socio-emotional functioning. *Child Development, 80*, 762–775.

Legerstee, M., Anderson, D., & Schaffer, A. (1998). Five- and eight-month-old infants recognise their faces and voices as familiar and social stimuli. *Child Development, 69*, 37–50.

Lehr, V. T., Zeskind, P. S., Ofenstein, J. P., Cepeda, E., & Aranda, J. V. (2007). Neonatal Facial Coding System scores and spectral characteristics of infant crying during newborn circumcision. *Clinical Journal of Pain, 23*, 417–424.

Leibenluft, E., & Stoddard, J. (2013). The developmental psychopathology of irritability. *Development and Psychopathology, 25*, 1473–1487.

Lemery, K. S., Essex, M. J., & Smider, N. A. (2002). Revealing the relation between temperament and behaviour problem symptoms by eliminating measurement confounding: Expert ratings and factor analyses. *Child Development, 73*, 867–882.

Lester, B. M. (1987). Developmental outcome prediction from acoustic cry analysis in term and preterm infants. *Pediatrics, 80*, 529–534.

Lewis, M., Alessandri, S. M., & Sullivan, M. W. (1990). Violation of expectancy, loss of control, and anger expressions in young infants. *Developmental Psychology, 26*, 745–761.

Lewis, M., Alessandri, S. M., & Sullivan, M. W. (1992). Differences in shame and pride as a function of children's gender and task difficulty. *Child Development, 63*, 630–638.

Lewis, M., Ramsay, D. S., & Sullivan, M. W. (2006). The relation of ANS and HPA activation to infant anger and sadness response to goal blockage. *Developmental Psychobiology, 48*, 397–405.

Lewis, M., Sullivan, M. W., Ramsay, D. S., & Alessandri, S. M. (1992). Individual differences in sad and angry expressions after extinction: Antecedents and consequences. *Infant Behavior and Development, 15*, 443–452.

Lichtenstein, P., & Annas, P. (2000). Heritability and prevalence of specific fears and phobias in childhood. *Journal of Child Psychology and Psychiatry, 41*, 927–936.

Lockwood, P. L., Sebastian, C. L., McCrory, E. J., Hyde, Z. H., Gu, X., De Brito, S. A., & Viding, E. (2013). Association of callous traits with reduced neural response to others' pain in children with conduct problems. *Current Biology, 23*, 901–905.

Luby, J. L., Belden, A., Sullivan, J., Hayen, R., McCadney, A., & Spitznagel, E. (2009). Shame and guilt in preschool depression: Evidence for elevations in self-conscious emotions in depression as early as age 3. *Journal of Child Psychology and Psychiatry, 50*, 1156–1166.

Luby, J. L., Heffelfinger, A. K., Mrakotsky, C., Brown, K. M., Hessler, M. J., Wallis, J. M., & Spitznagel, E. L. (2003). The clinical picture of depression in preschool children. *Journal of the American Academy of Child and Adolescent Psychiatry, 42*, 340–348.

Lyons-Ruth, K., Bronfman, E., & Parsons, E. (1999). Maternal frightened, frightening or atypical behaviour and infant disorganised attachment patterns. *Monographs of the Society for Research in Child Development, 64*(3), 67–96.

MacDonald, N. E., & Silverman, I. W. (1978). Smiling and laughter in infants as a function of level of arousal and cognitive evaluation. *Developmental Psychology, 14*, 235–241.

Main, M., Kaplan, N., & Cassidy, J. (1985). Security in infancy, childhood, and adulthood: A move to the level of representation. *Monographs of the Society for Research in Child Development, 50*(1/2).

Main, M., & Weston, D. R. (1981). The quality of the toddler's relationship to mother and to Father: Related to conflict behaviour and the readiness to establish new relationships. *Child Development, 52*, 932–940.

Malatesta, C. Z., & Haviland, J. M. (1982). Learning display rules: The socialization of emotion expression in infancy. *Child Development, 53*, 991–1003.

Malti, T. (2016). Toward an integrated clinical-developmental model of guilt. *Developmental Review, 39*, 16–36.

Malti, T., Ongley, S. F., Peplak, J., Chaparro, M. P., Buchmann, M., Zuffiano, A., & Cui, L. (2016). Children's sympathy, guilt, and moral reasoning in helping, cooperation, and sharing: A six-year longitudinal study. *Child Development, 87*, 1783–1795.

Mampe, B., Friederici, A. D., Christophe, A., & Wermke, K. (2009). Newborns' cry melody is shaped by their native language. *Current Biology, 19*, 1–4.

Marshall, P. J., & Meltzoff, A. N. (2015). Body maps in the infant brain. *Trends in Cognitive Sciences, 19*, 499–505.

Martin, G. B., & Clark, R. D. (1982). Distress crying in neonates: Species and peer specificity. *Developmental Psychology, 18*, 3–9.

Masciuch, S., & Kienapple, K. (1993). The emergence of jealousy in children 4 months to 7 years of age. *Journal of Personal and Social Relationships, 10*, 421–435.

Matheny, A. P., Jr. (1989). Children's behavioural inhibition over age and across situations: Genetic similarity for a trait during change. *Journal of Personality, 57*, 215–235.

Matias, A., & Cohn, J. (1993). Are Max-specified infant facial expressions during face-to-face interaction compatible with differential emotions theory? *Developmental Psychology, 29*, 524–531.

Matthiesen, A.-S., Ransjo-Arvidson, A.-B., Nissen, E., & Uvnas-Moberg, K. (2001). Postnatal maternal oxytocin release by newborns: Effects of infant hand massage and sucking. *Birth, 28*, 13–19.

Maynard, D. W. (1985). How children start arguments. *Language in Society, 14*, 1–29.

McDevitt, S. C., & Carey, W. B. (1978). The measurement of temperament in 3- to 7-year-old children. *Journal of Child Psychology and Psychiatry, 19*, 245–253.

Meltzer, H., Vostanis, P., Dogra, N., Doos, L., Ford, T., & Goodman, R. (2009). Children's specific fears. *Child: Care, Health and Development, 35*, 781–789.

Menesini, E., & Camodeca, M. (2008). Shame and guilt as behaviour regulators: Relationships with bullying, victimization and prosocial behaviour. *British Journal of Developmental Psychology, 26*, 183–196.

Messinger, D. S., Whitney, I. M., Mahoor, M. H., & Cohn, J. F. (2012). The eyes have it: Making positive expressions more positive and negative expressions more negative. *Emotion, 12*, 430–436.

Meunier, J. C., Bisceglia, R., & Jenkins, J. M. (2012). Differential parenting and children's behavioral problems: Curvilinear associations and mother – father combined effects. *Developmental Psychology, 48*, 987–1002.

Meunier, J. C., Boyle, M., O'Connor, T. G., & Jenkins, J. M. (2013). Multilevel mediation: Cumulative contextual risk, maternal differential treatment, and children's behaviour within families. *Child Development, 84*, 1594–1615.

Mezulis, A. H., Hyde, J. S., & Abramson, L. Y. (2006). The developmental origins of cognitive vulnerability to depression: Temperament, parenting, and negative life events in childhood as contributors to negative cognitive style. *Developmental Psychology, 42*, 1012–1025.

Mireault, G. C., Crockenberg, S. C., Sparrow, J. E., Cousineau, K., Pettinato, C., & Woodard, K. (2015). Laughing matters: Infant humor in the context of parental affect. *Journal of Experimental Child Psychology, 136*, 30–41.

Mireault, G. C., Poudre, M., Sargent-Hier, M., Dias, C., Perdue, B., & Myrick, A. (2012). Humour perception and creation between parents and 3- to 6-month-old infants. *Infant and Child Development, 21*, 338–347.

Mizugaki, S., Maehara, Y., Okanoya, K., & Myowa-Yamakoshi, M. (2015). The power of an infant's smile: Maternal physiological responses to infant emotional expressions. *PLOS One, 10*, e0129672.

Montague, D. P. F., & Walker-Andrews, A. S. (2001). Peekaboo: A new look at infants' perception of emotional expressions. *Developmental Psychology, 37*, 826–838.

Moore, G. A., Cohn, J. F., & Campbell, S. B. (2001). Infant affective responses to mother's still face at 6 months differentially predict externalising and internalising behaviors at 18 months. *Developmental Psychology, 37*, 706–714.

Morgan, L., Scourfield, J., Williams, D., Jasper, A., & Lewis, G. (2003). The Aberfan disaster: 33-year follow-up of survivors. *British Journal of Psychiatry, 182*, 532–536.

Morris, A. S., Silk, J. S., Morris, M. D. S., Steinberg, L., Aucoin, K. J., & Keyes, A. W. (2011). The influence of mother – child emotion regulation strategies on children's expression of anger and sadness. *Developmental Psychology, 47*, 213–225.

Moses, L. J., Baldwin, D. A., Rosicky, J. G., & Tidball, G. (2001). Evidence for referential understanding in the emotions domain at twelve and eighteen months. *Child Development, 72*, 718–735.

Motti, F., Cicchetti, D., & Sroufe, L. A. (1983). From infant affect expression to symbolic play: The coherence of development in Down Syndrome children. *Child Development, 54*, 1168–1175.

Muris, P., van der Heiden, S., & Rassin, E. (2008). Disgust sensitivity and psychopathological symptoms in non-clinical children. *Journal of Behaviour Therapy and Experimental Psychiatry, 39*, 133–146.

Murphy, L. B. (1937). *Social behaviour and child personality*. New York, NY: Columbia University Press.

Murray, L., De Pascalis, L., Bozicevic, L., Hawkins, L., Sclafani, V., & Ferrari, P. F. (2016). The functional architecture of mother-infant communication, and the development of infant social expressiveness in the first two months. *Scientific Reports, 6*, 39019.

Murray, L., De Rosnay, M., Pearson, J., Bergeron, C., Schofield, E., Royal-Lawson, M., & Cooper, P. J. (2008). Intergenerational transmission of social anxiety: The role of social referencing processes in infancy. *Child Development, 79*, 1049–1064.

Murray, L., Kempton, C., Woolgar, M., & Hooper, R. (1993). Depressed mothers' speech to their infants and its relation to infant gender and cognitive development. *Journal of Child Psychology and Psychiatry, 34*, 1083–1101.

Nachmias, M., Gunnar, M., Mangelsdorf, S., Parritz, R. H., & Buss, K. (1996). Behavioral inhibition and stress reactivity: The moderating role of attachment security. *Child Development, 67*, 508–522.

Nash, A. (1995). Beyond attachments: Toward a general theory of relationships in infancy. In K. E. Hood, G. Greenberg, & E. Tobach (Eds.), *Behavioral development: Concepts of approach / withdrawal and integrative levels* (pp. 287–328). New York, NY: Garland.

Natsuaki, M., Leve, L. D., Neiderheiser, J. M., & Shaw, D. S. (2013). Intergenerational transmission of risk for social inhibition: The interplay between parental responsiveness and genetic influences. *Development and Psychopathology, 25*, 261–274.

Nelson, C. A., & Dolgin, K. G. (1985). The generalised discrimination of facial expressions by seven-month-old infants. *Child Development, 56*, 58–61.

Nelson, N. L., Hudspeth, K., & Russell, J. A. (2013). A story superiority effect for disgust, fear, embarrassment, and pride. *British Journal of Developmental Psychology, 31*, 334–348.

Nelson, N. L., & Russell, J. A. (2012). Children's understanding of nonverbal expressions of pride. *Journal of Experimental Child Psychology, 111*, 379–385.

Newland, R. P., & Crnic, K. A. (2011). Mother-child affect and emotion socialization processes across the late preschool period: Predictions of emerging behaviour problems. *Infant and Child Development, 20*, 371–388.

Nicol-Harper, R., Harvey, A. G., & Stein, A. (2007). Interactions between mothers and infants: Impact of maternal anxiety. *Infant Behavior and Development, 30*, 161–167.

Nielsen, M., & Dissanayake, C. (2004). Pretend play, mirror self-recognition and imitation: A longitudinal investigation through the second year. *Infant Behavior and Development, 27*, 342–365.

Nock, M. K., Kazdin, A. E., Hiripi, E., & Kessler, R. C. (2007). Lifetime prevalence, correlates, and persistence of oppositional defiant disorder: Results from the National Comorbidity Survey Replication. *Journal of Child Psychology and Psychiatry, 48*, 703–713.

Nwokah, E. E., Hsu, H.-C., Dobrowolska, O., & Fogel, A. (1994). The development of laughter in mother-infant communication: Timing parameters and temporal sequences. *Infant Behavior and Development, 17*, 23–35.

Oaten, M., Stevenson, R. J., & Case, T. I. (2009). Disgust as a disease-avoidance mechanism. *Psychological Bulletin, 135*, 303–321.

Olatunji, B. O., Ebusutani, C., Kim, J., Riemann, B. C., & Jacobi, D. M. (2017). Disgust proneness predicts obsessive-compulsive disorder symptom severity in a clinical sample of youth: Distinctions from negative affect. *Journal of Affective Disorders, 213*, 118–125.

Ollendick, T. H., Yule, W., & Ollier, K. (1991). Fears in British children and their relation to manifest anxiety and depression. *Journal of Child Psychology and Psychiatry, 32*, 321–331.

Olson, S. (1992). Development of conduct problems and peer rejection in preschool children: A social systems analysis. *Journal of Abnormal Child Psychology, 20*, 327–350.

Olthof, T., Schouten, A., Kuiper, H., Stegge, H., & Jennekins-Schinkel, A. (2000). Shame and guilt in children: Differential situational antecedents and experiential correlates. *British Journal of Developmental Psychology, 18*, 51–64.

Orlandi, S., Garcia, C., Bandini, A., Donzelli, G., & Manfredi, C. (2016). Application of pattern recognition techniques to the classification of full-term and preterm infant cry. *Journal of Voice, 30*, 656–663.

Oster, H., Hegley, D., & Nagel, L. (1992). Adult judgments and fine-grained analysis of infant facial expressions: Testing the validity of a priori coding formulas. *Developmental Psychology, 28*, 1115–1131.

Paine, A. L., Pearce, H., van Goozen, S. H. M., de Sonneville, L. M. J., & Hay, D. F. (2018). Late, but not early, arriving younger siblings foster firstborns' understanding of second-order false belief. *Journal of Experimental Child Psychology, 166*, 251–265.

Pal, P., Iyer, A. N., & Yantorno, R. E. (2006). *Emotion detection from infant facial expressions and cries*. IEEE Proceedings of the International Conference on Acoustics, Speech and Signal Processing.

Parrott, W. G., & Gleitman, H. (1989). Infants' expectations in play: The joy of peek-a-boo. *Cognition and Emotion, 3*, 291–311.

Partty, A., & Kalliomaki, M. (2017). Infant colic is still a mysterious disorder of the microbiota-gut-brain axis. *Acta Paediatrica, 106*, 528–529.

Patterson, M. W., Mann, F. D., Grotzinger, A. D., Tackett, J. L., Tucker-Drob, E. M., & Harden, K. P. (2018). Genetic and environmental influences on internalizing psychopathology across age and pubertal development. *Developmental Psychology, 54*, 1928–1939.

Paul, R., Fuerst, Y., Ramsay, G., Chawarska, K., & Klin, A. (2011). Out of the mouths of babes: Vocal production in infant siblings of children with ASD. *Journal of Child Psychology and Psychiatry, 52*, 588–598.

Paulus, M. (2014). The emergence of prosocial behaviour: Why do infants and toddlers help, comfort, and share? *Child Development Perspectives, 8*, 77–81.

Pawlby, S., Hay, D. F., Sharp, D., Waters, C. S., & O'Keane, V. (2009). Antenatal depression predicts depression in adolescent offspring: Prospective longitudinal community-based study. *Journal of Affective Disorders, 113*, 236–243.

Pergamin-Hight, L., Bakermans-Kranenburg, M. J., van IJzendoorn, M. H., & Bar-Haim, Y. (2012). Variations in the promoter region of the serotonin transporter gene and biased attention for emotional information: A meta-analysis. *Biological Psychiatry, 71*, 373–379.

Perry-Parrish, C., & Zeman, J. (2011). Relations among sadness regulation, peer acceptance and social functioning in early adolescence: The role of gender. *Social Development, 20*, 135–153.

Peterson, C. C., Peterson, J. L., & Seeto, D. (1983). Developmental changes in ideas about lying. *Child Development, 54*, 1529–1535.

Pfeifer, Iacoboni, M., Mazziotta, J. C., & Dapretto, M. (2008). Mirroring others' emotions relates to empathy and interpersonal competence in children. *Neuroimage, 39*, 2076–2085.

Phillips, R. (2013). *Exploring the salience of anger for new mothers, their partners, and their young offspring* (PhD Thesis). Cardiff University, Cardiff, Wales, UK.

Piaget, J. (1962). *Play, dreams and imitation.* New York, NY: Norton.

Piaget, J. (1965). *The moral judgment of the child* (M. Gabain, Trans.). New York, NY: Free Press.

Plomin, R. L., Kagan, J., Emde, R. N., Reznick, J. S., Braungart, J. M., Robinson, J., . . . DeFries, J. C. (1993). Genetic change and continuity from fourteen to twenty months: The MacArthur Longitudinal Twin Study. *Child Development, 64*, 1354–1376.

Poggi Davis, E., Glynn, L. M., Dunkel Shetter, C., Hobel, C., Chicz-Demet, A., & Sandman, C. A. (2005). Corticotrophin-releasing hormone during pregnancy is associated with infant temperament. *Developmental Neuroscience, 27*, 299–305.

Porges, S. W., Doussard-Roosevelt, J. A., & Maiti, A. (1994). Vagal tone and the physiological regulation of emotion. *Monographs of the Society for Research in Child Development, 59*(2–3), 167–186.

Porter, F. L., Miller, R. H., & Marshall, R. E. (1986). Neonatal pain cries: Effects of circumcision on acoustic features and perceived urgency. *Child Development, 57*, 790–802.

Porter, F. L., Porges, S. W., & Marshall, R. E. (1988). Newborn pain cries and vagal tone: Parallel changes in response to circumcision. *Child Development, 59*, 495–505.

Potegal, M., & Davidson, R. J. (2003). Temper tantrums in young children. I. Behavioral composition. *Journal of Developmental and Behavioural Pediatrics, 24*, 140–147.

Potegal, M., Kosorok, M. R., & Davidson, R. J. (2003). Temper tantrums in young Children. II. Tantrum duration and temporal organisation. *Journal of Developmental and Behavioural Pediatrics, 24*, 148–154.

Preston, S. D., & de Waal, F. B. M. (2002). Empathy: Its ultimate and proximate bases. *Behavioural and Brain Sciences, 25*, 1–72.

Preyer, W. (1889). *The mind of the child* (H. W. Brown, Trans.). New York, NY: Appleton.

Prior, M., Smart, D., Sanson, A., & Oberklaid, F. (2000). Does shy-inhibited temperament in childhood lead to anxiety problems in adolescence? *Journal of the American Academy of Child and Adolescent Psychiatry, 39*, 461–468.

Protopapas, A., & Eimas, P. D. (1997). Perceptual differences in infant cries revealed by modifications of acoustic features. *Journal of the Acoustical Society of America, 102*, 3723.

Radke-Yarrow, M., Zahn-Waxler, C., & Chapman, M. (1983). Children's prosocial dispositions and behaviour. In P. H. Mussen (Ed.), *Handbook of child psychology*, Vol. 4, E. M. Hetherington (Volume Ed.), *Socialization, personality and social development* (pp. 469–545). New York, NY: Wiley.

Randell, A. C., & Peterson, C. C. (2009). Affective qualities of sibling disputes, mothers' conflict attitudes, and children's theory of mind development. *Social Development, 18*, 857–874.

Rapee, R. M. (2014). Preschool environment and temperament as predictors of social and nonsocial anxiety disorders in middle adolescence. *Journal of the American Academy of Child and Adolescent Psychiatry, 53*, 320–328.

Rapee, R. M., & Coplan, R. J. (2010). Conceptual relations between anxiety disorder and fearful temperament. *New Directions for Child and Adolescent Development, 127*, 17–31.

Raval, V. V., & Martini, T. S. (2009). Maternal socialization of children's anger, sadness, and physical pain in two communities in Gujarat, India. *International Journal of Behavioural Development, 33*, 215–229.

Raval, V. V., Martini, T. S., & Raval, P. H. (2007). "Would others think it is okay to express my feelings?" Regulation of anger, sadness and physical pain in Gujurati children in India. *Social Development, 16*, 79–105.

Recchia, H., Wainryb, C., & Pasupathi, M. (2013). "Two for flinching": Children's and adolescents' narrative accounts of harming their friends and siblings. *Child Development, 84*, 1459, 1474.

Redding, R. E., Morgan, G. A., & Harmon, R. J. (1988). Mastery motivation in infants and toddlers: Is it greatest when tasks are moderately challenging? *Infant Behavior and Development, 11*, 419–430.

Reddy, V. (2001). Infant clowns: The interpersonal creation of humour in infancy. *Enfance, 53*, 247–256.

Reijman, S., Bakermans-Kranenburg, M. J., Hiraoka, R., Crouch, J. L., Milner, J. S., Alink, L. R., & van IJzendoorn, M. H. (2016). Baseline functioning and stress reactivity in maltreating parents and at-risk adults. *Child Maltreatment, 21*, 327–342.

Reijneveld, S. A., Lanting, C. I., Crone, M. R., & van Wouwe, J. P. (2005). Exposure to tobacco smoke and infant crying. *Acta Paediatrica, 94*, 217–221.

Reiman, E. M., Lane, R. D., Ahern, G. L., Schwartz, G. E., Davidson, R. J., Friston, K. J., . . . Chen, K. (1997). Neuroanatomical correlates of externally and internally generated human emotion. *American Journal of Psychiatry, 154*, 918–925.

Reissland, N. (1994). The socialisation of pride in young children. *International Journal of Behavioural Development, 17*, 541–552.

Rhee, S. H., Boeldt, D. L., Friedman, N. P., Corley, R. P., Hewitt, J. K., Young, S. E., . . . Zahn-Waxler, C. (2013). The role of language in concern and disregard for others in the first years of life. *Developmental Psychology, 49*, 197–214.

Rheingold, H. L. (1956). The modification of social responsiveness in institutional babies. *Monographs of the Society for Research in Child Development, 21*(2).

Rheingold, H. L. (1969). The social and socializing infant. In D. A. Goslin (Ed.), *Handbook of socialization theory and research*. Chicago: Rand McNally.

Rheingold, H. L., & Eckerman, C. O. (1969). The infant's free entry into a new environment. *Journal of Experimental Child Psychology, 8*, 271–283.

Rheingold, H. L., & Eckerman, C. O. (1970). The infant separates himself from his mother. *Science, 168*, 78–83.

Rheingold, H. L., & Eckerman, C. O. (1973). Fear of the stranger: A critical examination. *Advances in Child Development and Behavior, 8*, 185–222.

Rheingold, H. L., & Emery, G. N. (1986). The nurturant acts of very young children. In D. Olweus, J. Block, & M. Radke-Yarrow (Eds.), *Development of antisocial and prosocial behaviour: Research, theories and issues* (pp. 75–96). London: Academic Press.

Rhoades, K. A., Leve, L., Harold, G. T., Neiderheiser, J. M., Shaw, D. S., & Reiss, D. (2011). Longitudinal pathways from marital hostility to child anger during toddlerhood: Genetic susceptibility and indirect effects via harsh parenting. *Journal of Family Psychology*, *25*, 282–291.

Rhoads, J., Collins, J., Fatheree, N. Y., Hashmi, S., Taylor, C. M., Luo, M., . . . Liu, Y. (2018). Infant colic represents gut inflammation and dysbiosis. *Journal of Pediatrics*, published online. doi: 10.1016/j.jpeds.2018.07.042

Richmond, M. K., & Stocker, C. M. (2008). Longitudinal associations between parents' hostility and children's externalizing behaviour in the context of marital discord. *Journal of Family Psychology*, *22*, 231–240.

Riem, M. M. E., Bakermans-Kranenburg, M. J., Pieper, S., Tops, M., Boksem, M. A. S., Vermeiren, R. R. J. M., . . . Rombouts, S. A. R. B. (2011). Oxytocin modulates amygdala, insula, and inferior frontal gyrus responses to infant crying: A randomised control trial. *Biological Psychiatry*, *70*, 291–297.

Robinson, J. L., Kagan, J., Reznick, S., & Corley, R. (1992). The heritability of inhibited and uninhibited behaviour: A twin study. *Developmental Psychology*, *28*, 1030–1037.

Rochat, P., & Striano, T. (2002). Who's in the mirror? Self-other discrimination in specular images by four- and nine-month-old infants. *Child Development*, *73*, 35–46.

Rodger, H., Vizioli, L., Ouyang, X., & Caldara, R. (2015). Mapping the development of facial expression recognition. *Developmental Science*, *18*, 926–939.

Rodrigues, S. M., Saslow, L. R., Garcia, N., John, O. P., & Keltner, D. (2009). Oxytocin receptor genetic variation relates to empathy and stress reactivity in humans. *PNAS*, *106*, 21437–21441.

Rosenberg, A., & Kagan, J. (1987). Iris pigmentation and behavioural inhibition. *Developmental Psychobiology*, *20*, 377–392.

Ross, H. S. (2013). Effects of ownership rights on conflicts between toddler peers. *Infancy*, *18*, 256–275.

Ross, H. S., & Goldman, B. D. (1977). Infants' sociability toward strangers. *Child Development*, *48*, 638–642.

Ross, H. S., & Lollis, S. P. (1987). Communication within infant social games. *Developmental Psychology*, *23*, 241–248.

Rothbart, M. K. (1973). Laughter in young children. *Psychological Bulletin*, *80*, 247–256.

Rothbart, M. K. (1986). Longitudinal observation of infant temperament. *Developmental Psychology*, *22*, 356–365.

Roth-Hanania, R., Davidov, M., & Zahn-Waxler, C. (2011). Empathy development from 8 to 16 months: Early signs of concern for others. *Infant Behavior and Development*, *34*, 447–458.

Rovee-Collier, C., Hartshorn, K., & DiRubbo, M. (1999). Long-term maintenance of infant memory. *Developmental Psychobiology*, *35*, 91–102.

Rowe, R., Costello, E. J., Angold, A., Copeland, W. E., & Maughan, B. (2010). Developmental pathways in oppositional defiant disorder and conduct disorder. *Journal of Abnormal Psychology*, *119*, 726–738.

Rozin, P., Fallon, A., & Augustoni-Ziskind, M. L. (1985). The child's conception of food: The development of contamination sensitivity to "disgusting" substances. *Developmental Psychology*, *21*, 1075–1079.

Rubin, K. H., Burgess, K. B., & Hastings, P. D. (2002). Stability and social-behavioral consequences of toddlers' inhibited temperament and parenting behaviors. *Child Development*, *73*, 483–495.

Ruch, W. (1993). Exhilaration and humour. In M. Lewis & J. Haviland (Eds.), *The handbook of emotion* (pp. 605–616). New York, NY: Guilford.

Russell, J. A. (2003). Core affect and the psychological construction of emotion. *Psychological Review, 110*, 145–172.

Rutter, M. L., Kreppner, J. M., & O'Connor, T. G. (2001). Specificity and heterogeneity in children's responses to profound institutional privation. *British Journal of Psychiatry, 179*, 97–103.

Rutter, M. L., Sonuga-Barke, E. J., Beckett, C., Castle, J., Kreppner, J., Kumsta, R., ... Gunnar, M. R. (2010). Deprivation-specific psychological patterns: Effects of institutional deprivation. *Monographs of the Society for Research in Child Development, 75*(1).

Saarni, C., Campos, J. J., Camras, L. A., & Witherington, D. (2006). Emotional development: Action, communication and understanding. In W. Damon & R. M. Lerner (Eds.), *Handbook of child psychology* (6th ed.), Vol. 3, N. Eisenberg (Vol. Ed.), *Social, emotional and personality development* (pp. 226–299). Hoboken, NJ: Wiley.

Sagi, A. (1981). Mothers' and non-mothers' identification of infant cries. *Infant Behavior and Development, 4*, 37–40.

Sagi, A., & Hoffman, M. L. (1976). Empathic distress in the newborn. *Developmental Psychology, 12*, 175–176.

Sauter, D. A., Panattoni, C., & Happé, F. (2013). Children's recognition of emotions from vocal cues. *British Journal of Developmental Psychology, 31*, 97–113.

Sayfan, V., & Lagattuta, K. H. (2009). Scaring the monsters away: What children know about managing fears of real and imaginary creatures. *Child Development, 80*, 1756–1774.

Schaffer, H. R., & Emerson, P. E. (1964). The development of social attachments in infancy. *Monographs of the Society for Research in Child Development, 29*(3).

Scherer, K. R., Zentner, M. R., & Stern, D. (2004). Beyond surprise: The puzzle of infants' expressive reactions to expectancy violation. *Emotion, 4*, 389–402.

Schneirla, T. C. (1959). An evolutionary and developmental theory of biphasic processes underlying approach and withdrawal. In M. R. Jones (Ed.), *Nebraska symposium on motivation* (pp. 1–42). Lincoln, NE: University of Nebraska Press.

Schulte-Ruther, M., Markowitsch, H. J., Shah, N. J., Fink, G. R., & Piefke, M. (2008). Gender differences in brain networks supporting empathy. *Neuroimage, 42*, 393–403.

Schwartz, A. N., Campos, J. J., & Baisel, E. J. (1973). The visual cliff: Cardiac and behavioral responses on the deep and shallow sides at five and nine months of age. *Journal of Experimental Child Psychology, 15*, 86–99.

Schwenck, C., Göhle, B., Hauf, J., Warnke, A., Freitag, C. M., & Schneider, W. (2013). Cognitive and emotional empathy in typically developing children: The influence of age, gender, and intelligence. *European Journal of Developmental Psychology, 11*, 63–76.

Serrano, J. M., Iglesias, J., & Loeches, A. (1995). Infants' responses to adult static facial expressions. *Infant Behavior and Development, 18*, 477–482.

Sheikh, W., & Janof-Bulman, R. (2010). The "shoulds" and "should nots" of moral emotions: A self-regulatory perspective on shame and guilt. *Personality and Social Psychology Bulletin, 36*, 213–224.

Sheinkopf, S. J., Iverson, J. M., Rinaldi, M. L., & Lester, B. M. (2012). Atypical cry acoustics in six-month-old infants at risk for Autism Spectrum Disorder. *Autism Research, 5*, 331–339.

Sheinkopf, S. J., Lester, B. M., & Silverman, H. F. (2015). *Accurate analysis tool and method for the quantitative acoustic assessment of infant cry.* US Patent Application US14633224.

Sherman, M. (1927). The differentiation of emotional responses in infants. II. The ability of observers to judge the emotional characteristics of the crying of infants, and of the voice of an adult. *Journal of Comparative Psychology, 7*, 335–351.

Shiller, V. M., Izard, C. E., & Hembree, E. A. (1986). Patterns of emotion expression during separation in the strange-situation procedure. *Developmental Psychology, 22*, 378–382.

Shinya, Y., Kawai, M., Niwa, F., & Myowa-Yamakoshi, M. (2014). Preterm birth is associated with an increased fundamental frequency of spontaneous crying in human infants at term-equivalent age. *Biology Letters, 10*, 20140350.

Shiota, M. N., Campos, B., & Keltner, D. (2003). The faces of positive emotion. *Annals of the New York Academy of Science, 1000*, 296–299.

Shipman, K. L., Zeman, J., Nesin, A. E., & Fitzgerald, M. (2003). Children's strategies for displaying anger and sadness: What works with whom? *Merrill-Palmer Quarterly, 49*, 100–122.

Shirley, M. (1933). *The first two years: A study of twenty-five babies.* Minneapolis, MN: University of Minnesota Institute of Child Welfare Monograph Series.

Shirtcliff, E. A., Vitacco, M. J., Graf, A. R., Gostisha, A. J., Merz, J. L., & Zahn-Waxler, C. (2009). Neurobiology of empathy and callousness: Implications for the development of antisocial behaviour. *Behavioural Sciences and the Law, 27*, 137–171.

Shore, G. N., & Rapport, M. D. (1998). The Fear Schedule for Children revised (FSSC-HI): Ethnocultural variations in children's fearfulness. *Journal of Anxiety Disorders, 12*, 437–461.

Shortt, J. W., Stoolmiller, M., Smith-Shine, J. N., Eddy, J. M., & Sheeber, L. (2010). Maternal emotion coaching, adolescent anger regulation, and siblings' externalizing symptoms. *Journal of Child Psychology and Psychiatry, 51*, 799–808.

Silverman, W. K., La Greca, A. M., & Wasserstein, S. (1995). What do children worry about? Worries and their relation to anxiety. *Child Development, 66*, 671–686.

Simner, M. L. (1971). Newborn's response to the cry of another infant. *Developmental Psychology, 5*, 136–150.

Smith, P. K. (1980). Shared care of young children: Alternative models to monotropism. *Merrill-Palmer Quarterly, 26*, 371–389.

Smith, P., Perrin, S., Yule, W., Hacam, B., & Stuvland, R. (2002). War exposure among children from Bosnia-Hercegovina: Psychological adjustment in a community sample. *Journal of Traumatic Stress, 15*, 147–156.

Snyder, J., Stoolmiller, M., Wilson, M., & Yamamoto, M. (2003). Child anger regulation, parents' response to children's anger displays, and early child antisocial behaviour. *Social Development, 12*, 335–360.

Sorce, J. F., Emde, R. N., Campos, J., & Klinnert, M. D. (1985). Maternal emotional signalling: Its effect on the visual cliff behaviour of 1-year-olds. *Developmental Psychology, 21*, 195–200.

Spence, M. J., & Freeman, M. S. (1996). Newborn infants prefer the maternal low-pass filtered voice, but not the maternal whispered voice. *Infant Behavior and Development, 19*, 199–212.

Spence, S. H., & McCathie, H. (1993). The stability of fears in children: A two-year prospective study; a research note. *Journal of Child Psychology and Psychiatry, 34*, 579–585.

Spinney, L. (2007). The science of swearing. *New Scientist, 196*, 51–53.

Sroufe, L. A. (1977). Wariness of strangers and the study of infant development. *Child Development, 48*, 731–746.

Sroufe, L. A. (1995). *Emotional development: The organisation of emotional life in the early years.* Cambridge: Cambridge University Press.

Sroufe, L. A., & Rutter, M. L. (1984). The domain of developmental psychopathology. *Child Development, 55*, 17–29.

Sroufe, L. A., & Wunsch, J. P. (1972). The development of laughter in the first year of life. *Child Development, 43*, 1326–1344.

Stahl, A. F., & Feigenson, L. (2015). Observing the unexpected enhances infants' learning and exploration. *Science, 348*, 91–94.

St James-Roberts, I. (1999). What is distinct about infants' "colic" cries? *Archives of Disease in Childhood, 80*, 56–61.

St James-Roberts, I., Conroy, S., & Wilsher, K. (1996). Bases for maternal perceptions of infant crying and colic behaviour. *Archives of Disease in Childhood, 75*, 375–384.

Steele, R. D., Waters, T. E. A., Bost, K. K., Vaughn, B. E., Truitt, W., Waters, H. S., . . . Roisman, G. I. (2014). Caregiving antecedents of secure base script knowledge: A comparative analysis of young adult attachment representations. *Developmental Psychology, 50*, 2526–2538.

Stenberg, C. R., Campos, J. J., & Emde, R. N. (1983). The facial expression of anger in seven-month-old infants. *Child Development, 54*, 178–184.

Stern, W. (1924). *Psychology of early childhood up to the sixth year of age* (3rd ed., A. Barwell, Trans.). New York, NY: Holt.

Stevenson-Hinde, J., & Marshall, P. J. (1999). Behavioral inhibition, heart period, and respiratory sinus arrhythmia: An attachment perspective. *Child Development, 70*, 805–816.

Stipek, D. J. (1983). A developmental analysis of pride and shame. *Human Development, 26*, 42–54.

Stocker, C., Dunn, J., & Plomin, R. (1989). Sibling relationships: Links with child temperament, maternal behaviour and family structure. *Child Development, 60*, 715–727.

Strathearn, L., Li, J., Fonagy, P., & Montague, P. R. (2008). What's in a smile? Maternal brain responses to infant facial cues. *Pediatrics, 122*, 40–51.

Stuewig, J., Tangney, J. P., Kendall, S., Folk, J. B., Reinsmith Meyer, C., & Dearing, R. L. (2015). Children's proneness to shame and guilt predict risky and illegal behaviours in young adulthood. *Child Psychiatry and Human Development, 45*, 217–227.

Suomi, S. J., Chaffin, A. C., & Higley, J. D. (2011). Reactivity and behavioural inhibition as personality traits in nonhuman primates. In A. Weiss, J. King, & L. Murray (Eds.), *Personality and temperament in nonhuman primates* (pp. 285–311). New York, NY: Springer.

Swedo, S. E., Rappoport, J. L., Leonard, H., Lenane, M., & Cheslow, D. (1989). Obsessive-Compulsive Disorder in children and adolescents: Clinical phenomenology of 70 consecutive cases. *Archives of General Psychiatry, 46*, 335–341.

Sylvester, C. M., Smyser, C. D., Smyser, T., Kenley, J., Ackerman, J. J., Jr., Shimony, J. S., . . . Rogers, C. E. (2017). Cortical functional connectivity evident after birth and behavioral inhibition at age 2. *American Journal of Psychiatry, 175*, 180–187.

Symons, D., & Moran, G. (1994). Responsiveness and dependency are different aspects of social contingencies: An example from mother and infant smiles. *Infant Behavior and Development, 17*, 209–214.

Taboas, W., Ojserkis, R., & McKay, D. (2015). Change in disgust reactions following cognitive-behavioral therapy for childhood anxiety disorders. *International Journal of Clinical and Health Psychology, 15*, 1–7.

Talge, N. M., Neal, C., & Glover, V. (2007). Antenatal maternal stress and long-term effects on child neurodevelopment: How and why? *Journal of Child Psychology and Psychiatry, 48*, 245–261.

Termine, N. T., & Izard, C. E. (1988). Infants' responses to their mothers' expressions of joy and sadness. *Developmental Psychology, 24*, 223–229.

Teti, D. M., & Ablard, K. E. (1989). Security of attachment and infant-sibling relationships: A laboratory study. *Child Development, 60*, 1519–1528.

Thomas, A., Chess, S., & Birch, H. G. (1970). The origin of personality. *Scientific American, 223*, 102–109.

Tikalsky, F. D., & Wallace, S. D. (1988). Culture and the structure of children's fears. *Journal of Cross-Cultural Psychology, 19*, 481–492.

Tomkins, S. S. (1963). *Affect, imagery, consciousness: II. The negative affects.* Oxford: Springer.

Tracy, J. L., Robins, R. W., & Lagattuta, K. H. (2005). Can children recognise pride? *Emotion, 5*, 251–257.

Triebenbacher, S. L. (1998). Pets as transitional objects: Their role in children's emotional development. *Psychological Reports, 82*, 191–200.

Troster, H., & Brambring, M. (1992). Early social-emotional development in blind infants. *Child: Care, Health and Development, 18*, 207–227.

Tustin, K., & Hayne, H. (2016). Early memories come in small packages: Episodic memory in young children and adults. *Developmental Psychobiology, 58*, 852–865.

Tuukkanen, T., Kankaanranta, M., & Wilska, T.-A. (2013). Children's life world as a perspective on their citizenship: The case of the Finnish Children's Parliament. *Childhood, 20*, 131–147.

Vagnoni, E., Lourenco, S. F., & Longo, M. R. (2012). Threat modulates perception of looming visual stimuli. *Current Biology, 22*, R826–R827.

Vaish, A., Carpenter, M., & Tomasello, M. (2016). The early emergence of guilt-motivated prosocial behaviour. *Child Development, 87*, 1772–1782.

Van Bakel, H. H. A., & Riksen-Walraven, J. M. (2004). Stress reactivity in 15-month-old infants: Links with infant temperament, cognitive competence, and attachment security. *Developmental Psychobiology, 44*, 157–167.

Van der Graff, J., Branje, S., de Wied, M., Hawk, S., van Leer, P., & Meeus, W. (2014). Perspective taking and empathic concern in adolescence: Gender differences in developmental changes. *Developmental Psychology, 50*, 881–888.

van der Meer, A. L. H., Svantesson, M., & van der Weel, F. R. R. (2012). Longitudinal study of looming in infants with high-density EEG. *Developmental Neuroscience, 34*, 488–501.

van der Pol, L. D., Groeneveld, M. G., van Berkel, S. R., Endendijk, J. J., Hallers-Haalboom, E. T., Bakermans-Kranenburg, M. J., & Mesman, J. (2015). Fathers' and mothers' emotion talk with their girls and boys from toddlerhood to preschool age. *Emotion, 15*, 854–864.

van der Weel, F. R. R., & van der Meer, A. L. H. (2009). Seeing it coming: Infants' brain responses to looming danger. *Naturwissenschaften, 96*, 1385.

Van Hulle, C., Zahn-Waxler, C., Robinson, J. L., Rhee, S. H., Hastings, P. D., & Knafo, A. (2013). Autonomic correlates of children's concern and disregard for others. *Social Neuroscience, 8*, 275–290.

van IJzendoorn, M. H., Belsky, J., & Bakermans-Kranenburg, M. (2012). Serotonin transporter genotype 5HTTLPR as a marker of differential susceptibility? A meta-analysis of child and adolescent gene-by-environment studies. *Translational Psychiatry, 2*, e147.

Vaughn, B. E., Coppolla, G., Verissimo, M., Monteiro, L., Santos, A. J., Posada, G., Carbonell, O. A., . . . Korth, B. (2007). The quality of maternal secure-base scripts predicts children's secure-base behavior at home in three sociocultural groups. *International Journal of Behavioural Development, 31*, 65–76.

Venezia, M., Messinger, D. S., Thorp, D., & Mundy, P. (2004). The development of anticipatory smiling. *Infancy, 6*, 397–406.

Veronese, G., & Castiglioni, M. (2015). "When the doors of Hell close": Dimensions of well-being and positive adjustment in a group of Palestinian children living amidst military and political violence. *Childhood, 22*, 6–22.

Vicari, S., Snitzer Reilly, J., Pasqualetti, P., Vizzotto, A., & Caltagirone, C. (2000). Recognition of facial expressions of emotions in school-age children: The intersection of perceptual and semantic categories. *Acta Paediatrica, 89*, 836–845.

Volling, B. L., & Elins, J. L. (1998). Family relationships and children's emotional adjustment as correlates of maternal and paternal differential treatment: A replication with toddler and preschool siblings. *Child Development, 69*, 1640–1656.

Vollmer, H. (1946). Jealousy in children. *American Journal of Orthopsychiatry, 16*, 660–671.

Wade, M., Moore, C., Astington, J. W., Frampton, K., & Jenkins, J. M. (2015). Cumulative contextual risk, maternal responsivity, and social cognition at 18 months. *Development and Psychopathology, 27*, 189–203.

Waller, R., Shaw, D. S., & Hyde, L. W. (2017). Observed fearlessness and positive parenting interact to predict childhood callous-unemotional behaviors among low-income boys. *Journal of Child Psychology and Psychiatry, 58*, 282–291.

Wang, Q. (2001). "Did you have fun?" American and Chinese mother-child conversations about shared emotional experiences. *Cognitive Development, 16*, 693–715.

Warneken, F., & Tomasello, M. (2006). Altruistic helping in human infants and young chimpanzees. *Science, 311*, 1301–1303.

Waters, C. S., van Goozen, S., Phillips, R., Swift, N., Hurst, S. L., Mundy, L., . . . Hay, D. F. (2013). Infants at familial risk for depression show a distinct pattern of cortisol response to experimental challenge. *Journal of Affective Disorders, 150*, 955–960.

Waters, E., & Deane, K. E. (1985). Defining and assessing individual differences in attachment relationships: Q-methodology and the organisation of behaviour in infancy and early childhood. *Monographs of the Society for Research in Child Development, 50*(1/2).

Waters, E., Vaughn, B. E., & Egeland, B. R. (1980). Individual differences in infant- mother attachment relationships at age one: Antecedents in neonatal behavior in an urban, disadvantaged sample. *Child Development, 51*, 208–216.

Waters, T. E. A., Bosmans, G., Vandevivere, E., Dujardin, A., & Waters, H. S. (2015). Secure base representations in middle childhood across two Western cultures: Associations with parental attachment representations and maternal reports of behaviour problems. *Developmental Psychology, 51*, 1013–1025.

Watson, J. S. (1972). Smiling, cooing and "the game". *Merrill-Palmer Quarterly, 18*, 323–339.

Waxer, M., & Morton, J. B. (2011). Children's judgments of emotion from conflicting cues in speech: Why 6-year-olds are so inflexible. *Child Development, 82*, 1648–1660.

Wazana, A., Moss, E., Jolicoeur-Martineau, A., Graffi, J., Tsabari, G., LeCompte, V., . . . Meaney, M. J. (2015). The interplay of birth weight, dopamine receptor D4 gene (DRD4), and early maternal care in the prediction of disorganized attachment at 36 months of age. *Development and Psychopathology, 27*, 1145–1161.

Weinfield, N. S., Sroufe, L. A., & Egeland, B. (2000). Attachment from infancy to Adulthood in a high risk sample: Continuity, discontinuity and their correlates. *Child Development, 71*, 695–702.

Weisz, J., Suwanlert, S., Chaiyasit, W., Weiss, B., Achenbach, T. M., & Trevathan, D. (1989). Epidemiology of behavioural and emotional problems among Thai and American children: Teacher reports for ages 6–11. *Journal of Child Psychology and Psychiatry, 30*, 471–484.

Wellman, H. M., & Banerjee, M. (1991). Mind and emotion: Children's understanding of the emotional consequences of beliefs and desires. *British Journal of Developmental Psychology, 9*, 191–214.

Wellman, H. M., & Woolley, J. D. (1990). From simple desires to ordinary beliefs: The early development of everyday psychology. *Cognition, 35*, 245–275.

White, L. K., Degnan, K. A., Henderson, H. A., Pérez-Edgar, K., Walker, O. L., Shechner, T., . . . Fox, N. A. (2017). Developmental relations among behavioural inhibition, anxiety, and attention biases to threat and positive information. *Child Development, 88*, 141–155.

Wichstrøm, P., Berg-Nielsen, T. S., Angold, A., Egger, H. L., Solheim, E., & Sveen, T. H. (2012). Prevalence of psychiatric disorders in pre-schoolers. *Journal of Child Psychology and Psychiatry, 53*, 695–705.

Widen, S. C. (2013). Children's interpretation of facial expressions: The long path from valence-based to specific discrete categories. *Emotion Review, 5*, 72–77.

Widen, S. C., & Russell, J. A. (2003). A closer look at preschoolers' freely produced labels for facial expressions. *Developmental Psychology, 39*, 114–128.

Widen, S. C., & Russell, J. A. (2008). Children acquire emotion categories gradually. *Cognitive Development, 23*, 291–312.

Widen, S. C., & Russell, J. A. (2013). Children's recognition of disgust in others. *Psychological Bulletin, 139*, 271–299.

Wiggins, S. (2013). The social life of "eugh": Disgust as assessment in family mealtimes. *British Journal of Social Psychology, 52*, 489–509.

Winnicott, D. W. (1960). The theory of the parent-infant relationship. *International Journal of Psychoanalysis, 41*, 585–595.

Witherington, D. C., Campos, J. J., Harriger, J. A., Bryan, C., & Margett, T. E. (2009). Emotion and its development in infancy. In J. G. Bremner & T. D. Wachs (Eds.), *The Wiley-Blackwell Handbook of Infant Development* (2nd ed.), Vol. 1, *Basic research* (pp. 568–591). Oxford: Wiley Blackwell.

Wolke, D., Bilgin, A., & Samara, M. (2017). Systematic review and meta-analysis: Fussing and crying durations and prevalence of colic in infants. *Journal of Pediatrics, 185*, 55–61.

Wong, Y., & Tsai, J. (2007). Cultural models of shame and guilt. In J. L. Tracy, R. W. Robins, & J. P. Tangney (Eds.), *The self-conscious emotions: Theory and research*. New York, NY: Guilford.

Wood, R. M., & Gustafson, G. E. (2001). Infant crying and adults' anticipated caregiving responses: Acoustic and contextual influences. *Child Development, 72*, 1287–1300.

Wormann, V., Holodynski, M., Kartner, J., & Keller, H. (2012). A cross-cultural comparison of the development of the social smile: A longitudinal study of maternal and infant imitation in 6- and 12-week-old infants. *Infant Behavior and Development, 35*, 335–347.

Yonas, A., Bechtold, A. G., Frankel, D., Gordon, F. R., McRoberts, G., Norcia, A., & Sternfels, S. (1977). Development of sensitivity to information for impending collision. *Perception and Psychophysics, 21*, 97–104.

Yule, W., Bolton, D., Udwin, O., & Boyle, S. (2000). The long-term psychological effects of a disaster experienced in adolescence: I. The incidence and course of PTSD. *Journal of Child Psychology and Psychiatry, 41*, 503–511.

Zachry, A. H., Goldman, R. L., Gordon, N. F., Lancaster, F. B., Simpson, K. B., & Springer, S. K. (2015). Differences in happiness after early crawling experience. *Journal of Educational and Developmental Psychology, 5*, 8–13.

Zahn-Waxler, C., Cole, P., Welsh, J. D., & Fox, N. A. (1995). Psychophysiological correlates of empathy and prosocial behaviors in preschool children with behavior problems. *Development and Psychopathology, 7*, 27–48.

Zahn-Waxler, C., Radke-Yarrow, M., Wagner, E., & Chapman, M. (1992). Development of concern for others. *Developmental Psychology, 28*, 126–136.

Zeanah, C. H., & Gleason, M. M. (2015). Annual research review: Attachment disorders in early childhood – clinical presentation, causes, correlates and treatment. *Journal of Child Psychology and Psychiatry, 56*, 207–222.

Zeifman, D. M. (2004). Acoustic features of infant crying related to intended caregiving Intervention. *Infant and Child Development, 13*, 111–122.

Zeskind, P. S., & Barr, R. G. (1997). Acoustic characteristics of cries of infants with "colic". *Child Development, 68*, 394–403.

Zeskind, P. S., Klein, L., & Marshall, T. R. (1992). Adults' perceptions of experimental modifications of durations of pauses and expiratory sounds in infant crying. *Developmental Psychology, 28*, 1153–1162.

Zeskind, P. S., Marshall, T. R., & Goff, D. M. (1996). Cry threshold predicts regulatory disorder in newborn infants. *Journal of Pediatric Psychology, 21*, 803–819.

Zeskind, P. S., Parker-Price, S., & Barr, R. G. (1993). Rhythmic organisation of the sound of infant crying. *Developmental Psychobiology, 26*, 321–333.

Zeskind, P. S., Platzman, K., Coles, C. D., & Schuetze, P. A. (1996). Crys analysis detects subclinical effects of prenatal alcohol exposure in newborn infants. *Infant Behavior and Development, 19*, 497–500.

INDEX

Note: Page numbers in *italic* indicate figures and page numbers in **bold** indicate tables on the corresponding pages.